Mastering Java

Mastering Computer Science

Series Editor: Sufyan bin Uzayr

Mastering Java: A Beginner's Guide
Divya Sachdeva and Natalya Ustukpayeva

Mastering Unreal Engine: A Beginner's Guide
Divya Sachdeva and Aruqqa Khateib

Mastering UI Mockups and Frameworks: A Beginner's Guide
Mohamed Musthafa MC and Kapil Kishnani

Mastering Ruby on Rails: A Beginner's Guide
Mathew Rooney and Madina Karybzhanova

Mastering Sketch: A Beginner's Guide
Mathew Rooney and Md Javed Khan

Mastering C#: A Beginner's Guide
Mohamed Musthafa MC, Divya Sachdeva, and Reza Nafim

For more information about this series, please visit: https://www.routledge.com/Mastering-Computer-Science/book-series/MCS

The "Mastering Computer Science" series of books are authored by the Zeba Academy team members, led by Sufyan bin Uzayr.

Zeba Academy is an EdTech venture that develops courses and content for learners primarily in STEM fields, and offers education consulting to Universities and Institutions worldwide. For more info, please visit https://zeba.academy

Mastering Java

A Beginner's Guide

Edited by Sufyan bin Uzayr

CRC Press
Taylor & Francis Group
Boca Raton London New York

CRC Press is an imprint of the
Taylor & Francis Group, an **informa** business

First edition published 2022
by CRC Press
6000 Broken Sound Parkway NW, Suite 300, Boca Raton, FL 33487-2742

and by CRC Press
2 Park Square, Milton Park, Abingdon, Oxon, OX14 4RN

CRC Press is an imprint of Taylor & Francis Group, LLC

ISBN: 9781032134109 (hbk)
ISBN: 9781032134086 (pbk)
ISBN: 9781003229063 (ebk)

DOI: 10.1201/9781003229063

Typeset in Minion
by KnowledgeWorks Global Ltd.

Contents

About the Editor

Sufyan bin Uzayr is a writer, coder, and entrepreneur with more than a decade of experience in the industry. He has authored several books in the past, pertaining to a diverse range of topics, ranging from History to Computers/IT.

Sufyan is the Director of Parakozm, a multinational IT company specializing in EdTech solutions. He also runs Zeba Academy, an online learning and teaching vertical with a focus on STEM fields.

Sufyan specializes in a wide variety of technologies, such as JavaScript, Dart, WordPress, Drupal, Linux, and Python. He holds multiple degrees, including ones in Management, IT, Literature, and Political Science.

Sufyan is a digital nomad, dividing his time between four countries. He has lived and taught in universities and educational institutions around the globe. Sufyan takes a keen interest in technology, politics, literature, history, and sports, and in his spare time, he enjoys teaching coding and English to young students.

Learn more at sufyanism.com.

CHAPTER 1

Introduction to Java

IN THIS CHAPTER

- ➤ What is Java, and why it is used
- ➤ Major features of Java
- ➤ Basic syntax

Java is one of the most widely used programming languages today. It all began in 1990 when an American firm at the forefront of the computer revolution decided to assemble its top engineers to design and create a product that would become a significant participant in the new Internet world. This book will look at java concepts, including their usage and critical features, and basic syntax.

DOI: 10.1201/9781003229063-1

WHAT IS JAVA?

Java is an object-oriented programming (OOP) language and software platform utilized on billions of devices, including laptop computers, mobile devices, game consoles, medical equipment, and more. Java's principles and grammar are based on the C and C++ programming languages.

The mobility of Java-based applications is a significant benefit. It's pretty simple to migrate code from a notebook computer to a mobile device after developing it in Java. The primary objective of the language, when it was created in 1991 by Sun Microsystems' James Gosling (later purchased by Oracle), was to "write once, run anywhere." It's also crucial to note that Java is not the same as JavaScript. The compilation is not required for JavaScript; however, it is needed for Java code.

Furthermore, JavaScript can only be used in web browsers, but Java may be used anywhere. New and improved software development tools replace existing technologies, previously believed to be necessary at a breakneck rate. Most back-end development projects, especially those requiring extensive data and Android development, employ Java as the server-side language. Java is also extensively used in gaming, numerical calculation, and desktop and mobile computers.

How Does Java Work?

Before we get into the reasons for Java's continued popularity, let's take a closer look at what Java is and why it's essential for corporate application development.

Java is a programming language, and a software platform all rolled into one. The Java Development Kit (JDK), available for Windows, macOS, and Linux, is required to develop a Java application. After writing the program in Java, a compiler converts it to Java bytecode, which is the instruction set for the Java Virtual Machine (JVM), part of the Java runtime environment (JRE).

Java bytecode runs unmodified on any system that supports JVMs, allowing us to run Java code on any platform. The JVM, the Java API, and a complete development environment make up the Java software platform. The JVM parses and executes (interprets) Java bytecode. The Java API includes many libraries, including fundamental objects, networking, security capabilities, Extensible Markup Language (XML) creation, and web services. The Java programming language and the Java software platform, when combined, provide a solid and well-proven solution for corporate software development.

Why Is Java Important?

Suppose we work as an enterprise application developer. In that case, we're probably already familiar with Java, and the company probably has hundreds, if not millions, of lines of production code written in the language. We'll almost certainly require some Java knowledge to debug, maintain, and upgrade the existing codebase.

However, thinking of Java exclusively in terms of old programs is a mistake. The Java programming language is at the heart of the Android operating system, which runs most smartphones worldwide. Java is also one of the most widely used programming languages for machine learning and data research. Java is the language of choice for Internet solutions in many corporate companies due to its robustness, simplicity of use, cross-platform capabilities, and security.

Java technology, in particular, provides an excellent platform for creating web apps, which are the cornerstone for every digital organization. Java application servers interact with databases and offer dynamic web content by acting as web containers for Java components, XML, and web services. With characteristics such as transaction management, security, clustering, performance, availability, connection, and scalability, Java application servers provide a reliable deployment environment for corporate applications.

Java's Technical Advantages Include

When selecting a programming language and environment for the next corporate application, several compelling technical reasons to choose Java include interoperability, scalability, and adaptability.

The most significant justification for using Java for new corporate applications is its fundamental concept of interoperability across various devices. The object-oriented architecture of Java allows us to construct modular programs and reusable code, which speeds up development and extends the life of corporate systems. Java's platform scalability is an important feature. With Java, we may utilize a single system to solve a wide range of problems. Existing desktop programs can simply be modified to run on smaller, resource-constrained devices. We also transfer apps from mobile to desktop by creating business apps for Android and then integrating them into existing desktop software, avoiding lengthy and costly development cycles.

Java also impresses strategic strategists with its adaptability to new use cases. Java, for example, is commonly regarded as an excellent platform for the Internet of Things (IoT). The typical IoT application links many different devices; a process made much easier because Java is installed on billions of devices. Furthermore, Java's large developer community is continually creating and sharing new libraries with features tailored to the creation of IoT applications.

Java's Advantages in the Workplace

Java has solid technical justifications and commercial arguments: a big talent pool, a low learning curve, and a wide choice of integrated development environments (IDEs).

The demand for talented developers is growing as more firms employ linked devices, machine learning algorithms, and cloud solutions. Many observers believe that there will be a scarcity of senior-level programmers shortly, making it challenging to staff new software ventures. Demand for mobile app developers might quickly outstrip supply in the near future.

A compelling argument to base considerable software efforts on Java is the enormous skill pool of Java engineers. When hiring managers advertise job vacancies for Java developers, they may anticipate receiving many eligible applicants and filling those jobs fast. Managers can also employ contract resources to complement in-house personnel for certain activities without hiring more people.

Major software projects need a significant number of junior contributors in addition to experienced engineers. While Java is still a common first programming language in university computer science programs, many graduates lack the necessary skills to be effective right away. Java is simpler to learn and master than many other programming languages, resulting in a shorter learning curve and quicker productivity ramp-up. Java's large online community of developer forums, tutorials, and user groups helps new programmers come up to speed while also providing seasoned programmers with useful, tried-and-true problem-solving solutions.

Java has several IDEs. Experienced Java developers may rapidly learn a new environment, allowing development managers to select the IDE that best suits the project type, budget, development process, and programmers' skill level. NetBeans, Eclipse, and IntelliJ IDEA are the best three IDEs for corporate application development by many experienced Java programmers. However, in certain situations, a lighter IDE, such as DrJava, BlueJ, JCreator, or Eclipse Che, is the better option.

THE JAVA PROGRAMMING LANGUAGE HAS THE FOLLOWING FEATURES

Java was created with versatility in mind, allowing programmers to build code that can run on any system or device, regardless of architecture or platform.[1] It is one of the most widely used programming languages on the planet, and it was designed to work reliably on every platform. Java BuzzWords are a set of Java features.[2]

---

[1] https://techvidvan.com/tutorials/features-of-java-programming-language/, Tech Vidvaan

[2] https://www.tutorialspoint.com/What-are-the-major-features-of-Java-programming, tutorialspoint

Sun MicroSystems officially describe Java as having the following features:

- Simple and well-known
- Compiled and interpreted the data
- Independent of the platform
- Portable
- Neutral in architecture
- Object-oriented
- Robust
- Safe
- Distributed
- Interactive and multi-threaded
- Outstanding performance
- Extensible and dynamic

Simple and Well-Known

Java is straightforward because:

- It has a very clear and easy-to-understand code style. It reduces complexity by excluding the following complex and challenging aspects found in other languages such as C and C++:
    - Explicit pointers concept
    - Classes for storing data
    - Header files and preprocessors

- Multiple inheritance
- Operator overloading
- Goto statements

Apart from eliminating these perplexing and unclear notions, there is an Automatic Garbage Collection feature that eliminates the need to delete unreferenced objects explicitly.

Java is well-known because:

- It is built on well-known languages such as C and C++, incorporating many of their capabilities.
- It eliminates the disadvantages, complexity, and perplexing aspects of C/C++. If you are familiar with C/C++, you will find Java quite friendly and simple to learn.

Compiled and Interpreted the Data

A computer language is often compiled or interpreted. The strength of compiled languages is combined with the flexibility of interpretable languages in Java.

Java compiler converts bytecode to java source code.

The JVM then runs this bytecode, which is portable and executable on various operating systems.

The following diagram depicts the procedure:

Working of JVM

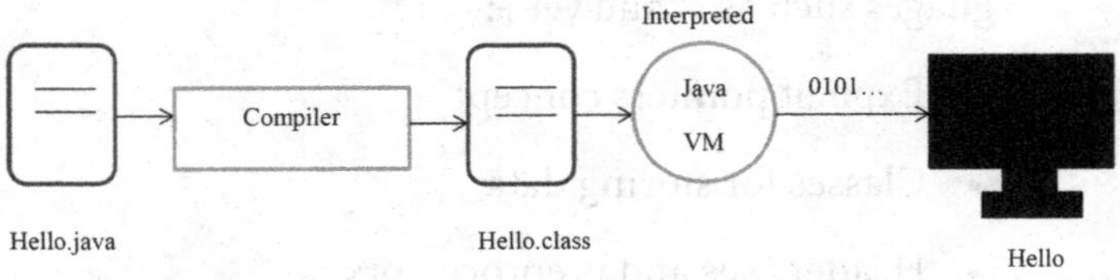

Independent of the Platform

Java's most important characteristic is that it enables platform freedom, which leads to portability, which is ultimately its greatest strength. Being platform-independent means that software written on one system may run without modification on any other machine in the world. Java uses the idea of the bytecode to achieve platform independence. Unlike the C/C++ compiler, the Java compiler never transforms source code to machine code.

Instead, it turns the source code into an intermediate code known as bytecode, translated into machine-dependent form by another software layer known as JVM. As a result, regardless of whatever machine created the bytecode, JVM may execute it on any platform or Operating System (OS) on which it is installed. This is where Java's motto "Write Once, Execute Anywhere" comes into play, implying that we may build programs in one environment and run them in another without changing the code.

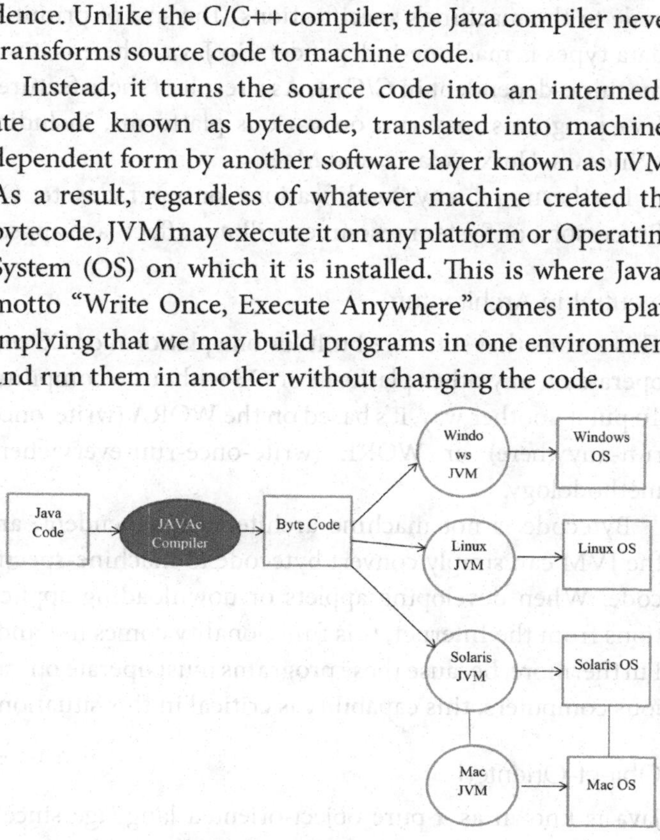

Java platform independence

Portable

The SE (Standard Edition) version of Java is referred to be "portable." The mobility is due to the architecture's neutrality.

The source code in C/C++ may execute somewhat differently on different hardware systems, but Java makes it easier to understand. Java bytecode can be executed on any device with a compatible JVM to convert the bytecode to the machine's specifications. The size of primitive data types is machine-independent in Java, whereas it was machine-dependent in C/C++. As a result of these features, Java programs may run on various platforms, including Windows, Unix, Solaris, and Mac.

Furthermore, any modifications or upgrades to OS, Processors, or System resources will not affect Java apps.

Neutral in Architecture

This means that software built for one platform or OS may operate on any other platform or OS without recompiling. To put it another way, it's based on the WORA (write-once-run-anywhere) or WORE (write-once-run-everywhere) methodology.

Bytecode is not machine architecture-dependent, and the JVM can simply convert bytecode to machine-specific code. When developing applets or downloading applications from the Internet, this functionality comes in handy. Furthermore, because these programs must operate on various computers, this capability is critical in this situation.

Object-Oriented

Java is known as a pure object-oriented language since it firmly supports the ideas of OOP. Encapsulation, abstraction, and inheritance are all aspects of OOP that Java provides. In Java, almost everything is an object. Objects and classes contain all applications and data. Java includes a modular collection of classes arranged into packages.

Robust

Java is robust because it can handle run-time failures, has automated garbage collection and exception handling, and does not use the explicit pointer notion. The memory management system in Java is rather good. It aids in the elimination of mistakes by checking the code both during build and execution. Java is a garbage-collected language, which means that the JVM automatically deallocates memory blocks, so programmers don't have to worry about manually removing memory as they do in C/C++. Exception handling is another feature of Java, which detects and removes runtime problems. Any runtime fault discovered by the JVM in Java is never communicated directly to the underlying system; instead, the application is terminated immediately, preventing it from inflicting any harm to the underlying system.

Safe

Because criminal actions and viruses are a hazard, security is a significant concern for every programming language. Java allows you to use access modifiers to monitor memory access and guarantee that no viruses get into your applet.

Java is a more secure language than C/C++ since it does not allow a programmer to construct pointers explicitly. As a result, if we do not correctly initialize a variable in Java, we will not access it. Virtual machines Sandbox is used to run programs. A distinct environment in which users may run their programs without impacting the underlying system. It has a bytecode validator that looks for unlawful code that violates the access right in code fragments.

Distributed

Because it enables users to develop distributed applications, Java is distributed. We can break a program into many pieces in Java and save them on various machines. A Java programmer sitting on one device can connect to another machine's software. This Java feature allows for distributed programming, which is particularly useful when working on massive projects. The concepts of RMI (Remote Method Invocation) and EJB (Enterprise JavaBeans) in Java enable us to do this (Enterprise JavaBeans). Java has an extensive collection of classes connecting via TCP/IP protocols like Hypertext Transfer Protocol (HTTP) and File Transfer Protocol (FTP), making network interactions easier than C/C++. It also allows programmers from many places to collaborate on the same project.

Interactive and Multi-Threaded

A thread is a separate execution route within a program that runs at the same time. Multithreaded refers to handling several tasks simultaneously or running various parts of the same program in parallel. Java's code is broken down into smaller chunks, which Java runs logically and timely.

Advantages:

- The primary benefit of multithreading is that it allows for the most efficient use of resources.
- Each thread does not take up memory. It has a shared memory space.

- It is unnecessary to wait for the application to complete one job before moving on to the next.
- The cost of maintenance has dropped. It also saves time.
- It boosts the efficiency of complicated applications.

Java is interactive because its code allows excellent Character User Interface (CUI) and Graphical User Interface (GUI) apps. It vastly increases graphical programs' interaction performance.

Outstanding Performance

Because of its intermediate bytecode, Java's speed is outstanding for an interpreted language. The Just In Time compiler in Java delivers excellent speed by compiling code on-demand, compiling just the methods that are being called. This saves time and increases efficiency. The Java architecture is also built in such a way that it lowers runtime overheads. The addition of multithreading to Java programs improves the overall speed of execution. Because the Java compiler generates highly efficient bytecodes, the JVM can process them considerably quicker.

Extensible and Dynamic

Java is dynamic and extensible, which means we may add classes and new methods to classes using OOPs and create new classes using subclasses. This makes it easy for us to expand and even change our classes. Java allows you to link new class libraries, methods, and objects dynamically. It is extremely dynamic since it can adapt to its changing surroundings. Java also allows for the use of functions written in other languages, such as C and C++, in Java projects. These are referred to as "native techniques." At runtime, these methods are dynamically connected.

BASIC SYNTAX

Each programming language has its own syntax. We'll go over the syntax for everything in Java that you should know before learning and familiarizing yourself with it.

The syntax refers to the format in which a Java program is written, and the commands used to compile and run it. It will be difficult for a programmer or learner to get the desired outputs from a program if they lack proper syntax knowledge.

What Is the Syntax of Java?

The collection of rules that determine how to construct and understand a Java program is referred to as Java syntax. Java's syntax is derived from C and C++. However, there are numerous differences, such as the lack of global variables in Java compared to C++.

In Java, the code belongs to objects and classes. To avoid programming errors, Java does not include some features such as operator overloading and the use of explicit pointers.

So let's start with java's basic syntax.[3]

Identifiers are the fundamental components of a Java program. Identifiers are used to give names to various parts

[3] https://www.baeldung.com/java-syntax, Baeldung

of a program, such as variables, objects, classes, methods, and arrays.

- **Objects:** Objects are made up of states and actions. A dog, for example, has states such as color, name, breed, and behavior such as wagging its tail, barking, and eating. A class's instance is an object.
- **Class:** A class is a pattern that describes the state that an object of its kind may support.
- **Methods:** The term "method" refers to a type of behavior. Many ways can be found in a single class. Methods are where logic is expressed, data is processed, and all actions are executed.
- **Instance Variables:** Each object has a collection of instance variables that are unique to it. The values supplied to these instance variables determine the state of an object.

First Java Program

Consider the following code, which prints the words Hello.

Example:

```
public class FirstJavaProgram {
   /* This is my first java program.
    * This will print 'Hello Everyone '
    */
   public static void main(String []
args) {
     System.out.println("Hello Everyone");
   }
}
```

Let's take a look at how to save the file, compile it, and run it. Please proceed with the steps below:

- Open notepad and add the code as above.
- Save the file as: FirstJavaProgram.java.
- Open a command prompt window and go to the directory where you saved the class. Assume it's C:\.
- Type "javac MyFirstJavaProgram.java" and press enter to compile your code. If there are no errors in code, the command prompt will take you to the following line (Assumption: The path variable is set).
- Now, type "java FirstJavaProgram" to run your program and we will be able to see "Hello Everyone" printed on the window.

Syntax for Beginners

It's critical to remember the following considerations while working with Java applications.

- Java is case sensitive, which implies that the identifiers Hello and hello have distinct meanings in Java.
- The initial letter of each class name should be capitalized. If a class name is made up of many words, the initial letter of each inner word should be in upper case.

  Example: FirstJavaClass is an example of a class.
- Method names should all begin with a lower case letter. If the method's name is made up of many words, the initial letter of each inner word should be capitalized.

Example: public void myMethodName is an example of a public void method ()

- The name of the program file should be identical to the name of the class.

  When saving the file, use the class name and attach ".java" to the end of the name (remember, Java is case sensitive) (if the file name and the class name do not match, your program will not compile).

  If the file does not include a public class, the file name may differ from the class name. It is also not required that the file have a public class.

  Example: Assume the class is called "FirstJavaProgram." Then, save the program as "FirstJavaProgram.java."

- Public static void main(String args[]): The main() method, which is a required part of any Java program, starts the processing of the program.

Identifiers in Java

The basic building elements of a Java program are identifiers. Identifiers are used to give names to various components of a program, such as variables, objects, classes, methods, arrays, etc.

The following are the guidelines for naming identifiers in Java:

1. Alphabets, numbers, underscore (_), and dollar ($) sign characters can all be used in identifiers.

2. They can't be a Java reserved term or keyword like true, false, while, and so on.

3. Identifiers can't start with a digit.

4. Identifiers can be as long as you want them to be.

5. Because Java is case sensitive, identifiers in uppercase and lowercase are handled differently.

Keywords in Java

Keywords are reserved words in Java that provide the compiler a particular interpretation. The keywords can't be used as regular identifier names; they must be used for a specific reason.[4]

The following are some Java keywords:

- **Abstract:** The abstract keyword in Java is used to declare an abstract class. The interface can be implemented using an abstract class. Both abstract and non-abstract methods may be used.

- **Boolean:** The boolean keyword in Java is used to define a Boolean type variable. It can only store True and False values.

- **Break:** The break keyword in Java is used to end a loop or switch expressions. It interrupts the program's current flow when certain criteria are met.

- **Byte:** The byte keyword in Java is used to create a variable containing 8-bit data values.

- **Case:** The case keyword in Java is used with switch statements to mark text blocks.

---

[4] https://www.javatpoint.com/java-keywords, javaTpoint

- **Catch:** The catch keyword in Java is used to capture exceptions thrown by try statements. It can only be used after the try block.
- **Char:** The char keyword in Java is used to create a variable containing unsigned 16-bit Unicode characters.
- **Class:** To declare a class in Java, use the class keyword.
- **Continue:** The continue keyword in Java is used to keep the loop going. It continues the program's current flow while skipping the remaining code at the given circumstance.
- **Default:** The default block of code in a switch statement is specified by the Java default keyword.
- **Do:** The do keyword in Java is used to identify a loop in the control statement. It can repeat a section of the program several times.
- **Double:** The double keyword in Java is used to create a variable containing a 64-bit floating-point value.
- **Otherwise:** In the if statement, the else keyword in Java is used to represent alternate branches.
- **Enum:** The enum keyword in Java is used to specify a set of fixed constants. Private or default constructors are always used in enum constructors.
- **Extend:** The extend keyword in Java is used to show that a class is inherited from another class or interface.
- **Final:** The final keyword in Java is used to denote that a variable has a constant value. It's used in

conjunction with a variable to prevent the user from changing the variable's value.

- **Finally:** The finally keyword in Java denotes a code block in a try-catch structure. Whether or not an exception is handled, this block is always performed.
- **Float:** The float keyword in Java is used to create a variable containing a 32-bit floating-point integer.
- **For:** The for keyword in Java is used to begin a for loop. When a condition is met, it is used to execute a set of instructions/functions repeatedly. If the number of iterations is fixed, the for loop is preferred.
- **If:** The if keyword in Java is used to test a condition. If the condition is true, the if block is executed.
- **Implements:** The term implements are used in Java to implement an interface.
- **Keyword:** The import keyword in Java makes classes and interfaces available to the current source code.
- **Instanceof:** The instanceof keyword in Java determines if an object is an instance of a particular class or implements an interface.
- **Int:** The int keyword in Java is used to declare a variable that can store a signed 32-bit integer.
- **Interface:** The interface keyword in Java is used to declare an interface. It is limited to abstract techniques.
- **Long:** The long keyword in Java is used to specify a variable that may store a 64-bit integer.

- **Native:** The Java native keyword indicates that a method is implemented using JNI (Java Native Interface) in native code.
- **New:** The new keyword in Java is used to create new objects.
- **Null:** The null keyword in Java is used to indicate that a reference refers to nothing. It gets rid of the trash value.
- **Package:** The term package in Java is used to declare a Java package that contains the classes.
- **Private:** The private keyword in Java is an access modifier. It's used to say that a method or variable may only be accessible in the class where it's declared.
- **Protected:** The protected keyword in Java is an access modifier. It can be accessed both within and outside the package, but only through inheritance. It isn't possible to use it with the class.
- **Public:** The public keyword in Java is an access modifier. It's a phrase that means anything may be found anyplace. Among all the modifiers, it has the broadest use.
- **Return:** When a method's execution is complete, the Java return keyword is used to exit the method.
- **Short:** The Java short keyword is used to declare a variable with a 16-bit integer capacity.
- **Static:** The static keyword in Java indicates that a variable or function belongs to a class. In Java, the static keyword is mainly used to control memory.

- **Strictfp:** To guarantee portability, Java strictfp is used to limit floating-point calculations.
- **Super:** The super keyword in Java is a reference variable that refers to parent class objects. It may be used to call the method of the immediate parent class.
- **Switch:** The switch keyword in Java includes a switch statement that executes code based on the test value. The switch statement compares several values to see whether they are equal.
- **Synchronised:** In multithreaded programming, the synchronized keyword is used to identify the critical portions or functions.
- **This:** In a method Java, this keyword can be used to refer to the current object.
- **Throw:** The throw keyword in Java is used to throw an exception explicitly. Throwing custom exceptions is the most common usage of the throw keyword. After that, there is an example.
- **Throws:** The throws keyword in Java is used to declare an exception. Throws can be used to propagate checked exceptions.
- **Transient:** In serialization, the Java temporary keyword is utilized. Any data member that is marked as transitory will not be serialized.
- **Try:** The try keyword in Java is used to begin a block of code that will be checked for errors. Either a catch or a final block must come after the try block.

- **Void:** The void keyword in Java is used to indicate that a method has no return value.
- **Volatile:** In Java, the volatile keyword is used to indicate that a variable may change asynchronously.
- **While:** The while keyword in Java is used to initiate a while loop. This loop repeats a section of the program several times. The while loop is recommended if the number of iterations is not fixed.

Modifiers in Java

Modifiers may be used to alter classes, methods, and other objects, much as in other languages. Modifiers are divided into two groups:

1. Default, public, protected, and private are the access modifiers.
2. Final, abstract, and strictfp are non-access modifiers.

Variables in Java

The kinds of variables in Java are as follows:

- Local Variables
- Class Variables (Static Variables)
- Instance Variable (Non-static Variables)

Enums in Java

In Java 5.0, enums were introduced. Enums limit a variable's value to one of a few preset options. Enums are the values in this enumerated list. It is possible to decrease the number of defects in your code by using enums.

For example, if we consider an application for a juice business, the glass sizes may be limited to small, medium, and large. This would ensure that no one could order anything other than a small, medium, or big size.

Literals in Java

Constants or data objects with fixed values are referred to as literals in Java. In Java, there are several sorts of Literals. Numeric, Floating, Character, Strings, Boolean, and Null are the types. They're also divided into subcategories. Let's take a look at each one separately:

1. **Numeric:** Numbers are represented via numeric literals. In Java, there are four different forms of numeric literals:
   i. **Integer Literals:** Integer literals are integers in base 10 that are entire numbers without any fractional parts. For instance, 108.
   ii. **Binary Literals:** A binary literal is an integer with a base of two, for instance, 011.
   iii. **Octal Literals:** The numbers with base 8 are known as octal literals. They can't have the numbers 8 or 9 in them. For instance, 565.
   iv. **Hexadecimal Literals:** Hexadecimal literals are integers that have a base of 16 characters. They can include numbers ranging from 0 to 9 as well as alphabets ranging from A to F. For instance, 24D6.
2. **Floating-point:** Floating-point literals are also known as real literals. Only a fractional point is used in the

floating-point literal to specify numeric values (.). They can take the shape of a fractional or exponential function. For instance, -15.6, 1.876, 11.4D08.

3. **Character:** Character literals deal with characters contained in a single quote. Within single quotes ' ' they can only contain one character. They are divided into the following categories:
   i. **Single quoted character:** A single-quoted character encloses all uni-length characters in single quotes. For example, 'b', 'p', 'S'.
   ii. **Escape Sequences:** These are the characters that appear after the backslash and perform a specific purpose on the screen, such as tabs, newlines, and so on. For example, 'b,' 'n,' 't'.
   iii. **Unicode Representation:** We may express it by putting the character's relevant Unicode value after the letter 'u'. For instance, 'u0057'.
4. **Boolean:** True and false are the two possible values for a boolean literal. ASCII letters are used to create these values. True or false, for example.
5. **String:** String-literals are multi-character constants enclosed in double quotes "." For example, "java-class," "Hello," "\cde," and so on.

Comments in Java

When programmers add documentation to a method or a line specified within the program, they can use comments. While compiling, the compiler does not read the comments and ignores them. The comments improve the program's readability and comprehension.

The following are the different sorts of comments:

- **Java Single-Line Comments:** These single-line comments are made up of a single line of text added after a code line to clarify what it means. We can designate a single-line comment with two backslashes(/), and it will be immediately ended when a new line is introduced into the editor.

  Example:

  ```
  int num = 4;
  //value defining
  System.out.println("The value is: "
  + number);
  //Printing
  ```

- **Multi-Line Comments in Java:** Throughout the program, multi-line comments cover many lines. To elaborate the algorithm, we can write them at the start of the program. Developers also use them to comment out code sections while debugging. We may utilize them by putting a starting tag(/*) and an ending tag(*/) in front of them.

  Example:

  ```
  int num = 4;
  System.out.println("The value is: "
  + number);
  /* The compiler will not execute it.
  Defining the value of numbers and
  printing the value. This is a multi-
  line comment. */
  ```

Blank Lines

A blank line is a line that has simply white space, maybe with a remark, and Java ignores it completely.

Inheritance

In Java, classes can be derived from other classes. Essentially, if you need to construct a new class and an existing class has part of the code you need, you may derive your new class from the current code.

This idea allows you to reuse existing class fields and functions without recreating the code in a new class. In this case, the current class is referred to as the superclass, and the derived class is referred to as the subclass.

Interfaces

In the Java programming language, an interface is a contract between objects that specifies how they communicate. When it comes to inheritance, interfaces are pretty important. An interface specifies which methods should be used by a derived class (subclass). However, it is entirely up to the subclass to implement the methods.

In this chapter, we discussed what Java is and how it works, why it is essential, and its benefits. We also learned about many features of the Java programming language. We also went through the fundamentals of Java syntax.

CHAPTER 2

Getting Started with Java

IN THIS CHAPTER

- ➤ How to Install and Run Java
- ➤ Java Primitive Types and Operators
- ➤ Control Structures
- ➤ A Guide to Java Loops
- ➤ A Guide to Java Packages

In the previous chapter, we discussed what Java is, why it's utilized, what its characteristics are, and what Java's core features are. In this chapter, we'll go through how to install and run Java on a Personal Computer (PC). What are the different sorts of operators and control structures, as well as whole packages?

DOI: 10.1201/9781003229063-2

HOW TO SETUP JAVA ON A WINDOWS COMPUTER

We may use this Java Development Kit (JDK) to write and run Java programs. It's feasible to have numerous JDK versions installed on the same computer. However, it is suggested that we install the most recent version of Java on Windows 10. Installing Java in Windows 10 for JDK 8 free download for 32 bit or JDK 8 free download for Windows 64 bit and installation are as follows:

- **Step 1:** Click on the link https://www.oracle.com/java/technologies/downloads/
  For Java, go to JDK Download and download JDK 8.
- **Step 2:** Accept the License Agreement.
  Download the Java 8 JDK for 32-bit or 64-bit operating systems.
- **Step 3:** A popup will appear when we click the Installation link. After clicking on it, I reviewed and accepted the Oracle Technology Network License Agreement for the Oracle Java Standard Edition (SE) development kit; we will be routed to the login page. If we don't already have an Oracle account, we can quickly create one by entering basic information.
- **Step 4:** After the Java JDK 8 download is finished, execute the exe to install the JDK. Next should be selected.
- **Step 5:** To install Java on Windows, choose the PATH… We may keep it at the default setting. Continue by pressing the next button.
- **Step 6:** When Java has been installed on Windows, click Close.

In Java, Here's How to Establish Environment Variables: Classpath and Path

The PATH variable specifies the location of executables such as javac and java, among others. We can start a program without providing the PATH but must give the entire path of the executable, such as C:\Program Files\Java\jdk1.8.0_271\bin\javacD.java instead of using basic javac, use javacD.java.

The CLASSPATH variable specifies where the Library Files are stored.

Let's look at how to establish the PATH and CLASSPATH variables.

- **Step 1:** Select the properties by right-clicking on My Computer.
- **Step 2:** Select Advanced System Settings from the drop-down menu.
- **Step 3:** To configure the Java runtime environment, choose Environment Variables.
- **Step 4:** Select the new User Variables Button.
- **Step 5:** In the Variable name field, type PATH.
- **Step 6:** In the JDK folder, copy the path to the bin folder.
- **Step 7:** In the Variable value, paste the path to the bin folder. Select the OK button.
  Note: If we already have a PATH variable set up on the computer, change it to PATH = <JDK installation directory>\bin;%PATH%;

- **Step 8:** To set CLASSPATH, use an exact procedure. Note: If Java installation fails after installing it, modify the classpath to CLASSPATH = <JDK installation directory>\lib\tools.jar;
- **Step 9:** Select the OK option.
- **Step 10:** Type javac instructions at the command prompt.

INSTALLING A JAVA INTEGRATED DEVELOPMENT ENVIRONMENT (IDE)

A step-by-step method to downloading and installing Eclipse IDE is provided below:

- **Step 1:** Installing Eclipse
  Type https://www.eclipse.org/ into the browser.
- **Step 2:** Select "Download" from the drop-down menu.
- **Step 3:** Select "Download 64 bit" from the drop-down menu.
- **Step 4:** Select "Download" from the drop-down menu.
- **Step 4:** Download and install Eclipse.
  - In the Windows file explorer, select "downloads."
  - Select the file "eclipse-inst-win64.exe" and double-click it.
- **Step 5:** Select the Run option.
- **Step 6:** Select "Eclipse IDE for Java Developers."
- **Step 7:** Select "INSTALL."
- **Step 8:** Select "LAUNCH" from the menu.

- **Step 9:** Again, Select "LAUNCH."
- **Step 10:** Select "Create a new Java project."
- **Step 11:** Create a new Java project
  - Name the project.
  - Select "Finish" from the drop-down menu.
- **Step 12:** Create a Java package.
  - Go to the "src."
  - Select "New."
  - Select "Package" from the drop-down menu.
- **Step 13:** Type in the package's name.
  - Put the package's name.
  - After that, click the Finish button.
- **Step 14:** Creating a Java Class
  - Select the package we've made.
  - Select "New."
  - Select "Class."
- **Step 15:** Create a Java Class
  - Put the name of the class.
  - Select the checkbox for "public static void main (String[] args)."
  - Select "Finish."
- **Step 16:** Press the "Run" button.

Internal Java Program Details

We must develop a Java program and learn how to compile and run it. We'll study what occurs when we build and run a Java application in this section.

What Occurs throughout the Compilation Process?

The Java file is converted by Java Compiler (which does not interface with the operating system) at compile-time, which turns the Java code into bytecode.

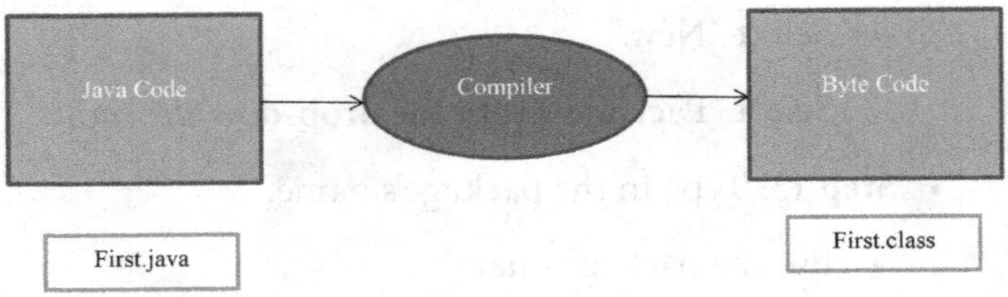

What Occurs When the Program Is Running?

The following stages are carried out at runtime:

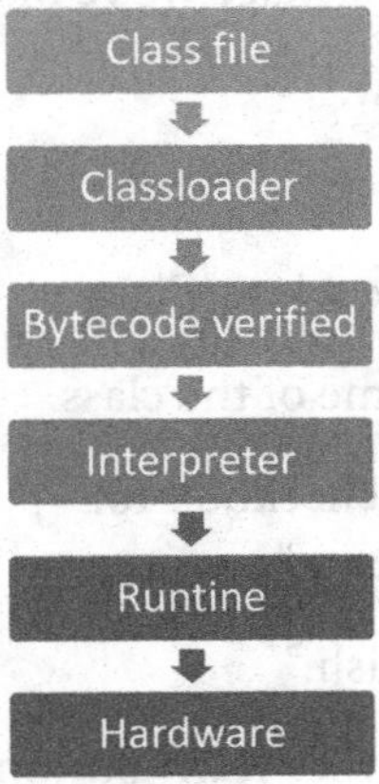

- **Classloader:** Classloader is a Java Virtual Machine (JVM) component that is responsible for loading class files.
- **Bytecode Verifier:** Checks code fragments for criminal code that might compromise object access privileges.
- **Interpreter:** The interpreter reads the bytecode stream and then executes the commands.

TYPES OF PRIMITIVE DATA

- Java basic data types and related topics such as variables, constants, data types, operators, and expressions will be covered.
- We'll learn how to create programs with basic data kinds, input, and computations.

Simple Programs to Write

- Designing algorithms and data structures and converting algorithms into programming code are all part of the process of writing a program.
- An algorithm defines how to solve a problem regarding the activities to be performed and the sequence they should be performed.
- Calculating the area of a circle. The following is a description of the program's algorithm:

  1. Take a look at the radius
  2. Calculate the area using the formula below.
     Area = radius * radius * ∏
  3. Make the area visible.

- Integers, floating-point numbers, characters, and Boolean kinds are all represented by data types in Java. Primitive data types are what they're called.
- When we code, we convert an algorithm into a programming language that the computer can understand.
- The following is a summary of the program:

```
//Area.Java: calculate the area

public class Area
{
public static void main(String[] args
{
double radius; // variable and data type
double area;

// radius assign
radius = 20;

// Calculate area
area = radius * radius * 3.14159;

// Display results
System.out.println("The area for the
circle:" +
radius + " is " + area);
}
}
```

- The radius must be represented by a variable symbol, which must be declared in the program. In the software, variables are utilized to store data and computational results.

- Instead of a and b, use descriptive labels. Use radius to represent radius and area to represent the area. Indicate if their data types are integer, float, or anything else to tell the compiler what radius and area are.
- Radius and area are declared as double-precision variables in the program. The reserved word double indicates that radius and area are stored in the computer as double-precision floating-point numbers.

Identifiers

- Variables, constants, methods, classes, and packages are named using special symbols called identifiers in programming languages.
- The guidelines for naming identifiers are as follows:
    - An identifier is a string of letters, underscores (_), digits, and dollar signs ($) composed of letters, digits, underscores (_), and dollar signs ($).
    - An identifier must begin with a letter, underscore (_), or dollar symbol ($). It must not start with a digit.
    - A reserved term cannot be used as an identifier. (For a list of reserved terms, see Appendix A, "Java Keywords").
    - An identifier can't be true, false, or null at the same time.
    - The length of an identifier is irrelevant.

- Examples of legal IDs include $4, ComputeArea, area, radius, and showMessageDialog.
- Examples of illegal IDs are 4A and d+8.
- Because Java is case-sensitive, the letters A and an are distinct identifiers.

Variables

- Variables are used to store data in a program.
- We may use the following code to calculate the area for various radii:

Example:

```
// Calculate the first area radius
area = radius*radius*3.14159;
System.out.println("Area " + area +
" for radius "+radius);

// Calculate the second area radius
area = radius*radius*3.14159;
System.out.println("Area " + area +
" for radius "+radius);
```

Variable Declaration

- Variables are used to represent specific types of data.
- To use a variable, we must first define it by telling the compiler its name and the kind of data it represents. Variable declaration is the term for this.

- Declaring a variable instructs the compiler to allocate memory to the variable depending on its data type. Variable declarations can be seen in the following examples:

```
int a;
char c;
radius r
```

- If two variables are of the same type, they can be defined as a single variable using the short-hand form: var1, var2,..., varn are datatypes.

Assignments Expressions and Assignment Statements

- We may use an assignment statement to assign a value to a variable after it has been declared. The assignment statement has the following syntax:

```
variable = expr;
x = 3;  // Assign 3 to x;
radius = 2.0;  // Assign 2.0 to radius;
d = 'D';  // Assign 'D' to d;
```

- We may use the variable in the expression as well.

```
y = y + 3;  // the result of y + 3 is
assigned to x;
```

- The variable name must be on the left of the assignment operator to assign a value to it.

```
4 = y would be wrong.
```

- An assignment statement in Java can also be considered an expression that evaluates the value being assigned to the variable on the left-hand side of the assignment operator. As a result, an assignment statement is also known as an assignment expression, and the assignment operator is the symbol =.

```
System.out.println(y = 6); which is
equivalent to
y = 6;
System.out.println(y);
The following statement is also
correct: a = b = c = 2;
which is equivalent to c = 2; b = c;
a = b;
```

In a Single Step, Declare and Initialize Variables

```
int y = 1;
This is equivalent to the next two
statements: int y;
y = 1;
// shorthand form to declare and initialize
vars of same type
int a = 1, b = 2;
```

Constants

- A variable's value may vary throughout the program's execution, while a constant represents permanent data that never changes.

- The following is the syntax for declaring a constant:

Syntax:

```
final datatype CONSTANTNAME = VALUE;
```

Example:

```
final double pi = 3.14; // Declare a
constant
final int size = 6;
```

- Before a constant can be used, it must be declared and initialized. We can't modify the value of a constant after it's been declared. Constants are named in uppercase by convention.

Example:

```
//Area.Java: calculate the area of a
circle
public class Area  // Class Name
{
public static void main(String[] args)
// Main Method signature
{
final double pi = 3.14;   // declare a
constant double radius = 10;  // assign
a radius

// Compute area
double area = radius * radius * pi;
```

```
// Results display
System.out.println("Area for the circle
" + radius + " is " + area);
}
}
```

Numerical Data Types and Operations

- Every data type has a set of values that it can hold. According to the data type of each variable or constant, the compiler allocates memory space.
- Six numeric types are available in Java: four for integers and two for floating-point values.

Name	**Storage Size**	**Range**
byte	8 bits	-2^7 (-128) to $2^7 - 1$ (127)
short	16 bits	-2^{15} (-32768) to $2^{15} - 1$ (32767)
int	32 bits	-2^{32} (-2147483648) to 2^{31} −1(2147483647)
long	64 bits	-2^{63} to 2^{63} - 1
float	32 bits	6 – 7 significant digits of accuracy
double	64 bits	14 – 15 significant digits of accuracy

Numerical Operators

+, -, *, /, and %

5/2	yields	an integer	2
5.0/2	yields	a double value	2.5
-5/2	yields	an integer value	-2
-5.0/2	yields	a double value	-2.5
-7 % 3	yields	-1	
-12 % 4	yields	0	
-26 % -8	yields	-2	
20 % -13	yields	7	

Numeric Literals

- A literal is a constant value[1] that appears in a program on its own. In the following statements, for example, 64 and 2.0 are literals:

```
int a = 64;
double d = 2.0;
```

Integer Literals

- As long as an integer literal fits within an integer variable, it can be assigned to it. If the literal were too large for the variable to contain, a compilation error would result.
- The expression byte a = 10000, for example, would result in a compilation error since 10000 cannot be stored in a byte type variable.
- The value of an integer literal is presumed to be in the range of -231 (-2147483648) to 231–1. (2147483647).
- Append the letter L or one to an integer literal of the long type to signify it (lowercase L).
- The following code, for example, displays the decimal value 65535 for the hexadecimal integer FFFF.

Example:

```
System.out.println(0xFFFF);
```

[1] https://www.geeksforgeeks.org/literals-in-java/, GeeksforGeeks

Floating-Point Literals

- A decimal point is used in floating-point literals. A floating-point literal is interpreted as a double type value by default.
- For example, 2.0 is a double value rather than a float number.
- A float is created by attaching the letter f or F to a number, while a double is created by appending the letter d or D to a number.
- For a float number, use 201.2f or 201.2F, and for a double number, use 201.2d or 201.2D.
- Values of the double type are more precise than those of the float type.

  Example:

  ```
  System.out.println("value is " + 2.0 /
  5.0);
  Output will be value is 0.4
  ```

Notations in Scientist

Scientific notation may be used to specify floating-point literals; for example, 1.23456e+2, which is the same as 1.23456e2, is identical to 123.456, while 1.23456e-2 is equivalent to 0.0123456. An exponent is represented by the letter E (or e), written in lowercase or uppercase.

Arithmetic Expressions

- Consider, the arithmetic expression (5 + 4 * x)/4 – 10 * (y - 4)*(a + b + c)/x + 8 *(5/x + (8 + x)/y)
- The operators included in parenthesis are evaluated first.

- Parentheses can be nested, in which case the inner parentheses' expression is evaluated first.
- After that, the multiplication, division, and remainder operators are used. From left to right, the order of operations is followed. Subtraction and addition are done last.

Shortcut Operators

Operator	Example	Equivalent
+=	i+=8	i = i+8
-=	f-=8.0	f = f-8.0
*=	i*=8	i = i*8
/=	i/=8	i = i/8
%=	i%=8	i = i%8

- For incrementing and decrementing a variable by one, there are two more shortcut operators. ++ and — are the two operators. They can be written as prefixes or suffixes.

Suffix	x++; // Same as x = x + 1;
Prefix	++x; // Same as x = x + 1;
Suffix	x--; // Same as x = x - 1;
Prefix	--x; // Same as x = x - 1;

Operators for increment and decrement:

- **++var (pre-increment):** After incrementing var by one, the expression (++var) evaluates the new value in var.
- **var++ (post-increment):** The expression (var++) returns the original value of var and increases it by one.

- **<u>–var</u> (pre-decrement):** After decrementing var by one, the expression (—var) evaluates the new value in var.
- **<u>.var–</u> (post-decrement):** The expression (var–) evaluates the *original* value in <u>var</u> and decrements <u>var</u> by 1.

Example:

```
double a = 2.0; double b = 7.0;
double d = a-- + (++b);
```

- Using the increment and decrement operators shorten expressions but makes them more complicated and challenging to interpret. Avoid using these operators in expressions like int h = ++i + i, which alter several variables or the same variable numerous times.

Numeric Type Conversions

- Take a look at the following statements:

```
byte i = 300;
long k = i*4+5;
double d = i*4.1+k/3;
```

Are these statements correct?

- When executing a binary operation with two operands of different kinds, Java transforms the operand automatically according to the following rules:

1. If one of the operands is double, the other is double as well.
2. If one of the operands is float, the other is changed to float as well.

3. If one of the operands is long, the other gets changed to long as well.
4. If neither operand is int, both operands are changed to int.

- As a result, the 1/2 result is 0, and the 1.0/2 result is 0.5.
- Typecasting is the process of converting one data type's value into another data type's value.
- Casting a variable with a limited range to a variable of a wider range is referred to as enlarging a type without explicit casting; a type can be automatically widened.
- Casting a variable of a type having an extensive range to a variable with a smaller range is referred to as a narrowing. The process of narrowing a type must be done explicitly.
- Caution: Casting is required if we're assigning a value to a variable with a narrower type range. If casting is not utilized in instances like these, a compilation fault will result. Casting should be used with caution. Inaccurate findings might come from lost data.

```
float f = (float) 11.1;
 int i = (int) g;

double c = 3.5;
int i =(int)c;  // c is not changed
System.out.println("c " + c + " i " +
i);
```

```
Implicit casting
double c = 4;  // type widening

Explicit casting
int i = (int)4.0; // type narrowing

What's wrong?
int i = 1;
byte b = i;  // Error because explicit
casting required
```

Character Data Type and Operations

- The character data type char represents a single character.
- A single quote mark surrounds a character literal.

```
char letter = 'D'; / Assigns the letter
D to the char variable (ASCII)
char numChar = '6'; / Numeric character
6 is assigned to numChar
```

- Use caution when using a literal string since it must be wrapped in quotation marks. A single character contained in single quotation marks is referred to as a character literal. So “D” is a character, and “D” is a string.

Unicode and ASCII Code

- Unicode is a 16-bit encoding method developed by the Unicode Consortium to facilitate the exchange, processing, and display of written texts in various languages throughout the world.

- Unicode requires two bytes, precoded by u and represented in four hexadecimal numbers ranging from "u0000" to "uFFFF." The word "coffee" is translated into Chinese using two characters; for example. "u5496u5561" is the Unicode for these two characters.

```
char letter = '\u0041'; (Unicode è
16-bit encoding scheme)
char numChar = '\u0034'; (Unicode)
```

- Because FFFF is 65535 in hexadecimal, Unicode can represent 65,536 characters.
- Most computers use the (ASCII) American Standard Code for Information Interchange is a 7-bit encoding method representing all capital and lowercase letters, numbers, punctuation marks, and control characters.
- ASCII code ranges from "u0000" to "u007F," equivalent to 128 ASCII characters.
- **Note:** To retrieve the next or previous Unicode character, use the increment and decrement operators on char variables.
- The following statements, for example, show character c:

```
char ch = 'c';
System.out.println(++ch);
```

Special Character Escape Sequences

Description	Escape Sequence	Unicode
Backspace	\b	\u0008
Tab	\t	\u0009
Linefeed	\n	\u000A
Carriage return	\r	\u000D
Backslash	\\	\u005C
Single Quote	\'	\u0027
Double Quote	\"	\u0022

- Let's say we wish to publish the following message:

  ```
  he remarked, "Java is entertaining."
  ```

  The following is an example of how to write the statement:

  ```
  System.out.println(he remarked\ "Java
  is entertaining\")
  ```

Casting between Char and Numeric Types

- Any numeric type may be cast into a char and vice versa.
- If the result of a casting fits inside the target variable, implicit casting can be utilized. Otherwise, precise casting is required.
- The char operands can be used with any numeric operation.
- If the other operand is a number or a character, the char operand is converted to a number.

- The character is concatenated with the string if the other operand is a string.

```
int i = 'a'; // Same as int i =
(int)'a'; // (int) a is 97

char c = 99; // Same as char c =
(char)99;
```

String Type

- The char type represents a single character. Use the String data type to express a string of characters.

  Example:

  ```
  String message = "Welcome to Java";
  ```

- Like the System class and JOptionPane classes, the String class is a predefined class in the Java library.

- The String data type isn't a primitive data type. A reference type is what it's called. Any Java class can be used as a variable's reference type.

String Concatenation

- If one operand is a string, the plus sign (+) is the concatenation operator.

- If one operand is a non-string (for example, a number), it is transformed into a string and concatenated with the other string.

Example:

```
String message = "Welcome" + "to " +
"MyJava";
message += " and Java is fun"; //
message = Welcome to MyJava and Java
is fun
```

Converting a String to a Number

String to Integers Conversion

- The input returned from the input dialog box is a string. If we enter a numeric value such as 123, it returns "123." To obtain the input as a number, we have to convert a string into a number.
- To convert a string into an int value, we can use the static parseInt method in the Integer class as follows:

  ```
  int val = Integer.parseInt(intString);
  ```

  Where intString is a numeric string such as "132."

Strings to Doubles Conversion

- We may use the static parseDouble function in the Double class to convert a string to a double value as follows:

  ```
  double val = Double.
  parseDouble(doubleString);
  ```

  where doubleString is a numeric string such as "132.42."

Using the Console for Input

Using a Scanner to Getting Information

- Creation of Scanner object

```
Scanner scan = new Scanner(System.in);
```

- To get a string, byte, short, int, long, float, double, or boolean value, use the methods next (), nextByte (), nextShort (), nextInt (), nextLong (), nextFloat (), nextDouble (), or nextBoolean (). As an example,

```
System.out.print("Enter double value: ");
Scanner scan = new Scanner(System.in);
double db = scan.nextDouble( );
```

Source Code:

```
import java.util.Scanner;

public class testscan {
public static void main(String args[])
{

// Create a Scanner
System.out.print("Enter an integer: ");
 int value = scanner.nextInt();
System.out.println("Entered the integer
" + value);

// user to enter a value
System.out.print("Enter double value: ");
double dvalue = scanner.nextDouble();
System.out.println("Entered the double
value "+ dvalue);
```

```
// user to enter a string
System.out.print("Enter string without
space: ");
String str = scanner.next();
System.out.println("You entered the
string " + str);
}
}
```

Documentation and Programming Style

- Programming Style is concerned with the appearance of programs.
- A program's documentation is the collection of explanatory notes and comments.
- As essential as code is the programming style and documentation. They make it simple to follow the programs.

Appropriate Comments and Style of Comments

- At the start of the program, provide a description that explains what the program does, its significant features, supporting data structures, and distinctive approaches it employs.
- Include comments that introduce each critical step and clarify anything challenging to read in an extensive program.
- Make comments brief, so they don't clog up the show or make it difficult to follow.
- The program's start includes your name, class section, date, instructor, and a brief description.

Conventions for Naming

- For variables and methods, use lowercase. If a name is made up of many words, concatenate them all into one, lowercase the first word, then uppercase the first letter of each succeeding word. showInputDialog, for example.
- Pick names that are both significant and descriptive. The variables radius and area, as well as the procedure computeArea, are examples.
- In the class name, capitalize the initial letter of each word. Take, for example, the ComputeArea class.
- In constants, capitalize all letters. Consider the constant Process Integration (PI).
- Don't use names for classes that are already in the Java library. The constants PI and MAX_VALUE, for example.

Spacing Lines and Proper Indentation

- Indentation is used to show how the program's components or statements are connected structurally.
- Indent each subcomponent two spaces more than the structure into which it is nested.
- On both sides of a binary operator, use a single space.

```
boolean bn = 4 + 3 * 3 > 5 * (3 + 4)
```

- Use a blank line to divide code parts.

Block Styles

- A block is a collection of statements encircled by braces. For braces, use the end-of-line or next-line style.

New-line style

```
public class Test
{
public static void
main(String[] args)
{
System.out.println("Block
Styles");
}
}
```

End-of-line style

```
public class Test {
public static void
main(String[] args) {
System.out.println("Block
Styles");
}
}
```

Errors in Programming

Syntax Problems "Compilation Errors"

- Syntax errors or compilation mistakes are errors that occur during compilation.
- Syntax errors are caused by mistakes in code composition, such as mistyping a term, deleting essential punctuation, or using an opening brace without a closing brace.

- These mistakes are easy to see since the compiler informs you of their location and causes.

  Example:

```
public class ShowErrors {
public static void main(String[] args)
{ i = 20;
System.out.println(i+5);
}
}
```

Runtime Errors

- Runtime mistakes are errors that cause a program to crash unexpectedly.
- Runtime errors arise when the environment identifies an action that cannot be completed while executing the program.
- An input error, for example, happens when a user inputs an unexpected input value that the software is unable to handle. The application should remind the user to enter the right kind of data to avoid input mistakes.
- Division by zero is another example of a run-time mistake.

```
public class ShowErrors {
public static void main(String[] args)
{ int i = 1 / 0;
}
}
```

Logic Errors

- When a program doesn't work as it should, it's called a logic error.
- For example, the program is free of syntax and run-time problems, but it fails to output the expected result.

```
// Program contains a logic error
import javax.swing.JOptionPane;

public class ShowErrors
{
public static void main(String[] args)
{
// Add number1 to number2
int number1 = 3; int number2 = 3;
number2 += number1 + number2;
System.out.println("number2 " + number2);
}
}
```

Debugging

- Finding logic mistakes, or "bugs," is a difficult task, and the process of locating and resolving problems is known as debugging.
- You may either hand-trace the program or use print statements to display the values of the variables or the program's execution sequence.
- The most effective way for debugging an extensive, complex program is to utilize a debugger tool.

CONTROL STRUCTURES

The Java compiler runs the code from beginning to end. The statements in the code are executed in the order that they occur in the code.[2] Java, on the other hand, Statements that can be used to regulate the flow of Java code are available. Control flow statements are what they're called. It is one of Java's most important aspects since it ensures a smooth program flow.

There are three different sorts of control flow statements in Java.

1. Decision Making statements
    - if statements
    - switch statement
2. Loop statements
    - do-while loop
    - while loop
    - for loop
    - for-each loop
3. Jump statements
    - break statement
    - continue statement

[2] https://www.javatpoint.com/control-flow-in-java, javaTpoint

- **Decision-Making statements:** Making decision in programming is comparable to making decisions in real life. We also come into instances in programming when we want a specific block of code to be run when a particular condition is met.

  Regulate statements are used in programming languages to control a program's execution flow based on specific criteria. These are used to force the execution flow to progress and branch in response to changes in a program's state.

  - If
    - Simple if
    - if-else
    - nested-if
    - if-else-if
  - switch-case

If

if Statement

The if statement is the simplest way to make a choice. It is used to determine if a statement or a block of statements will be executed or not, i.e., if a condition is true, a block of statements will be performed; otherwise, it will not.

Syntax:

```
if(condition)
{
statement; //it executes when condition
is true
}
```

Example:

```
public class stud {
public static void main(String[] args)
{
int x = 13;
int y = 11;
if(x+y > 15) {
System.out.println("x + y is greater
than 15");
}
}
}
```

Output:

```
x + y is greater than 15
```

if-else Statement

The if-else statement is an expansion of the if-statement that employs the else block of code. If the if-condition block is assessed as false, the else block is performed.

Syntax:

```
if(condition)
{
statement one; //executes when
condition is true
}
else
{
statement two; //executes when the
condition is false
}
```

Example:

```
public class Stud
{
public static void main(String[] args) {
int x = 13;
int y = 11;
if(x+y < 12) {
System.out.println("x + y is less than
12");
}
else
{
System.out.println("x + y is greater
than 17");
}
}
}
```

Output:

```
x + y is greater than 17
```

if-else-if Ladder

The if-else-if statement is made up of an if statement and many else-if statements. In other words, a decision tree is created by a sequence of if-else statements in which the computer can enter the block of code when the condition is true. At the conclusion of the chain, we may also define an else statement.

Syntax:

```
if(condition 1)
{
statement 1; //executes when condition
1 is true
```

```
}
else if(condition 2)
{
statement 2; //executes when condition
2 is true
}
else
{
statement 2; //when all the conditions
are false then executes
}
```

Example:

```
public class main
{
  public static void main(String[]
args) {

    int num = 0;

    // checks
    if (num > 0) {
      System.out.println(" positive
number ");
    }

    // checks
    else if (num < 0) {
      System.out.println(" negative
number ");
    }

    // if both condition is false
```

```
    else
{
      System.out.println("Number is 0 ");
    }
  }
}
```

Output:

```
Number is 0
```

Nested if Statement

The if statement can include an if or if-else statement within another if or else-if statement in nested if-statements.

Syntax:

```
if(condition 1) {
statement 1; //executes when condition
1 is true
if(condition 2) {
statement 2; //executes when condition
2 is true
}
else{
statement 2; //executes when condition
2 is false
}
}
```

Example:

```
public class main {
  public static void main(String[] args)
{
```

```
    // declaring double variables type
    Double d1 = -2.0, d2 = 5.5, d3 =
-6.3, large;

    // checks if d1 is greater than or
equal to d2
    if (d1 >= d2) {

      // if...else statement inside
the if block
      if (d1 >= d3) {
        large = d1;
      }

      else {
        large = d3;
      }
    } else {

      // if..else statement inside
else block
      // checks if d2 is greater than
or equal to d3
      if (d2 >= d3)
{
        large = d2;
      }

      else {
        large = d3;
      }
    }
```

```
        System.out.println("Largest Number:
" + large);
    }
}
```

Output:

```
Largest Number: 5.5
```

Switch Statement

Switch statements in Java are comparable to if-else-else statements. A single case is performed based on the variable being switched in the switch statement, which comprises numerous blocks of code called cases. Instead of using if-else-if statements, you may use the switch statement. It also improves the program's readability.

There are a few things to keep in mind with the switch statement:

- Integers, shorts, bytes, chars, and enumerations can all be used as case variables. Since Java version 7, the string type has also been supported.
- Cases are unique and cannot be duplicated.
- When the value of the expression does not meet any of the circumstances, the default statement is used. It's a decision.
- When the condition is met, the break statement ends the switch block.
- If it is not utilized, the following case is executed.

- We must remember that the case expression will be the same type as the variable when employing switch statements. It will, however, be a constant value.

Syntax:

```
switch (expression)
{
    case val1:
     statement1;
     break;
     .
     .
     .
    case valN:
     statementN;
     break;
    default:
    default statement;
}
```

Example:

```
public class Main {
  public static void main(String[]
args) {
    int day = 5;
    switch (day)
{
      case 1:
        System.out.println("monday");
        break;
      case 2:
        System.out.println("tuesday");
        break;
      case 3:
```

```
                System.out.println("wednesday");
                break;
            case 4:
                System.out.println("thursday");
                break;
            case 5:
                System.out.println("friday");
                break;
            case 6:
                System.out.println("saturday");
                break;
            case 7:
                System.out.println("sunday");
                break;
        }
    }
}
```

Output:

```
friday
```

We must remember that the case expression will be the same type as the variable when employing switch statements. It will, however, be a constant value. Only int, string, and enum type variables are allowed to be used with this option.

Loop Statements

In programming, we may need to run a code several times while a condition evaluates to true. Loop statements, on the other hand, are used to repeat the set of instructions. The execution of the set of instructions is contingent on a specific circumstance.[3]

[3] https://www.sitesbay.com/java/java-looping-statement, Sitesbay.com

In Java, there are three different forms of loops that all work in the same way. However, there are variations in their syntax and the time it takes to check for conditions.

1. for and for each loop
2. while loop
3. do-while loop

Let's take a look at each loop statement individually.

1. **For loop:** In java, for loop is similar to C and C++. In a single line of code, we may initialize the loop variable, verify the condition, and increment/decrement. We only use the for loop when we know exactly how many times we want to run a code block.

   Syntax:

   ```
   for(initialization, condition,
   increment/decrement)
   {
   //statements block
   }
   ```

   Example:

   ```
   public class Cal
   {
   public static void main(String[] args)
   {
   int sum = 0;
   for(int c = 1; c<=10; c++) {
   ```

```
sum = sum + c;
}
System.out.println("sum of 10 natural
numbers: " + sum);
}
}
```

Output:

```
The sum of first 10 natural numbers is 55
```

2. **for-each loop:** Java provides an enhanced for loop to traverse the data structures like array or collection. In the for-each loop, we don't need to update the loop variable. The syntax to use the for-each loop in java is given below.

Syntax:

```
for(data_type var : array_name){
//statement
}
```

Example:

```
public class Cal {
public static void main(String[] args)
{
String[] names = {"C","C++","Java","Ja
vaScript"};
System.out.println("Printing the
content:\n");
for(String name:names) {
System.out.println(name);
}
}
}
```

Output:

```
Printing the content:
C
C++
Java
JavaScript
```

3. **while loop:** The while loop may also be used to iterate over a set of statements repeatedly. We should use a while loop if we don't know the number of iterations ahead of time. In contrast to the loop, the initialization and increment/decrement do not happen inside the while loop statement.

   Because the condition is verified at the start of the loop, it's also known as the entry-controlled loop. The loop body will be run if the condition is true; else, the statements after the loop will be executed.

Syntax:

```
while(condition){
//looping statements
}
```

Example:

```
public class Cal
{
public static void main(String[]
args)
{
int c = 0;
```

```
System.out.println("Print list of 10
even numbers \n");
while(c<=10) {
System.out.println(c);
c = c + 2;
}
}
}
```

Output:

```
Print list of 10 even numbers

0
2
4
6
8
10
```

4. **do-while loop:** After running the loop statements, the do-while loop verifies the condition at the conclusion of the loop. We can use a do-while loop when the number of iterations is unknown, and we need to run the loop at least once.

   Because the condition is not verified in advance, it is also known as the exit-controlled loop. The do-while loop's syntax is seen below.

   Syntax:

```
do
{
//statement
} while (condition);
```

Example:

```
public class Cal
{
public static void main(String[] args)
{
// Auto-generated method stub
int c = 0;
System.out.println("Print the list of
10 even numbers \n");
do {
System.out.println(c);
c = c + 2;
}while(c<=10);
}
}
```

Output:

```
Print the list of 10 even numbers
0
2
4
6
8
10
```

Jump Statements

Jump statements are used to move the program's control to particular statements. Jump statements, in other words, move the execution control to another portion of the program. In Java, there are two sorts of jump statements:

1. Break
2. Continue

1. **Break statement:** As its name implies, the break statement is used to interrupt the program's current flow and transfer control to the following statement outside of a loop or switch statement. In the event of a nested loop, however, it just breaks the inner loop.

   In a Java program, the break statement cannot be used on its own; it must be put inside a loop or switch statement.

   Example:

```
public class breakex
{
public static void main(String[] args)
{
// Auto-generated method
for(int c = 0; c<= 10; c++)
{
System.out.println(c);
if(c==8)
{
break;
}
}
}
}
```

   Output:

```
0
1
2
3
4
```

```
5
6
7
8
```

2. **Continue statement:** In comparison to the break statement, the continue statement does not break the loop; instead, it skips the specified section of the loop and immediately goes to the next iteration of the loop.

Example:

```
public class ContinueEx
{

public static void main(String[] args)
{
// Auto-generated method

for(int c = 0; c<= 3; c++)
{

for (int d = c; d<=6; d++)
{

if(d == 5)
{
continue;
}
System.out.println(d);
}
}
}
}
```

Output:

```
0
1
2
3
4
6
1
2
3
4
6
2
3
4
6
3
4
6
```

A GUIDE TO JAVA PACKAGES

As the name implies, a package is a collection of classes, interfaces, and other packages. Packages are used in Java to arrange classes and interfaces. In Java, there are built-in packages and packages that we may construct (also known as a user-defined package).

We have numerous built-in packages in Java; for example, when we need user input, we import the following package:

Syntax:

```
import java.util.Scanner
```

- Java is the top-level package, whereas util is a sub-package.
- The scanner is a class included in the util package.

Let's look at the benefits of utilizing a package before we look at how to make one in Java.

The following are some of the benefits of using packages in Java:

- **Reusability:** When working on a Java project, we frequently notice a few things that we repeat in our code. You may build such things in classes inside a package and then import that package and use the class anytime you need to execute the same operation.
- **Better Organization:** In big java projects with hundreds of classes, it is usually necessary to arrange similar types of classes into a meaningful package name to better organize your project and find and utilize what you need quickly increasing efficiency.
- **Name Conflicts:** We may create two classes with the same name in distinct packages; thus, we can utilize packages to avoid name collisions.

Package Kinds in Java

There are two sorts of packages in Java.

1. **User-defined package:** The package we make is referred to as a "user-defined package."
2. **Built-in package:** Built-in packages are pre-defined packages such as java.io.*, java.lang.*, and so on.

Example 1: Java packages

Within the package letcalculate, we've built a class called Calculator. Declare the package name in the first sentence of your program to create a class inside it. There may only be one package declaration per class.

```
package letcalculate;

public class Calc {
   public int add(int x, int y){
  return x+y;
   }
   public static void main(String
args[]){
  Calc obj = new Calc();
  System.out.println(obj.add(20, 30));
   }
}
```

Let's look at how to use this package in another program.

```
import letcalculate.Calc;
public class Demo{
   public static void main(String
args[]){
  Calc obj = new Calc();
  System.out.println(obj.add(200,
300));
   }
}
```

We've imported the package letcalculate to utilize the Calculator class. We've named the package letcalculate in the above application. The calculator is the only class that this imports. However, if the package letcalculate has many classes, we may import it to utilize all of the package's classes.

```
import letcalculate.*;
```

Example 2: While importing another package, create a class within the package.

Both package declaration and package import should be the initial statement in your Java application, as we've seen. Let's look at the sequence in which we should create a class within a package while importing another package.

```
//Declaring a package
package anotherpackage;
//importing a package
import letcalculate.Calc;
public class Example{
   public static void main(String
args[]){
  Calc obj = new Calc();
  System.out.println(obj.add(200,
300));
   }
}
```

Example 3: When importing a class, use the fully qualified name.

To eliminate the import statement, we can use a fully qualified name.

Example:

Calc.java

```
package letcalculate;
public class Calc {
    public int add(int x, int y){
  return x+y;
    }
    public static void main(String
args[]){
  Calc obj = new Calc();
  System.out.println(obj.add(20, 30));
    }
}
```

Exp.java

```
//package declaration
package anotherpackage;
public class Exp{
    public static void main(String
args[]){
          //Using fully qualified name
instead of import
  letcalculate.Calc obj =
    new letcalculate.Calc();
  System.out.println(obj.add(200, 300));
    }
}
```

Instead of importing the package, we created its object using the entire qualified name such as package_name.class_name in the Exp class.

Subpackages in Java

A subpackage is a package that is contained within another package. For example, if a package is created within the letcalculate package, it is referred to as a subpackage.

Let's pretend we've added another package to letcalculate, and the name of the subpackage is multiply. So, if we build a class in this subpackage, it should start with the following package declaration:

Syntax:

```
package letcalculate.multiply;
```

Multiplication.java

Example:

```
package letmecalculate.multiply;
public class Multipli {
  int product(int x, int y){
    return x*y;
  }
}
```

If we want to utilize this Multiplication class, we must either import the package as follows:

Syntax:

```
import letcalculate.multiply;
```

This chapter taught us how to install Java on a Windows computer and set up Environment Variables. We also learnt how to set up an IDE and about the internal workings of a Java application. In addition, we learnt about Java's primitive classes and operations. Later on, we discussed control structures and loops, as well as their many forms. Finally, we learnt about Java packages through several examples.

CHAPTER 3

Object-Oriented Programming

IN THIS CHAPTER

- ➢ Java OOP's Concept
- ➢ Java Classes and Objects
- ➢ Access Modifiers and Constructors
- ➢ Interfaces
- ➢ A Guide to Inheritance
- ➢ Java Enums

In the previous chapter, we covered a complete guide to installing and executing Java and the primitives. In addition, we learned about Java's control structures and various packages. In this chapter, we'll learn about object-oriented

DOI: 10.1201/9781003229063-3

programming, including what classes and objects are, as well as modifiers and interfaces. We'll also go over inheritance and enums in detail.

JAVA OBJECT-ORIENTED PROGRAMMINGS (OOPs) CONCEPTS

Inheritance, data binding, polymorphism, and other notions are all part of the Object-Oriented Programming (OOP) paradigm.

The OOP language Simula is regarded as the first. An utterly OOP language is a programming paradigm in which everything is represented as an object.

Smalltalk is widely regarded as the first OOP language.

OOPs

A real-world entity such as a pen, chair, table, computer, watch, and so on is referred to as an object. OOP is a programming approach or paradigm that uses classes and objects to create a program. It makes software development and maintenance more accessible by introducing the following concepts:

- Object
- Class
- Inheritance
- Polymorphism
- Abstraction
- Encapsulation

Aside from these ideas, there are a few more words used in Object-Oriented design:

- Coupling
- Cohesion
- Association
- Aggregation
- Composition

Object

An object is any entity that has a state and behavior. For instance, a pen, table, chair, bicycle, and so forth. It might be physical or intellectual.

An instance of a class can be declared as an Object. An object has an address and takes up memory. Even if they are ignorant of one other's data or code, objects can communicate. The only thing that matters is the type of message accepted and the type of response that the objects provide.

A dog, for example, is an object since it has states such as color, name, breed, and actions such as waving the tail, barking, and eating.

Class

The term "class" refers to a group of things. It's a logical thing.

A class may alternatively be thought of as a blueprint from which an individual object can be created. Class doesn't take up any room.

Inheritance

When one object inherits all of its parent object's properties and behaviors, this is known as inheritance. It allows for code reuse. It's utilized to achieve polymorphism at runtime.

Polymorphism

Polymorphism refers to the notion that the same task may be completed in a number of different ways. To persuade a consumer in a new way, draw a form, triangle, rectangle, or another object.

To accomplish polymorphism in Java, we employ method overloading and method overriding.

Another example is to say anything; for example, a cat meows, a dog barks woofs, and so on.

Abstraction

Abstraction is the process of concealing internal information while displaying functionality. We don't know the internal processes of a phone call, for example. To accomplish abstraction in Java, we utilize abstract classes and interfaces.

Encapsulation

Encapsulation is the process of binding (or wrapping) code and data together into a single entity. A capsule, for example, is coated with several medications.

Encapsulation is demonstrated through a Java class. Because all data members are private in a Java bean, it is a fully enclosed class.

Coupling

Another class's knowledge, information, or reliance is referred to as coupling. It occurs when students are aware of one another's existence. There is strong coupling when a class possesses the detailed information of another class. To display the visibility level of a class, method, or field in Java, we utilize the private, protected, and public modifiers. Because there is no real implementation, you may use interfaces for the lesser coupling.

Cohesion

The degree of a component that performs a single well-defined duty is referred to as cohesion. A very coherent technique is used to complete a single well-defined job. The work will be divided into different sections using the weakly cohesive approach. Because it contains I/O-related classes and interfaces, the java.io package is relatively coherent. The java.util package, on the other hand, is a disjointed collection of classes and interfaces.

Association

The link between the items is represented through association. One item can be linked to one or more objects in this case. There are four different types of object associations:

1. One to One
2. One to Many
3. Many to One, and
4. Many to Many

Aggregation

Aggregation is a technique for achieving Association. Aggregation refers to a connection in which one object's state includes other things. It symbolizes a shaky connection between items. In Java, it's known as a has-a connection. The is-a connection, for example, is represented by inheritance. It's yet another way to recycle items.

Composition

Association can also be achieved through composition. The composition denotes a connection in which one item includes other objects as part of its state. The enclosing item and the dependent object have a strong connection. It is the state in which the items that make up the container have no independent existence. If you delete the parent object, it will be followed by the deletion of all child objects.

In Java, What Is the Difference between an Object and a Class?

In OOP, a Class is a blueprint or prototype that specifies the variables and methods (functions) that are shared by all Java Objects of a particular kind.[1]

In OOPs, an object is a class specimen. Software objects are frequently used to simulate real-world things seen in daily life.

Advantages of OOPs over Procedure-Oriented Programming Languages

- OOPs make development and maintenance more accessible, but procedure-oriented programming languages are difficult to handle as project sizes expand.

[1] https://www.guru99.com/java-oops-class-objects.html, Guru99

- Data hiding is provided by OOPs, whereas global data may be accessed from anywhere in a procedure-oriented programming language.
- OOPs significantly improve the capacity to replicate real-world events. If we use the OOP language, we may give a solution to a real-world problem.

Java Naming Conventions

A naming convention in Java is a set of rules to follow when naming identifiers such as classes, packages, variables, constants, methods, etc.

It is not, however, obligatory to follow. As a result, it is referred to as a convention rather than a regulation. Several Java groups, including Sun Microsystems and Netscape, have recommended these norms.

According to the Java naming convention, the Java programming language's classes, interfaces, packages, methods, and fields are all named. If you don't follow these rules, you could end up with some ambiguous or incorrect code.

Benefits of Java Naming Conventions

Using standard Java naming conventions makes your code easier to read for both you and other programmers. The readability of a Java program is crucial. It means that less effort is spent deciphering what the code accomplishes.

The following are the fundamental rules that any identifier must follow:

- There must be no white spaces in the name.
- Special characters such as & (ampersand), $(dollar), and _ (underscore) should not be used in the name.

Class

- The class should begin with an uppercase letter.
- Color, Button, System, Thread, and so on are examples of nouns.
- Instead of acronyms, use relevant words.

Example:

```
public class Emp
{
//code
}
```

Interface

- The interface should begin with an uppercase letter.
- An adjective like Runnable, Remote, or Action Listener should be used.
- Instead of acronyms, use relevant words.

Example:

```
interface Print
{
//code
}
```

Method

- It should begin with a lowercase letter.
- It must be a verb like main(), print(), or println ().

- If the name has more than one word, begin with a lowercase letter and then an uppercase letter, such as actionPerformed ().

  Example:

```
class Emp
{
//method
void draw()
{
//code
}
}
```

Variable

- It should begin with a lowercase letter, for example, id or name.
- It should not begin with special characters such as (&) ampersand, ($) dollar, and underscore (_).
- If the name has more than one word, begin with a lowercase letter and then an uppercase letter, such as firstName and lastName.
- Avoid using one-character variables such as a, b, and c.

  Example:

```
class Emp
{
//variable
int name;
//code
}
```

Package

- It should start with a lowercase letter, like java or lang.
- If the name comprises multiple terms, such as java.util or java.lang, the dots (.) should be used to separate them.

Example:

```
package com.javatpoint;
class Emp
{
//code
}
```

Constant

- It should be written in capital letters, such as RED.
- If the name comprises several words, an underscore (_) should separate them, such as MAX PRIORITY.
- It may have digits but not as the first letter.

Example:

```
class Emp
{
//constant
 static final int min_age = 13
//code
}
```

Java Objects and Classes

We create a program utilizing objects and classes in OOP.

In Java, an object is both a physical and a logical thing, whereas a class is simply a logical entity.

In Java, What Is an Object?

An object is a physical item with a state and activity, such as a chair, a bike, a marker, a pen, a table, a car, and so on. It might be either physical or logical (tangible and intangible). The financial system is an example of an intangible thing.

There are three qualities of an object:

1. **State:** The data (value) of an object is represented by its state.
2. **Behavior:** The behavior (functionality) of an object, such as deposit, withdrawal, and so on, is characterized by the term behavior.
3. **Identify:** A unique ID is generally used to represent an object's identification. The value of the ID is hidden from the outside user. The Java Virtual Machine (JVM), on the other hand, uses it internally to identify each object uniquely.

Pen, for instance, is an object. Reynolds is its name, and the color white is its condition. It's accustomed to writing, so that's what it does.

A class's instance is an object. A class is a blueprint or template from which things are built. As a result, an object is a class's instance.

In Java, What Is a Class?

A class is a collection of objects with similar characteristics. It's a blueprint or template from which things are made. It's a logical thing. It can't be a physical problem.

In Java, a class can have the following elements:

- Fields
- Methods
- Constructors
- Blocks
- Nested class and interface

Syntax:

```
class <classname>
{
     field;
     method;
}
```

In Java: Instance Variable

In Java, an instance variable is a variable that is generated within a class but outside of a method. At compilation time, memory is not allocated to instance variables. When an object or instance is formed, it obtains memory at runtime. As a result, it's referred to as an instance variable.

In Java: Method

A method in Java is similar to a function in that it is used to expose an object's behavior.

The method has an advantage:

- Reusability of code
- Optimization of the code

In Java: New Keyword

At runtime, the new keyword is used to allocate memory. In the Heap memory region, all things receive memory.

Example of an Object and a Class: Main within the Class: We've constructed a Student class in this example, with two data members: id and name. The object of the Student class is created using the new keyword, and the object's value is printed.

Inside the class, we're going to create a main() function.

Source Code:

```
// Class Declaration
class dog
{
     String breed;
     int age;
     String color;

     // method 1
     public String getinfo() {
          return ("Breed: "+breed+"
Age:"+age+" color: "+color);
     }
}
public class Exec{
     public static void main(String[]
args) {
          dog bulldog = new dog();
          bulldog.breed=" bulldog ";
          bulldog.age=3;
          bulldog.color="brown";
          System.out.println(bulldog.
getinfo());
     }
}
```

Output:

```
Breed: bulldog Age:3 color: brown
```

There are three ways to initialize an object in java.

1. By reference variable
2. By method
3. By constructor

1. **By reference variable:** When we construct a class object (instance), heap memory space is reserved. Let's look at an example to assist us to comprehend.[2]

   Syntax:

   ```
   demo d1 = new demo();
   ```

   We construct a Pointing element, also known as a Reference variable, which simply indicates where the Object is located.

   Identifying the Reference Variable

   - A reference variable is a type of the variable used to point to an object or a set of data.
   - In Java, reference types include classes, interfaces, arrays, enumerations, and annotations. In Java, reference variables are used to store the objects/values of reference types.

[2] https://www.geeksforgeeks.org/reference-variable-in-java/, geeksforgeeks

- A null value can be stored in a reference variable. If no object is given to a reference variable, it will default to storing a null value.
- Using dot syntax, you may access object members using a reference variable.

Syntax:

```
<reference variablename >.<instance
variablename / methodname>
```

Example:

```
// Java program to explain reference
variable in java

import java.io.*;
class demo {
  int y = 20;
  int display()
  {
    System.out.println("y = " + y);
    return 0;
  }
}

class Main {
  public static void main(String[] args)
  {
    demo dm1 = new demo();

    System.out.println(dm1);

    System.out.println(dm1.display());
  }
}
```

Output:

```
demo@6a6824be
y = 20
0
```

2. **Initialization through the method:** In this example, we're creating two Student objects and using the insertRecord method to set their values. By using the displayInformation() function, we may see the status (data) of the objects.

Example:

```
class student{
 int rollnum;
 String name;
 void insertRecord(int rn, String num)
{
  rollnum=rn;
  name=num;
 }
 void displayInformation()
{
System.out.println(rollnum+" "+name);
}
}
public class test
{
 public static void main(String args[])
{
  student s1=new student();
  student s2=new student();
  s1.insertRecord(11,"Kirti");
```

```
    s2.insertRecord(22,"Adii");
    s1.displayInformation();
    s2.displayInformation();
  }
}
```

Output:

```
11 Kirti
22 Adii
```

3. **Initialization through a constructor**

Example:

```
class Emp
{
    int id;
    String name;
    float salary;
    void insert(int d, String nm, float
sr) {
        id=d;
        name=nm;
        salary=sr;
    }
   void display()
{
System.out.println(id+" "+name+"
"+salary);
}
}
public class Test
{
```

```
public static void main(String[]
args)
{
     Emp e1=new Emp();
     Emp e2=new Emp ();
     Emp e3=new Emp();
     e1.insert(11,"aman",65000);
     e2.insert(12,"isha",35000);
     e3.insert(13,"nitin",25000);
     e1.display();
     e2.display();
     e3.display();
}
}
```

Output:

```
11 aman 65000.0
12 isha 35000.0
13 nitin 25000.0
```

What Are the Many Methods of Creating an Object in Java?

In Java, there are several ways to construct an object. They are as follows:

- By new keyword
- By newInstance() method
- By clone() method
- By deserialization
- By factory method

Anonymous Object

The term "anonymous" simply means "without a name." An anonymous object does not have a reference. It can only be used when creating an item.

An anonymous object is an excellent choice if you need to utilize it once. Consider the following scenario:

```
new Calc();
```

Using a reference to call a method:

```
Calc c=new Calc();
c.fact(6);
```

Using an anonymous object to call a method:

```
new Calc().fact(6);
```

Example:

```
public class Calc
{
 void fact(int  n){
  int fact=2;
  for(int c=2;c<=n;c++){
   fact=fact*c;
  }
 System.out.println("factorial is
"+fact);
}
public static void main(String args[])
{
 new Calc().fact(6);
}
}
```

Output:

```
factorial is 1440
```

Creating many objects with a single type:
As with primitives, we may generate several objects with a single type.

Primitive variable initialization:

```
int c=20, d=30;
```

Reference variables are set up as follows:

```
rectangle rn1=new rectangle(), rn2=new
rectangle();
```

Example:

```
class rectangle
{
int len;
 int wid;
 void insert(int ln,int wd)
{
  len=ln;
  wid=wd;
 }
 void calculateArea()
{
System.out.println(len*wid);}
}
class TestRectangle2
```

```
{
 public static void main(String args[])
{
 rectangle rn1=new rectangle(),
 rn2=new rectangle();//creating two
objects
  rn1.insert(12,6);
  rn2.insert(4,15);
  rn1.calculateArea();
  rn2.calculateArea();
}
}
```

CONSTRUCTORS

A function in Java is a piece of code that is comparable to a method. When a new instance of the class is created, this method is invoked. Memory for the object is allocated in the memory when the constructor is called. It's a unique kind of method that's used to set up an object.

At least one constructor is invoked every time an object is created with the new() keyword. If no constructor is provided in the class, it uses the default constructor. In this situation, the Java compiler automatically creates a default constructor.

In Java, there are two types of constructors: no-arg and parameterized constructors.

It's called a constructor because it creates the values when the object is created. A constructor does not have to be written for a class. It's because if the class doesn't have one, the Java compiler will produce one.

Rules for Writing a Java Constructor:
Two rules specify the constructor.

- The constructor's name must match the class's name.
- There must be no explicit return type in a constructor.
- An abstract, static, final, and synchronized Java constructor is not possible.

Constructors in Java are divided into two categories:

- Default constructor (no-arg constructor)
- Parameterized constructor

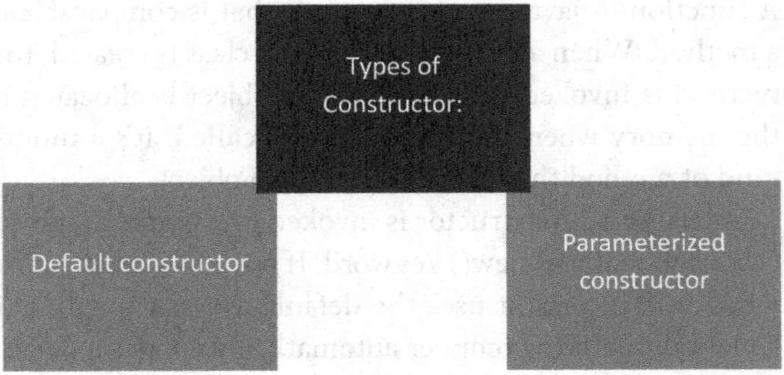

Default Constructor

A constructor is classified "Default Constructor" when it doesn't have any parameter.

Syntax:

```
<classname> (){}
```

Example:

```
// Program to create & call default
constructor
class bike{
// default constructor
bike()
{
System.out.println("created bike ");
}
//main method
public static void main(String args[])
{
//calling a default constructor
bike bk=new bike();
}
}
```

Output:

```
created bike
```

What Is a Default Constructor's Purpose?

The default constructor gives the object default values like 0, null, and so on, depending on the type.

Example:

```
public class student
{
int id;
String name;
// display the value
void display()
```

```
{
System.out.println(id+" "+name);
}
public static void main(String args[])
{
//create objects
student st1=new student();
student st2=new student();
//displaying values
st1.display();
st2.display();
}
}
```

Output:

```
0 null
0 null
```

Explanation: In the above class, we are not making any constructor, so the compiler gives you a default constructor. Here 0 and invalid qualities are given default constructor.

Parameterized Constructor

A constructor which has a particular number of parameters is known as a parameterized constructor.

Why Utilize the Parameterized Constructor?

The parameterized constructor is utilized to give various qualities to distinct objects. In any case, we can provide a similar value moreover.

Example:

In this model, we have made the constructor of the Student class that has two boundaries. We can have quite a few limitations in the constructor.

```
public class student
{
    int id;
    String name;
    // parameterized constructor
    student(int c,String nm)
{
    id = c;
    name = nm;
    }
    // display values
    void display()
{
System.out.println(id+" "+name);
}

    public static void main(String args[])
{
    // object creation and passing values
    student st1 = new student(11,"Kiran");
    student st2 = new student(22,"Arav");
    //calling method
    st1.display();
    st2.display();
  }
}
```

Output:

```
11 Kiran
22 Arav
```

Constructor Overloading

A constructor is similar to a method in Java, except it does not have a return type. It, like Java methods, can be overloaded.

In Java, constructor overloading is the practice of having many constructors with different argument lists. They're organized such that each a constructor does something distinct. The compiler distinguishes them based on the number of arguments in the list and their kinds.

Example:

```
// program for overload constructors
public class student
{
    int id;
    String name;
    int age;
    // two arg constructor creation
    student(int c,String nm)
{
    id = c;
    name = nm;
    }
    // three arg constructor creation
    student(int c,String nm,int ag)
{
    id = c;
    name = nm;
    age=ag;
    }
    void display()
{
System.out.println(id+" "+name+" "+age);
}
```

```
      public static void main(String
  args[])
  {
      student st1 = new
  student(11,"Kiran");
      student st2 = new
  student(22,"Arav",25);
      st1.display();
      st2.display();
    }
  }
```

Output:

```
11 Kiran 0
22 Arav 25
```

In Java, What Is the Difference between a Constructor and a Method?

The distinctions between constructors and methods are many. Below is a list of them.

Java Constructor	Java Method
An object's state is initialized using a constructor.	A method is used to reveal an object's behavior.
There can't be a return type in a constructor.	A return type is required for a method.
Implicitly, the constructor is called.	The method is explicitly called.
If a class lacks a compiler, the Java compiler offers a default compiler.	In any instance, the compiler does not supply the method.
The constructor must have the same name as the class.	The method name and the class name may or may not be the same.

Copy Constructor in Java

Java doesn't have a copy constructor. However, using the copy f constructor in C++, we may copy data from one object to another.

In Java, there are several methods for copying the values of one object to another. They are as follows:

- By constructor
- By assigning values from one item to another.
- By using the Object class's clone() function.

Example:

```
public class student
{
    int id;
    String name;
    //constructor to initialize
integer and string
    student(int c,String nm)
{
    id = c;
    name = nm;
    }
    //constructor to initialize object
    student(student st)
{
    id = st.id;
    name =st.name;
    }
    void display()
{
System.out.println(id+" "+name);}
```

```
    public static void main(String
args[]){
    student st1 = new
student(11,"Kiran");
    student st2 = new student(st1);
    st1.display();
    st2.display();
   }
}
```

Output:

```
11 Kiran
11 Kiran
```

Copying Values without Constructor

We may replicate the values of one object into another without using a constructor by assigning the object's values to another object. There is no need to build the constructor in this situation.

Example:

```
public class student
{
    int id;
    String name;
    student(int c,String nm)
{
    id = c;
    name = nm;
    }
    student(){}
    void display()
```

```
{
System.out.println(id+" "+name);
}

    public static void main(String args[])
{
    student st1 = new student(11,"Kiran");
    student st2 = new student();
    st2.id=st1.id;
    st2.name=st1.name;
    st1.display();
    st2.display();
   }
}
```

Output:

```
11 Kiran
11 Kiran
```

STATIC KEYWORD

In Java, the static keyword is mainly used for memory management. With variables, methods, blocks, and nested classes, we may use the static keyword. The static keyword refers to a class rather than a specific instance of that class.

The static can take the form of:

- Variable
- Method
- Block
- Nested class

1. **Static variable in Java:** A static variable has been declared as static.

   The static variable can be used to refer to a property that is shared by all objects (but not unique to each object), such as an employee's business name or a student's college name.

   The static variable is only stored in memory once in the class area when the class is loaded.

   Static variables provide the following advantages: They conserve memory in your application (i.e., it saves memory).

   Without a static variable, it is possible to comprehend the situation.

```
class students
{
     int roll_no;
     String name;
     String college="TTS";
}
```

   If the college has 300 students, all instance data members will receive memory each time the object is created. Because each student has a unique roll number and name, an instance data member is helpful in this situation. The term "college" denotes a quality that all things share. This field will only get the memory once if we make it static.

   Example:

```
class students
{
   int roll_no; //instancevariable
```

```
    String name;
    static String college ="TTS"; //
staticvariable
    //constructor
    students(int rn, String nm){
    roll_no = rn;
    name = nm;
    }
    // display values methods
    void display ()
{
System.out.println(roll_no+" "+name+"
"+college);
}
}
//Test class
public class Test
{
 public static void main(String
args[])
{
 students st1 = new
students(11,"Kiran");
 students st2 = new
students(22,"Arya");
 st1.display();
 st2.display();
  }
}
```

Output:

```
11 Kiran TTS
22 Arya TTS
```

Counter Program with No Static Variables

We've established a count instance variable in this example, which is increased in the constructor. Each object will have a copy of the instance variable since it receives memory at the moment of object creation. It will not reflect other objects if it is increased. As a result, the count variable will have the value 1 for each item.

Example:

```
public class counter
{
int counts=0; // When an instance is
created, it will acquire memory each time.

counter()
{
counts++; // value incrementing
System.out.println(counts);
}

public static void main(String args[])
{
// objects creating
counter c1=new counter();
counter c2=new counter();
counter c3=new counter();
}
}
```

Output:

```
1
1
1
```

Counter Program with Static Variables

As previously stated, a static variable will only get memory once; nevertheless, if any object changes the value of the static variable, it will maintain its value.

Example:

```
Public class counter
{
static int counts=0; // will only
receive memory once and keep its value

counter()
{
counts++; //incrementing value
System.out.println(counts);
}

public static void main(String args[])
{
//creating objects
counter c1=new counter();
counter c2=new counter();
counter c3=new counter();
}
}
```

Output:

```
1
2
3
```

2. **Static method in Java:** A static method is created by using the static keyword with any method.

A class's static method, rather than the class's object, belongs to the class.

A static method can be called without having to create a class instance.

A static method can access and alter the value of a static data member.

Example:

```
class student
{
      int roll_no;
      String name;
      static String college = "TTS";
      // To modify the value of a static
variable, use the static method.
      static void change()
{
      college = "TTDIT";
      }
      // initialize the variable
      student(int rn, String nm)
{
      roll_no = rn;
      name = nm;
      }
      // display values method
      void display()
{
System.out.println(roll_no+" "+name+"
"+college);
}
}
//Test class
public class Test
```

```
{
    public static void main(String
args[])
{
    student.change();  //change method
calling
    // objects creating
    student st1 = new
student(11,"Kiran");
    student st2 = new
student(22,"Arav");
    student st3 = new
student(33,"Sonali");
    // display method calling
    st1.display();
    st2.display();
    st3.display();
    }
}
```

Output:

```
11 Kiran TTDIT
22 Arav TTDIT
33 Sonali TTDIT
```

Static method constraints:

There are two primary constraints for the static method. They are as follows:

- A static method cannot utilize non-static data members or directly invoke non-static methods.
- In a static environment, this and super aren't allowed to be used.

Example:

```
class B{
 int x=30;//non static

 public static void main(String
args[])
{
  System.out.println(x);
 }
}
```

Output:

```
Compile Time Error
```

3. **Static Block in Java**

 - The static data member is initialized using the Java static block.
 - It is called before the main function when the class is loaded.

Example:

```
public class B2
{
  static{System.out.println("invoked
static block");
}
  public static void main(String args[])
{
   System.out.println("Hello");
  }
}
```

Output:

```
invoked static block
Hello
```

IN JAVA, "THIS" KEYWORD

"This" keyword in Java can be used in a variety of ways. This is a reference variable in Java that points to the current object.

The following is an example of how to use the Java keyword:

This keyword is used in six different ways in Java:

1. "this" may be used to refer to the current instance variable of a class.
2. "this" may be used to invoke the method of the current class.
3. "this()" can be used to invoke the constructor call of the current class.
4. In the method call, "this" can be provided as an argument.
5. "this" can be given to the constructor call as an argument.
6. "this" may be used to get the current instance of the class from a method.

1. **this: to refer to the current instance variable of the class:** This keyword can be used to refer to the existing instance variable of a class. If there is any misunderstanding between the instance variables and arguments, this keyword resolves the ambiguity.

   Without this term, it is impossible to comprehend the situation.

Let's look at an example to see what happens if we don't utilize this keyword:

Example:

```
class student
{
int roll_no;
String name;
float fees;
student(int roll_no,String name,float
fees)
{
roll_no= roll_no;
name=name;
fees=fees;
}
void display()
{
System.out.println(roll_no+" "+name+"
"+fees);
}
}
public class Test
{
public static void main(String args[])
{
student st1=new
student(11,"ankita",4500);
student st2=new
student(12,"sunita",5000);
st1.display();
st2.display();
}
}
```

Output:

```
0 null 0.0
0 null 0.0
```

Parameters and instance variables are the same in the example above. As a result, we use this term to distinguish between local and instance variables.

This keyword can be used to solve the above problem:

```
class student
{
int roll_no;
String name;
float fees;
student(int roll_no,String name,float
fees)
{
this.roll_no=roll_no;
this.name=name;
this.fees=fees;
}
void display()
{
System.out.println(roll_no+" "+name+"
"+fees);}
}

public class Test
{
public static void main(String args[])
{
student st1=new
student(11,"ankita",7000);
```

```
student st2=new
student(12,"sunita",9000);
st1.display();
st2.display();
}
}
```

Output:

```
11 ankita 7000.0
12 sunita 9000.0
```

There is no need to use this keyword if local and instance variables are distinct, like in the following program:

This keyword is not necessary for this program.

```
class student
{
int roll_no;
String name;
float fees;
student(int rn,String nm,float fs)
{
roll_no=rn;
name=nm;
fees=fs;
}
void display()
{
System.out.println(roll_no+" "+name+"
"+fees);
}
}
```

```
public class Test
{
public static void main(String args[])
{
student st1=new
student(11,"ankita",4000);
student st2=new
student(12,"sunita",5000);
st1.display();
st2.display();
}
}
```

Output:

```
11 ankita 4000.0
12 sunita 5000.0
```

2. **this: to call the current class method:** "this" keyword can be used to call a method in the current class. If you don't use the "this" keyword, the compiler will add it when you call the method. Let's look at an example.

Example:

```
class B
{
void x()
{
System.out.println("hello x");
}
void y()
{
System.out.println("hello y");
//x(); //same as this.x()
```

```
this.x();
}
}
public class Test
{
public static void main(String args[])
{
B b=new B();
b.y();
}
}
```

Output:

```
hello y
hello x
```

3. **this(): to call the constructor of the current class:** The current class can be called using this() constructor call. Its purpose is to allow the constructor to be reused. To put it another way, it's utilized to link constructors.

Using a parameterized constructor to call the default constructor:

Example:

```
class B
{
B()
{
System.out.println("hello b");}
B(int y){
this();
```

```
System.out.println(y);
}
}
public class Test
{
public static void main(String args[])
{
B b=new B(20);
}
}
```

Output:

```
hello b
20
```

Using the default constructor to call the parameterized constructor:

Example:

```
class B
{
B()
{
System.out.println("hello b");}
B(int y)
{
this();
System.out.println(y);
}
}
public class Test
{
public static void main(String args[])
```

```
{
B b=new B(20);
}
}
```

Output:

```
hello b
20
```

4. **this() constructor call real usage:** To reuse the constructor from the constructor, use this() constructor call. It is used for constructor chaining and maintains the chain between the constructors.

   Example:

```
class student
{
int roll_no;
String names,courses;
float fees;
student(int roll_no,String names,String
courses)
{
this.roll_no=roll_no;
this.names=names;
this.courses=courses;
}
student(int roll_no,String names,String
courses,float fees)
{
this(roll_no,names,courses); //reusing
constructor
this.fees=fees;
}
```

```
void display()
{
System.out.println(roll_no+" "+names+"
"+courses+" "+fees);
}
}
public class Test
{
public static void main(String args[])
{
student st1=new
student(11,"ankita","java");
student st2=new student(12,"sunita","j
ava",7000);
st1.display();
st2.display();
}}
```

Output:

```
11 ankita java 0.0
12 sunita java 7000.0
```

5. **this: to be passed as an argument to the method:** "this" keyword can also be used as an argument in a method. It is mainly used in event management. Let's look at an example:

Example:

```
public class D2
{
  void b(D2 obj)
{
  System.out.println("method invoked");
  }
```

```
  void c()
{
  b(this);
  }
  public static void main(String
args[]){
  D2 d1 = new D2();
  d1.c();
  }
}
```

Output:

```
method invoked
```

6. **this: to use in the constructor call as a parameter:** "this" keyword can also be sent to the constructor. It comes in handy when we need to utilize the same object in numerous classes. Let's look at an example:

Example:

```
class C
{
  D4 obj;
  C(D4 obj)
{
    this.obj=obj;
  }
  void display(){
    System.out.println(obj.data); //
using D4 class data member
  }
}
```

```
public class D4{
  int data=20;
  D4(){
   C c=new C(this);
   c.display();
  }
  public static void main(String
args[]){
   D4 a=new D4();
  }
}
```

Output:

```
20
```

7. **"this" keyword may be used to get the current instance of a class:** "this" keyword can be returned as a statement from the method. In this situation, the method's return type must be the class type (non-primitive). Let's look at an example:

Syntax:

```
returntype methodname()
{
return this;
}
```

Example:

```
class B
{
B getB()
{
```

```
return this;
}
void msg()
{
System.out.println("Hello");
}
}
public class Test
{
public static void main(String args[])
{
new B().getB().msg();
}
}
```

Output:

```
Hello
```

JAVA ENUM'S

In a programming language, enumerations are used to express a set of named constants. The four suits in a deck of playing cards, for example, might be four enumerators named Club, Diamond, Heart, and Spade, all of which belong to the enumerated type Suit. Natural enumerated types are another example (like the planets, days of the week, colors, directions, etc.).

Enums are used when all potential values are known at compile-time, such as menu options, rounding modes, command line settings, and so on. The set of constants in an enum type does not have to be fixed at all times.[3] Enums

[3] https://docs.oracle.com/javase/tutorial/java/javaOO/enum.html, Oracle

are represented in Java by the enum data type. Enums in Java is more powerful than enums in C/C++. We may also include variables, methods, and constructors in Java. Enum's primary goal is to allow us to design our data types.

In Java, an enum is declared as follows:

- Enum declaration is possible both outside and inside a Class, but not inside a Method.

Example 1:

```
// enum example where the enum is
declared outside a class

enum colors
{
  BLUE, YELLOW, ORANGE;
}

public class test1
{
  // Driver method
  public static void main(String[]
args)
  {
    colors cr1 = colors.ORANGE;
    System.out.println(cr1);
  }
}
```

Output:

```
ORANGE
```

Example 2:

```
// declaration of enum inside a class

public class test1
{
  enum colors
  {
    BLUE, YELLOW, ORANGE;
  }

  // Driver method
  public static void main(String[] args)
  {
    colors cr1 = colors.ORANGE;
    System.out.println(cr1);
  }
}
```

Output:

```
ORANGE
```

- The first line should be a list of constants, followed by methods, variables, and constructors inside the enum.
- Constants should be named with full capital letters, according to Java naming standards.

Example:

```
//Java program to demonstrate working
on enum

import java.util.Scanner;
```

```
// Enum class
enum Days
{
  MONDAY, TUESDAY, WEDNESDAY,
  THURSDAY, FRIDAY, SATURDAY, SUNDAY;
}

public class test1
{
  Days days;

  // Constructors
  public test1(Days days)
  {
    this.days = days;
  }

  // Prints
  public void dayIsLike()
  {
    switch (days)
    {
    case TUESDAY:
      System.out.println("Tuesday is
bad.");
      break;
    case THURSDAY:
      System.out.println("Thursday
are better.");
      break;
    case FRIDAY:
    case SUNDAY:
      System.out.println("Weekends
best.");
      break;
```

```
      default:
         System.out.println("Midweek
so-so.");
         break;
      }
   }

   // Driver method
   public static void main(String[] args)
   {
     String st = "TUESDAY";
     test1 ts1 = new test1(Days.
valueOf(st));
     ts1.dayIsLike();
   }
}
```

Output:

```
Tuesday is bad.
```

- Every enum constant is public static final by default. We may use the enum Name to access it because it is static. We can't make child enums since it's final.
- The main() function can be declared inside the enum. As a result, we may use the Command Prompt to call enum.

Inheritance and Enumeration

- Java.lang is implicitly extended by all enums.
- Enum class. Because in Java, a class can only extend one parent, an enum can't extend anything else.

- In java.lang, the function toString() is overridden.
- Enum class that returns the name of an enum constant.
- Many interfaces may be implemented with enum.

Methods values(), ordinal(), and function valueOf()

- These methods may be found in the java.lang.enum.
- The values() function of an enum may be used to return all of the values in the enum.
- In enums, the order is crucial. Each enum constant index may be determined using the ordinal() function, much like an array index.
- If an enum constant for the supplied string valueof() exists, the function returns it.

Example:

```
//Demonstrate working of values(),
ordinal() and valueOf()
enum colors
{
  BLUE, YELLOW, ORANGE;
}

public class test1
{
  public static void main(String[]
args)
  {
    // values() calling
    colors arr[] = colors.values();
```

```
        // with loop enum
        for (colors colr : arr)
        {

          System.out.println(colr + " at
    index "
                    + colr.ordinal());
        }

      // Using the function valueOf()
    returns a Color object with the
    specified constant.

        System.out.println(colors.
    valueOf("ORANGE"));

      }
    }
```

Output:

```
BLUE at index 0
YELLOW at index 1
ORANGE at index 2
ORANGE
```

Constructor and Enum

- A constructor can be included in an enum, and it is run independently for each enum constant when the enum class is loaded.
- We can't explicitly build enum objects; therefore, we can't call the enum constructor directly.

Enumeration and Methods

- Both concrete and abstract methods can be found in an enum. If an enum class has an abstract method, it must be implemented by each instance of the enum class.

Example:

```
// enums can have constructor and
concrete methods, as seen in this
program.

enum colors
{
  ORANGE, GREEN, RED;

  // for each constant enum constructor
called separately
  private colors()
  {
    System.out.println("Constructor
called: " +
    this.toString());
  }

  public void colorInfo()
  {
    System.out.println("Color
Universal");
  }
}

public class test1
{
```

```
  // Driver method
  public static void main(String[]
args)
  {
    colors cr1 = colors.ORANGE;
    System.out.println(cr1);
    cr1.colorInfo();
  }
}
```

Output:

```
Constructor called: ORANGE
Constructor called: GREEN
Constructor called: RED
ORANGE
Color Universal
```

In this chapter, we learned about OOPs concepts such as java objects and classes and how to use modifiers and constructors in Java. In addition, we learned what interfaces are and a complete tutorial on inheritance and enums in Java.

CHAPTER 4

Creating and Using Java Strims

IN THIS CHAPTER

- ➢ Introductory to String in Java
- ➢ Comparing Strings
- ➢ Java String Conversions

In Chapters 1 to 3, we covered Object-Oriented Programming (OOPs) and classes and objects, as well as access modifiers, constructors, and interfaces. Moreover, we discussed guidance to inheritance and java enums. In this chapter, we will learn about the complete introduction to strings and the string comparisons and conversions.

DOI: 10.1201/9781003229063-4

A BEGINNER'S GUIDE TO STRINGS

It is a collection of char values represented by an object. A character array works in the same way as a Java string does. Consider the following scenario: "hello java" is a string containing a sequence of characters 'h', 'e', 'l', 'l', 'o', 'j', 'a', 'v', and 'a'.

In Java, double quotes are used to denote a string. As an example,

```
// string creation
String type = " hello Java ";
```

The Java String class has several methods for working with strings, including compare(), concat(), equals(), split(), length(), replace(), compareTo(), intern(), substring(), and so on.

Serializable, Comparable, and CharSequence interfaces are implemented by the java.lang.String class.

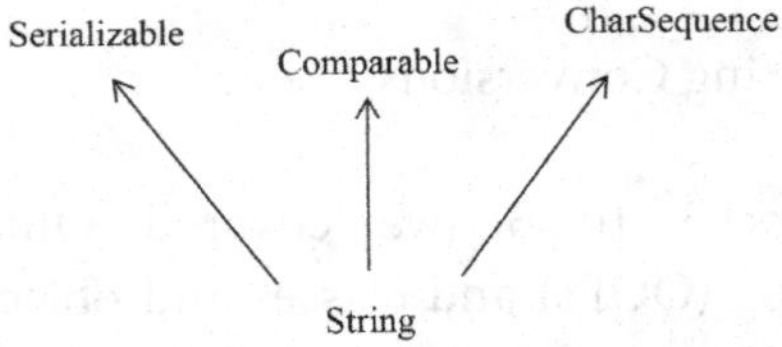

Interface for CharSequence

To represent a series of characters, the CharSequence interface is utilized. It is implemented by the String, StringBuffer, and StringBuilder classes. This indicates that these three classes can be used to produce strings in Java.[1]

[1] https://www.javatpoint.com/java-string, javaTpoint

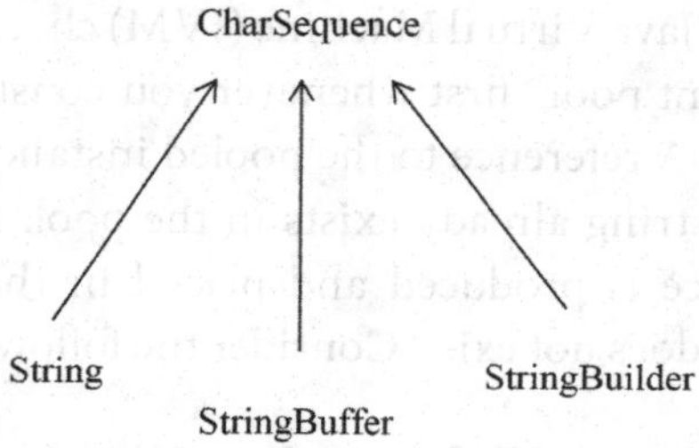

The Java String is immutable, meaning it cannot be modified. A new instance is produced every time we alter a string. You may use the StringBuffer and StringBuilder classes to create mutable strings.

Immutable strings will be discussed later. Let's start by learning what a String is in Java and how to make a String object.

In Java, What Is a String?

A string, in general, is a collection of characters, whereas a Java object is a string of characters. The java.lang package. A string object is created using the String class.

What Is the Best Way to Make a String Object?

String objects can be created in two ways:

- Using a string literal
- By using a new keyword

1. **Using a string literal:** Double quotes are used to produce a Java String literal. Consider the following scenario:

```
String s="welcome";
```

The Java Virtual Machine (JVM) checks the "string constant pool" first whenever you construct a string literal. A reference to the pooled instance is returned if the string already exists in the pool. A new string instance is produced and placed in the pool if the string does not exist. Consider the following scenario:

```
String s1="Welcome Everyone";
String s2="Welcome Everyone"; //doesn't
create a new instance
```

Only one object will be generated in the case above. First, JVM will generate a new object since it cannot locate a string object with the "Welcome Everyone" value in the constant string pool. After that, it will search the collection for the string "Welcome Everyone" and return a reference to the same instance rather than creating a new one.

Why does Java utilize the String literal concept?

To improve Java's memory efficiency (because no new objects are created if it exists already in the constant string pool).

2. **By using a new keyword**

```
String s=new String("Welcome
Everyone"); //one reference variable
and creates two objects
```

The literal "Welcome" will be stored in the constant string pool, and JVM will construct a new string object in regular (non-pool) heap memory. The variable s will be used to refer to a heap object (non-pool).

Example of String:

```
public class StringEx
{
public static void main(String
args[])
{
String st1="java program"; //by Java
string literal creating string
char chr[]={'s','t','r','i','n','g'};
String st2=new String(chr);//char array
to string convertion
String st3=new String("eg"); // Java
string by new keyword  creating
System.out.println(st1);
System.out.println(st2);
System.out.println(st3);
}}
```

Output:

```
java program
string
eg
```

The code above creates a String object from a char array. The println() function displays the String objects st1, st2, and st3 on the console.

Methods of the String Class in Java

Many useful methods for performing operations on a series of char values are available in the java.lang.String class.

No.	Method	Description
1	char charAt(int index)	For each index, it returns a char value.
2	int length()	It returns the length of a string.
3	static String format(String format, Object... args)	It returns a string that has been formatted.
4	static String format(Locale l, String format, Object... args)	It returns a formatted string in the locale specified.
5	String substring(int beginIndex)	For a specified begin index, it returns a substring.
6	String substring(int beginIndex, int endIndex)	It returns a substring for the specified begin and end indexes.
7	boolean contains(CharSequences)	After matching the sequence of char values, it returns true or false.
8	connect static Strings (CharSequence delimiter, CharSequence... elements)	It gives you a connected string as a result.
9	static String join(CharSequence delimiter, Iterable<?extends CharSequence> elements)	It gives you a connected string as a result.
10	boolean equals(Object another)	It compares the string to the provided object to see whether they are equal.
11	boolean isEmpty()	It determines if the string is empty.
12	String concat(String str)	The supplied string is concatenated.
13	String replace(char old, char new)	All occurrences of the supplied char value are replaced.
14	String replace(CharSequence old, CharSequence new)	All occurrences of the provided CharSequence are replaced.
15	static String equalsIgnoreCase(String another)	It makes a comparison with another string. It does not do a case check.

(Continued)

No.	Method	Description
16	String[] split(String regex)	It returns a split string that matches the regex pattern.
17	String[] split(String regex, int limit)	It gives you a split string that matches the regex and the limit.
18	String intern()	It returns a string that has been interned.
19	int indexOf(int ch)	It returns the index of the specified char value.
20	int indexOf(int ch, int fromIndex)	It starts with the provided index and returns the specified char value index.
21	int indexOf(String substring)	It returns the substring index that was given.
22	int indexOf(String substring, int fromIndex)	It returns the provided substring index, beginning at index.
23	String toLowerCase()	It returns a lowercase string.
24	String toLowerCase(Locale l)	It returns a lowercase string in the provided locale.
25	String toUpperCase()	It returns an uppercase string.
26	String toUpperCase(Locale l)	It returns an uppercase string in the provided locale.
27	String trim()	This string's starting and ending spaces are removed.
28	static String valueOf(int value)	It turns any type into a string. It's an approach that's been overloaded.

IMMUTABLE STRING IN JAVA

When developing any application software, a String is an inevitable type of variable. Various characteristics such as usernames, passwords, and so on are stored via string references. String objects are immutable in Java. Immutable simply means that it cannot be changed or modified.

The data or state of a String object can't be altered once it's been formed; instead, a new String object is generated.

Let's use the following example to grasp the idea of immutability better:

Example 1:

```
public class immutablestringTest
{
 public static void main(String args[])
{
   String st="Sunita";
   st.concat(" palkar "); //concat()
   System.out.println(st); //print
 }
}
```

Output:

```
Sunita
```

Example 2:

```
public class immutablestringTest
{
 public static void main(String args[])
{
   String st=" Sunita ";
   st=st.concat("palkar ");
   System.out.println(st);
 }
}
```

Output:

```
Sunita palkar
```

Why Are String Objects in Java Immutable?

The idea of a string literal is used in Java. Assume there are five reference variables, all of which relate to the same object, "Sunita." All reference variables will be impacted if one reference variable alters the value of the object. As a result, String objects in Java are immutable.

The properties of String that make String objects immutable are listed below.

1. **ClassLoader:** A String object is passed as an input to a Java ClassLoader. Consider that if the String object is changeable, the value might change, and the class intended to be loaded could change.

   The string is immutable to avoid this type of misunderstanding.
2. **Thread Security:** We don't have to worry about synchronization when sharing an item across many threads since the String object is immutable.
3. **Security:** Immutable String objects, like class loading, avoid additional problems by loading the right class. As a result, the application software becomes more secure. Consider banking software as an example. Because String objects are immutable, no intruder can change the username or password. This can improve the security of the application program.
4. **Heap Space:** String's immutability helps to keep heap memory use to a minimum. The JVM checks if the value already exists in the String pool when defining a new String object. If it already exists, the new object is given the same value. This feature helps Java to make effective use of memory space.

Why Is the String Class in Java Final?

The String class is final because no one can override the String class's methods to give the same functionality to both new and old String objects.

STRING COMPARISON

In Java, we may compare Strings based on their content and references.

It's utilized for things like authentication (by equals() method), sorting (by compareTo() method), reference matching (by == operator), etc.

In Java, there are three techniques to compare strings:

- By using the equals() method
- Using the == operator
- By using the compareTo() method

1. **Using the equals() method:** The equals() function of the String class compares the string's original content. It compares string values for equality. Two methods are available in the String class:
    - This string is compared to the provided object using public boolean equals(Object another).
    - This string is compared to another string using equalsIgnoreCase(String another), which ignores the case.

Example:

```
public class stringcomparisonTest
{
 public static void main(String args[])
{
   String st1="Sunita";
   String st2="Sunita";
   String st3=new String("Sunita");
   String st4="Saurabh";
   System.out.println(st1.equals(st2));
//true
   System.out.println(st1.equals(st3));
//true
   System.out.println(st1.equals(st4));
//false
  }
}
```

Output:

```
true
true
false
```

2. **By using == operator:** The == operator compares references rather than values.

Example:

```
public class stringcomparisonTest
{
 public static void main(String args[])
{
```

```
    String st1="Sunita";
    String st2="Sunita";
    String st3=new String("Sunita");
    System.out.println(st1==st2); //true
    System.out.println(st1==st3); //
false
 }
}
```

Output:

```
true
false
```

3. **Using compareTo() method:** The compareTo() function of the String class compares data lexicographically and returns an integer value indicating whether the first string is smaller, equal to, or larger than the second string.

   Assume that s1 and s2 are two different String objects.

   If:

   - The function returns 0 if s1 == s2
   - The function delivers a positive result if s1 > s2
   - The method returns a negative number. s1 < s2

Example:

```
public class stringcomparisonTest
{
 public static void main(String args[])
{
```

```
    String st1="Sunita";
    String st2="Sunita";
    String st3="Rita";
    System.out.println(st1.
compareTo(st2));
    System.out.println(st1.
compareTo(st3));
    System.out.println(st3.
compareTo(st1));
  }
}
```

Output:

```
0
1
-1
```

STRING CONCATENATION

String concatenation in Java creates a new String that combines several strings. In Java, there are two techniques to concatenate strings:

- By + (String concatenation) operator is used to join two strings together.
- By using the concat() function.

1. **by (+) String concatenation operator**

Example:

```
public class StringConcatenationTest
{
 public static void main(String args[])
```

```
{
   String st="Sunita"+" Palkar";
   System.out.println(st);
 }
}
```

Output:

```
Sunita Palkar
```

The above code is transformed into this by the Java compiler:

```
String st=(new StringBuilder()).
append("Sunita").append(" Palkar").
toString();
```

The StringBuilder (or StringBuffer) class and its add function are used to concatenate strings in Java. By adding the second argument to the end of the first operand, the String concatenation operator creates a new String. Not just Strings but also primitive items may be concatenated using the String concatenation operator.

Example:

```
public class StringConcatenationTest
{
 public static void main(String args[])
{
   String st=40+60+"Sunita"+30+20;
   System.out.println(st);
 }
}
```

Output:

```
100Sunita3020
```

2. **Concatenation of strings using the concat() method:** Concatenates the supplied text to the end of the current string with the String concat() function.

   Syntax:

   ```
   public String concat(String_another)
   ```

   Example:

   ```
   public class StringConcatenationTest
   {
    public static void main(String
   args[])
   {
      String st1="Sunita ";
      String st2="Palkar";
      String st3=st1.concat(st2);
      System.out.println(st3);
     }
   }
   ```

   Output:

   ```
   Sunita Palkar
   ```

There are a few more options for concatenating Strings in Java:

1. **Concatenation of strings using the StringBuilder class:** The append() function of the StringBuilder class is used to execute concatenation operations. Objects,

StringBuilder, int, char, CharSequence, boolean, float, and double inputs are all accepted by the add() function. In Java, StringBuilder is the most common and fastest method of concatenating strings. Because it is a mutable class, values saved in StringBuilder instances can be modified or altered.

Example:

```
public class Strbuild
{
    /* Code */
    public static void main(String
args[])
    {
        StringBuilder st1 = new
StringBuilder("Hello");
        StringBuilder st2 = new
StringBuilder(" Everyone");
        StringBuilder st = st1.
append(st2);
            System.out.println(st.
toString());  //result display
    }
}
```

Output:

```
Hello Everyone
```

2. **Concatenation of strings using the format() method:** The String.format() function concatenate multiple strings using format specifiers such as % and string values or objects.

Example:

```
public class Strform
{
    /* Code */
    public static void main(String
args[])
    {
        String st1 = new String("Hello");
        String st2 = new String("
Everyone");
        String st = String.
format("%s%s",st1,st2);
             System.out.println(st.
toString());
    }
}
```

Output:

```
Hello Everyone
```

3. **Concatenation of strings using the String.join() method:** The String.join() function is present in Java version 8 and all versions higher. String.join() takes two arguments: a separator and an array of String objects.

Example:

```
public class StrgJoin
{
    /* Code */
    public static void main(String
args[])
    {
        String st1 = new String("Hello");
```

```
        String st2 = new String("
Everyone");
        String st = String.
join("",st1,st2);
            System.out.println(st.
toString());  // result
    }
}
```

Output:

```
Hello Everyone
```

4. **String concatenation with the StringJoiner class:** The StringJoiner class contains all of the String.join() method's functionality. Its function constructor can optionally receive optional parameters, such as prefix and suffix, in advance.

Example:

```
public class StringJoin
{
    public static void main(String[]
args)
{
        String st = String.join("/",
"2021", "9", "29");
        System.out.println(st);
    }
}
```

Output:

```
2021/9/29
```

5. **Using Collectors.joining() method in String concatenation:** Collectors class has a joining() method that concatenates the input components in the same order in which they appear.

Example:

```
import java.util.*;
import java.util.stream.Collectors;
public class CollJoin
{
    /* Code */
    public static void main(String
args[])
    {
        List<String> liststrg = Arrays.
asList("xyx", "abc", "ghi");
        String st = liststrg.stream().
collect(Collectors.joining(", ")); //
performs
        System.out.println(st.
toString()); //Displays result
    }
}
```

Output:

```
xyx, abc, ghi
```

IN JAVA SUBSTRING

Substring, in other terms, is a subset of another String. The built-in substring() method of the Java String class extracts a substring from a specified string using the index values supplied as an argument. StartIndex is inclusive, and endIndex is exclusive when using the substring() technique.

One of two techniques can be used to extract a substring from a String object:

1. **public String substring(int startIndex):** This function returns a new String object with the substring of the given string beginning at the specified startIndex. When the startIndex is greater than the length of String or less than zero, the procedure raises an IndexOutOfBoundException.
2. **public String substring(int startIndex, int endIndex):** This method returns a new String object with the substring of the provided string from startIndex to endIndex. When the startIndex is less than zero, the startIndex is higher than the endIndex, or the endIndex is greater than the String length, the function raises an IndexOutOfBoundException.

When it comes to String:

- startIndex: inclusive.
- endIndex: exclusive.

Let's look at the code below to see how startIndex and endIndex work:

```
String st="hello everyone";
System.out.println(st.substring(1,3));
```

Example:

```
public class SubstringTest
{
 public static void main(String args[])
{
```

```
 String st="SunitaPalkar";
 System.out.println("OriginalString: "
+ st);
 System.out.println("Substringstarting
from index 5: " +st.substring(5));
 System.out.println("Substringstarting
from index 0 to 7: "+st.
substring(0,7));
 }
}
```

Output:

```
OriginalString: SunitaPalkar
Substringstarting from index 5: aPalkar
Substringstarting from index 0 to 7:
SunitaP
```

METHODS OF JAVA STRING CLASS

The java.lang.String class in Java has a variety of built-in methods for manipulating strings. We may execute String objects using these methods, such as cutting, concatenating, converting, comparing, and replacing strings.

Because everything is regarded as a String when you submit any form in a windowed, web-based, or mobile application, Java String is a powerful notion.

Let's look at some of the String class's most significant functions:

Methods toUpperCase() and toLowerCase() in Java String

This String is converted to the uppercase letter using the Java String toUpperCase() method and lowercase letter using the String toLowerCase() method.

Example:

```
public class Stringop
{
public static void main(String ar[])
{
String st="Sunita";
System.out.println(st.toUpperCase());
System.out.println(st.toLowerCase());
System.out.println(st);
}
}
```

Output:

```
SUNITA
sunita
Sunita
```

Method to Java String trim():

The trim() function of the String class removes white spaces from both before and after the String.

Example:

```
public class Stringop
{
public static void main(String ar[])
{
String st="  Sunita  ";
System.out.println(st);
System.out.println(st.trim());
}
}
```

Output:

```
  Sunita
Sunita
```

The Methods startsWith() and endsWith() in Java String

The method startsWith() determines if the String begins with the letters provided as arguments, while the method endsWith() determines if the String ends with the letters passed as arguments.

Example:

```
public class Stringop
{
public static void main(String ar[])
{
String st="Sunita";
 System.out.println(st.
startsWith("Su"));
 System.out.println(st.endsWith("a"));
}
}
```

Output:

```
true
true
```

Method to Java String charAt()

The charAt() function of the String class in Java returns a character at the provided index.

Example:

```
public class Stringop
{
public static void main(String ar[])
{
String st="Sunita";
System.out.println(st.charAt(0));
System.out.println(st.charAt(3));
}
}
```

Output:

```
S
i
```

Method to Java String length()

The length() function of the String class returns the length of the supplied String in Java.

Example:

```
public class Stringop
{
public static void main(String ar[])
{
String st="Sunita";
System.out.println(st.length());
}
}
```

Output:

```
6
```

Method to Java String intern()

The class String keeps a private pool of strings, which is initially empty.

When the intern method is used, the String from the pool is returned if it already has a String equal to this String object as determined by the equals(Object) function. Otherwise, a reference to this String object is returned, which is added to the pool.

Example:

```
public class Stringop
{
public static void main(String ar[])
{
String st=new String("Sunita");
String st2=st.intern();
System.out.println(st2);
}
}
```

Output:

```
Sunita
```

Method to Java String valueOf()

The function valueOf() of the String class converts any type into String, including int, long, float, double, boolean, char, and char array.

Example:

```
public class Stringop
{
public static void main(String ar[])
```

```
{
int b=20;
String st=String.valueOf(b);
System.out.println(st+20);
}
}
```

Output:

```
2020
```

Method to Java String replace ()

The replace() function of the String class replaces all occurrences of the first sequence of characters with the second sequence of characters.

Example:

```
public class Stringop
{
public static void main(String ar[])
{
String st1="Java programming language
and Java is a platform.";
String replaceString=st1.
replace("Java","Hello");
System.out.println(replaceString);
}
}
```

Output:

```
Hello programming language and Hello
is a platform.
```

STRINGBUFFER CLASS IN JAVA

The StringBuffer class is used to construct mutable (modifiable) String objects in Java. In Java, the StringBuffer class is similar to the String class except that it is changeable, meaning that it may be modified.

StringBuffer Class's Important Constructors

- **StringBuffer():** It produces an empty string buffer with a size of 16 by default.
- **StringBuffer(String str):** It creates a string buffer with the string given.
- **StringBuffer(int capacity):** It generates an empty string buffer with a length equal to the provided capacity.

StringBuffer's Most Important Methods

Modifier and Type	Method	Description
public synchronized StringBuffer	append(String st)	It's used to add this string to the supplied string. Append(char), append(boolean), append(int), append(float), append(double), and so on are all overloaded versions of the append() function.
public synchronized StringBuffer	insert(int offsets, String st)	Its purpose is to insert the supplied string at the defined location. Insert(int, char), insert(int, boolean), insert(int, int), insert(int, float), insert(int, double), and so on are all overloaded versions of the insert() function.

(Continued)

(Continued) StringBuffer's Most Important Methods

Modifier and Type	Method	Description
public synchronized StringBuffer	replace(int startindex, int endindex, String st)	It's used to replace a string starting at startindex and ending at endindex.
public synchronized StringBuffer	delete(int startindex, int endindex)	It's used to remove the string from the startindex and endindex given.
public synchronized StringBuffer	reverse()	It's used to turn the string around.
public int	capacity()	It's used to get the current capacity.
public void	ensureCapacity(int mincapacity)	It's used to make sure the capacity is at least as high as the specified minimum.
public char	charAt(int indexs)	It's used to get the character back at the given location.
public int	length()	It's used to get the string's length or the total amount of characters.
public String	substring(int beginindex)	It's used to get the substring from the beginindex value.
public String	substring(int beginindex, int endindex)	It's used to get the substring from the beginindex and endindex parameters.

Mutable String

Mutable Strings are strings that can be altered or modified. For generating mutable strings, the StringBuffer and StringBuilder classes are utilized.

1. **Method of StringBuffer Class append():** The append() function joins this String with the supplied input.

Example:

```
public class ExampleStringBuffer
{
public static void main(String
args[])
{
StringBuffer stb=new
StringBuffer("Hello Everyone ");
stb.append("Javapro"); //original
string is changed now
System.out.println(stb); //print Hello
Javapro
}
}
```

Output:

```
Hello Everyone Javapro
```

2. **Method to StringBuffer insert():** The insert() function replaces the provided String at the specified location with the given String.

Example:

```
public class ExampleStringBuffer
{
public static void main(String
args[])
{
StringBuffer stb=new
StringBuffer("Hello Everyone ");
```

```
stb.insert(1,"Javapro"); //original
string is changed now
System.out.println(stb);
}
}
```

Output:

```
HJavaproello Everyone
```

3. **Method to StringBuffer replace():** The replace() function replaces the provided beginIndex and endIndex with the given String.

Example:

```
Public class ExampleStringBuffer
{
public static void main(String
args[])
{
StringBuffer stb=new
StringBuffer("Hello Everyone");
stb.replace(1,3,"Javapro");
System.out.println(stb);
}
}
```

Output:

```
HJavaprolo Everyone
```

4. **Method to StringBuffer delete():** The StringBuffer class's delete() function deletes the String from the provided beginIndex to endIndex.

Example:

```
public class ExampleStringBuffer
{
public static void main(String args[])
{
StringBuffer stb=new
StringBuffer("Hello Everyone");
stb.delete(1,3);
System.out.println(stb);
}
}
```

Output:

```
Hlo Everyone
```

5. **Method to StringBuffer reverse():** The StringBuilder class's reverse() function reverses the current String.

Example:

```
public class ExampleStringBuffer
{
public static void main(String args[])
{
StringBuffer stb=new
StringBuffer("Hello Everyone");
stb.reverse();
System.out.println(stb);
}
```

Output:

```
enoyrevE olleH
```

6. **Method to StringBuffer capacity():** The StringBuffer class's capacity() function returns the buffer's current capacity. The buffer's default capacity is 16. If the number of characters exceeds the existing limit, the capacity increases by (oldcapacity*2)+2. If your current capacity is 16, for example, (16*2)+2=34.

   Example:

```
public class ExampleStringBuffer
{
public static void main(String args[])
{
StringBuffer stb=new StringBuffer();
System.out.println(stb.capacity());
stb.append("Hello Everyone");
System.out.println(stb.capacity());
stb.append("java high level language");
System.out.println(stb.capacity());
}
}
```

   Output:

```
16
16
38
```

7. **Method to StringBuffer ensureCapacity():** The StringBuffer class's ensureCapacity() function assures that the specified capacity is equal to or less than the existing capacity. It raises the capacity by (oldcapacity*2)+2 if larger than the existing capacity if your current capacity is 16, for example, (16*2)+2=34.

Example:

```
public class ExampleStringBuffer
{
public static void main(String args[])
{
StringBuffer stb=new StringBuffer();
System.out.println(stb.capacity());
stb.append("Hello Everyone");
System.out.println(stb.capacity());
stb.append("java high level language");
System.out.println(stb.capacity());
stb.ensureCapacity(20);
System.out.println(stb.capacity());
stb.ensureCapacity(40);
System.out.println(stb.capacity());
}
}
```

Output:

```
16
16
38
38
78
```

STRINGBUILDER CLASS IN JAVA

To build mutable (modifiable) Strings, the Java StringBuilder class is utilized. The StringBuilder class in Java is similar to the StringBuffer class; however, it is non-synchronized. Since Java Development Kit (JDK) 1.5, it has been accessible.[2]

[2] https://www.geeksforgeeks.org/stringbuilder-class-in-java-with-examples/, geeksforgreeks

StringBuilder's Most Important Constructors

Constructor	Description
StringBuilder()	It generates an empty string Builder with a capacity of 16 by default.
StringBuilder(String st)	With the supplied string, it produces a String Builder.
StringBuilder(int len)	It generates an empty string Builder with the length provided as capacity.

StringBuilder's Most Essential Methods

Method	Description
public StringBuilder append(String st)	It's used to add this string to the supplied string. Append(char), append(boolean), append(int), append(float), append(double), and so on are all overloaded versions of the append() function.
public StringBuilder insert(int offsets, String st)	Its purpose is to insert the supplied string at the defined location. Insert(int, char), insert(int, boolean), insert(int, int), insert(int, float), insert(int, double), and so on are all overloaded versions of the insert() function.
public StringBuilder replace(int startindex, int endindex, String st)	It's used to replace a string starting at startIndex and ending at endIndex.
public StringBuilder delete(int startindex, int endindex)	It's used to remove the string from the startIndex and endIndex given.
public StringBuilder reverse()	It's used to turn the string around.
public int capacity()	It's used to get the current capacity of the system.

(Continued)

(Continued) StringBuilder's Most Essential Methods

Method	Description
public void ensureCapacity(int mincapacity)	It's used to make sure the capacity is at least as high as the specified minimum.
public char charAt(int Index)	It's used to get the character back at the given location.
public int leng()	It's used to get the string's length or the total amount of characters.
public String substring(int beginindex)	It's used to get the substring starting at the provided beginindex.
public String substring(int beginindex, int endindex)	It's used to get the substring from the beginindex and endindex parameters.

Examples of StringBuilders

1. **Method StringBuilder append():** The append() function of the StringBuilder concatenates the provided argument with this String.

Example:

```
public class ExampleStringBuilder
{
public static void main(String args[])
{
StringBuilder stb=new
StringBuilder("Hello Everyone ");
stb.append("Javapro");
System.out.println(stb);
}
}
```

Output:

```
Hello Everyone Javapro
```

2. **Method StringBuilder insert():** The StringBuilder insert() function replaces the provided string at the specified location with this string.

Example:

```
public class ExampleStringBuilder
{
public static void main(String args[])
{
StringBuilder stb=new
StringBuilder("Hello Everyone");
stb.insert(1,"Javapro");
System.out.println(stb);
}
}
```

Output:

```
HJavaproello Everyone
```

3. **Method StringBuilder replace():** The replace() function of the StringBuilder replaces the provided string with the defined beginIndex and endIndex.

Example:

```
public class ExampleStringBuilder
{
public static void main(String args[])
{
StringBuilder stb=new
StringBuilder("Hello Everyone");
stb.replace(1,3,"Javapro");
System.out.println(stb);
}
}
```

Output:

```
HJavaprolo Everyone
```

4. **Method to StringBuilder delete():** The StringBuilder class's delete() function removes the string from the provided beginIndex to endIndex.

Example:

```
public class ExampleStringBuilder
{
public static void main(String args[])
{
StringBuilder stb=new
StringBuilder("Hello Everyone");
stb.delete(1,3);
System.out.println(stb);
}
}
```

Output:

```
Hlo Everyone
```

5. **Method to StringBuilder reverse():** The StringBuilder class's reverse() function reverses the current string.

Example:

```
public class ExampleStringBuilder
{
public static void main(String args[])
{
StringBuilder stb=new
StringBuilder("Hello Everyone");
```

```
stb.reverse();
System.out.println(stb);
}
}
```

Output:

```
enoyrevE olleH
```

6. **Method to StringBuilder capacity():** The capacity() function of the StringBuilder class returns the Builder's current ability. The Builder's default capacity is 16. If the number of characters exceeds the existing limit, the capacity increases by (oldcapacity*2)+2. If your current capacity is 16, for example, (16*2)+2=34.

Example:

```
public class ExampleStringBuilder
{
public static void main(String args[])
{
StringBuilder stb=new StringBuilder();
System.out.println(stb.capacity());
stb.append("Hello Everyone");
System.out.println(stb.capacity());
stb.append("Java high programming
language");
System.out.println(stb.capacity());
}
}
```

Output:

```
16
16
44
```

7. **Method to StringBuilder ensureCapacity():** The StringBuilder class's ensureCapacity() function guarantees that the supplied capacity is equal to or less than the existing capacity. It raises the capacity by (oldcapacity*2)+2 if larger than the existing capacity if your current capacity is 16, for example, (16*2)+2=34.

Example:

```
public class ExampleStringBuilder
{
public static void main(String
args[])
{
StringBuilder stb=new StringBuilder();
System.out.println(stb.capacity());
stb.append("Hello Everyone");
System.out.println(stb.capacity());
stb.append("Java high programming
language");
System.out.println(stb.capacity());
stb.ensureCapacity(20);
System.out.println(stb.capacity());
stb.ensureCapacity(60);
System.out.println(stb.capacity());
}
}
```

Output:

```
16
16
44
44
90
```

DIFFERENCE BETWEEN STRINGBUFFER AND STRING

String and StringBuffer are two different types of strings.

The distinctions between String and StringBuffer are many. The following is a list of the differences between String and StringBuffer:

Sr No.	String	StringBuffer
(1)	Immutability is a property of the String class.	StringBuffer is a changeable class.
(2)	When we concatenate too many strings, it takes longer and uses more memory since it produces a new instance each time.	When concatenating t strings, StringBuffer is faster and uses less memory.
(3)	The String class overrides the Object class's equals() method. As a result, the equals() function may be used to compare the contents of two strings.	The StringBuffer class does not override the Object class's equals() method.
(4)	When executing a concatenation operation, the String class is slower.	When performing concatenation operations, the StringBuffer class is quicker.
(5)	The String class is used. The pool of string constants.	StringBuffer uses heap memory.

String and StringBuffer Performance Tests

Example:

```
public class TestConcat
{
    public static String
concatWithString()
{
```

```
        String st = "Javapro";
        for (int c=0; c<10000; c++)
{
            st = st + "Tpoint";
        }
        return st;
    }
    public static String
concatWithStringBuffer()
{
        StringBuffer stb = new
StringBuffer("Javapro");
        for (int c=0; c<10000; c++){
            stb.append("Tpoint");
        }
        return stb.toString();
    }
    public static void main(String[]
args)
{
        long starttime = System.
currentTimeMillis();
        concatWithString();
        System.out.println("Concating
with String takes time: "+(System.
currentTimeMillis()-starttime)+"mts");
        starttime = System.
currentTimeMillis();
        concatWithStringBuffer();
        System.out.println("Concating
using StringBuffer takes time: "+(System.
currentTimeMillis()-starttime)+"mts");
    }
}
```

Output:

```
Concating with String takes time: 192mts
Concating using StringBuffer takes time:
2mts
```

HashCode Test for Strings and StringBuffers

As shown in the example below, when String does concatenation, it returns a new hashcode, whereas the StringBuffer class returns the same hashcode.

Example:

```
public class TestInstance
{
    public static void main(String args[])
{
        System.out.println("Test of
Hashcode String:");
        String sr="java";
        System.out.println(sr.hashCode());
        sr=sr+"tpoint";
        System.out.println(sr.hashCode());

        System.out.println("StringBuffer
Hashcode test:");
        StringBuffer stb=new
StringBuffer("javapro");
        System.out.println(stb.
hashCode());
        stb.append("tpoint");
        System.out.println(stb.
hashCode());
    }
}
```

Output:

```
Test of Hashcode String:
3254818
229541438
StringBuffer Hashcode test:
88579647
885796475
```

Difference between StringBuilder and StringBuffer?

To express a series of characters, Java provides three classes: String, StringBuffer, and StringBuilder. The string is an immutable class, whereas StringBuffer and StringBuilder are changeable classes. There are several distinctions between StringBuffer and StringBuilder. Since JDK 1.5, there has been a StringBuilder class.

The following are the distinctions between StringBuffer and StringBuilder:

No.	StringBuffer	StringBuilder
1.	StringBuffer is thread-safe since it is synchronized. It indicates that two threads cannot call StringBuffer methods at the same time.	StringBuilder is non-synchronized, which means it is not thread-safe. It indicates that two threads can call StringBuilder methods at the same time.
2.	StringBuffer is inefficient in comparison to StringBuilder.	StringBuilder outperforms StringBuffer in terms of efficiency.
3.	StringBuffer first appeared in Java 1.0.	StringBuilder first appeared in Java 1.5.

Example of StringBuffer

```
public class TestBuffer
{
    public static void main(String[]
args)
{
        StringBuffer buf=new
StringBuffer("hello everyone");
        buf.append("javapro");
        System.out.println(buf);
    }
}
```

Output:

```
hello everyonejavapro
```

Example of StringBuilder

```
public class TestBuilder
{
    public static void main(String[]
args)
{
        StringBuilder build=new
StringBuilder("hello everyone");
        build.append("javapro");
        System.out.println(build);
    }
}
```

Output:

```
hello everyonejavapro
```

HOW CAN WE MAKE AN IMMUTABLE CLASS?

String, Boolean, Byte, Short, Integer, Long, Float, Double, and other immutable classes exist. In summary, all wrapper classes, including the String class, are immutable. We may also construct immutable classes by defining final classes with final data members, as seen in the example below:

Example:

```
final class Emp
{
final String pancardnumb;
public Emp(String pancardnumb)
{
this. pancardnumb = pancardnumb;
}
public String getPancardNumber()
{
return pancardnumb;
}
}
public class Immutabledemo
{
public static void main(String ar[])
{
Emp ep = new Emp("CDE1231");
String st1 = ep.getPancardNumber();
System.out.println("Pancard number: "
+ st1);
}
}
```

Output:

```
Pancard number: CDE1231
```

The above-mentioned class is immutable because:

- The class' instance variable is final, so we cannot alter its value after creating an object.
- Because the class is final, we cannot build a subclass.
- There are no setter methods; therefore, we can't alter the value of the instance variable.

The Function toString() Method in Java

The function toString() function is available if we wish to express any object as a string.

The function toString() returns the object's string representation.

The Java compiler calls the function toString() method on the object internally when we print an object. Overriding the function toString() returns the desired output, which can be the state of an object or anything else depending on our implementation.

Benefit

We can return values from the object by overriding the function toString() function of the Object class, so we don't need to write any code.

Understanding the situation in the absence of the function toString() function:

```
public class students
{
 int roll_no;
 String names;
 String city;
```

```
 students(int roll_no, String names, String
city)
{
 this.roll_no=roll_no;
 this.names=names;
 this.city=city;
 }

 public static void main(String args[]){
   students st1=new
students(11,"Rajiv","london");
   students st2=new
students(12,"Vicky","delhi");

   System.out.println(st1);
   System.out.println(st2);
 }
}
```

Output:

```
students@7960847b
students@6a6824be
```

Printing st1 and st2 output the hashcode values of the objects, as seen in the preceding example, but we want to publish the values of these objects. Because the Java compiler invokes the function toString() method internally, overriding this method returns the supplied values. Let's look at an example to help us understand:

Java function toString() method example:

```
public class students
{
 int roll_no;
```

```
 String names;
 String city;

 students(int roll_no, String names, String
city)
{
 this.roll_no=roll_no;
 this.names=names;
 this.city=city;
 }

 public String toString()
{
  return roll_no+" "+names+" "+city;
 }
 public static void main(String args[])
{
   students st1=new students
(11,"Rajiv","ludhiana");
   students st2=new students
(12,"Vicky","noida");

   System.out.println(st1);
   System.out.println(st2);
 }
}
```

Output:

```
11 Rajiv ludhiana
12 Vicky Noida
```

In the above example, the Java compiler uses the internal function toString() method; overriding this method returns the given values of the student class's st1 and st2 objects.

Java StringTokenizer

The java.util.StringTokenizer class allows you to tokenize a String. It is a straightforward method for breaking a String. It is a Java legacy class.[3]

It does not support differentiating between integers, quoted strings, identifiers, and so on, like the StreamTokenizer class, does. In Chapter 3, we will go through the StreamTokenizer class.

The delimiters in the StringTokenizer class can be given at the time of creation or one by one to the tokens.

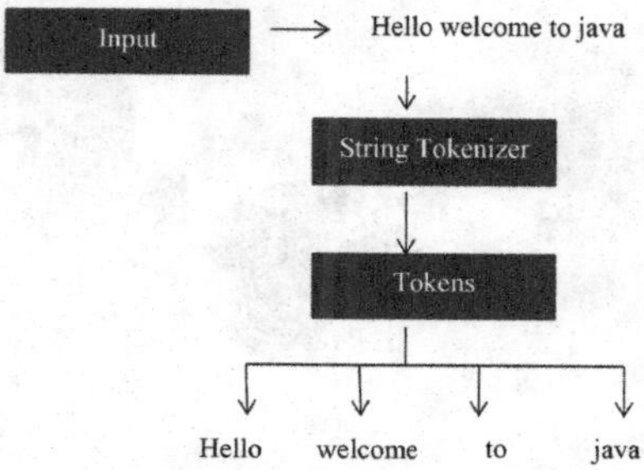

StringTokenizer Constructors

The StringTokenizer class defines three constructors.

Constructor	Description
StringTokenizer(String st)	It generates a StringTokenizer from the supplied string.
StringTokenizer(String st, String deli)	StringTokenizer is created using the supplied string and delimiter.
StringTokenizer(String st, String deli, boolean returnVal)	StringTokenizer is created using the provided string, delimiter, and returnValue. If the return value is true, delimiter characters are treated as tokens. If true, delimiter characters are used to separate tokens.

[3] https://techvidvan.com/tutorials/java-stringtokenizer/, TechVidvaan

StringTokenizer Class Methods

The StringTokenizer class has six helpful methods, which are as follows:

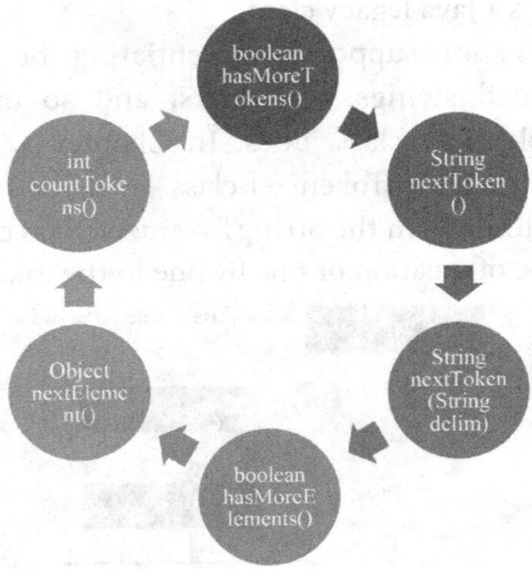

Example:

```
import java.util.StringTokenizer;
public class simplestng
{
 public static void main(String args[])
{
   StringTokenizer str = new
StringTokenizer("Java programs "," ");
     while (str.hasMoreTokens())
{
         System.out.println(str.
nextToken());
     }
   }
}
```

Output:

```
Java
programs
```

Example of nextToken method:

```
import java.util.*;

public class testing
{
   public static void main(String[] args)
{
        StringTokenizer str = new
StringTokenizer("Java pro is important");

       // next token printing
       System.out.println("Next token:
" + str.nextToken(","));
   }
}
```

Output:

```
Next token: Java pro is important
```

In this chapter, we studied the Introduction to Strings in Java and the many types of strings and methods available in Java. Concatenation is a string and comparison. Furthermore, we discussed the distinctions between string and string buffer, as well as stringbuffer and stringbuilder.

CHAPTER 5

Collections, Lists, and Java's Built-in APIs

IN THIS CHAPTER

- ➤ Arrays
- ➤ Sets
- ➤ Lists
- ➤ Maps
- ➤ Iterating with Collections

In the previous chapter, we discovered the basics of Java Strings, including string types and methods. Furthermore, Concatenation is a string and a comparison. It also explains

DOI: 10.1201/9781003229063-5

the distinctions between string and string buffer, as well as stringbuffer and stringbuilder.

This chapter will talk about arrays, sets, lists, and maps in Java and iterating with the collection.

WHAT ARE JAVA ARRAYS?

An array is often a collection of comparable types of items with contiguous memory locations.

An array in Java is an object that includes items of the same data type. Furthermore, array items are kept in a continuous memory region. It is a data structure in which related components are stored. A Java array can only hold a fixed number of items.[1]

In Java, arrays are index-based; the first member of the array is kept at the 0th index, the second element at the 1st index, etc.

In Java, an array is a dynamically created class object. The Object class is inherited by the Java array, which implements the Serializable and Cloneable interfaces. In Java, we may store primitive values or objects in an array. In Java, we can build single-dimensional or multidimensional arrays in the same way we do in C/C++.

Furthermore, Java has the characteristic of unnamed arrays, which C/C+ does not have.

Advantages

- **Code Optimization:** It optimizes the code so that we can obtain or sort the dta more efficiently.

[1] https://www.dummies.com/programming/java/what-are-java-arrays/, dummies.

- **Random Access:** We can obtain any data that is situated at an index point using random access.

Disadvantages

- **Size Restriction:** We can only store elements of a fixed size in the array. It does not expand in size during running. In Java, a collection framework that grows automatically is utilized to overcome this problem.

Array Types in Java

There are two types of arrays:

1. Multidimensional Array
2. Single Dimensional Array

Java Single Dimensional Array

Syntax:

```
dataType arr[];
```

In Java, you may create an array by instantiating it.

```
arrayRefVari=new datatype[size];
```

Example:

```
public class arrayTest
{
public static void main(String args[])
{
int b[]=new int[5];
```

```
 b[0]=20;
b[1]=40;
b[2]=50;
b[3]=70;
b[4]=10;
// array traversing
for(int c=0;c<b.length;c++)
System.out.println(b[c]);
}
}
```

Output:

```
20
40
50
70
10
```

Java Array Declaration, Instantiation, and Initialization

We may declare, instantiate, and initialize a Java array by doing the following:

Syntax:

```
int b[]={43,5,41,52}; //declaration,
instantiation and initialization
```

Example:

```
public class arrayTest
{
public static void main(String args[])
{
```

```
int b[]={43,5,41,52}; //declaration,
instantiation and initialization
// array printing
for(int c=0;c<b.length;c++)//length is
the property of array
System.out.println(b[c]);
}
}
```

Output:

```
43
5
41
52
```

Java Array for Each Loop

We can use a for each loop to display the Java array. The array elements are printed one by one using Java for each loop. It stores an array element in a variable before executing the loop's body.

Syntax:

```
for(datatype variable_array)
{
//body
}
```

Example:

```
public class arrayTest
{
public static void main(String args[])
{
```

```
int arr[]={43,5,41,52};
//printing
for(int c:arr)
System.out.println(c);
}
}
```

Output:

```
43
5
41
52
```

Passing an Array to a Method

We may provide a java array to a method to reuse the same logic on any array.

Let's look at a basic example of utilizing a method to retrieve the smallest integer in an array.

Example:

```
public class arrayTest
{
//creating method
static void min(int arr[])
{
int mini=arr[0];
for(int c=1;c<arr.length;c++)
 if(mini>arr[c])
  mini=arr[c];

System.out.println(mini);
}
```

```
public static void main(String args[])
{
int b[]={43,5,41,52};// array declaring
and initializing
min(b);
}
}
```

Output:

```
5
```

In Java, an anonymous array is defined as follows:

Because Java provides the anonymous array feature, you don't need to declare the array when giving it a function.

Example:

```
public class AnonymousArrayTest
{
// which receives an array as a
parameter creating that method
static void printArray(int arra[])
{
for(int c=0;c<arra.length;c++)
System.out.println(arra[c]);
}

public static void main(String args[])
{
printArray(new int[]{12,20,54,67}); //
passing anonymous array
}
}
```

Output:

```
12
20
54
67
```

Method Returning an Array

In Java, we may also return an array from the method.

Example:

```
public class ReturnArrayTest
{
// which receives an array as a parameter
creating that method
static int[] get()
{
return new int[]{20,40,80,10,30};
}
public static void main(String args[])
{
int arra[]=get();
//printing
for(int c=0;c<arra.length;c++)
System.out.println(arra[c]);
}
}
```

Output:

```
20
40
80
10
30
```

ArrayIndexOutOfBoundsException

The JVM (Java Virtual Machine) throws an ArrayIndex-OutOfBoundsException if the length of the array is negative, larger than, or equivalent to the array size when traversing the array

Example:

```
public class ArrayExceptionTest
{
public static void main(String args[])
{
int arra[]={55,40,80,90};
for(int c=0;c<=arra.length;c++)
{
System.out.println(arra[c]);
}
}
}
```

Output:

```
55
40
80
90
```

Exception in thread "main" java.lang.ArrayIndexOutOf BoundsException: Index 4 out of bounds for length 4

```
at ArrayExceptionTest.
main(ArrayExceptionTest.java:8)
```

Java Multidimensional Array

In this scenario, data is kept in a row and column index.

Syntax:

```
dataType []arrayRefVar[];
```

In Java, here's an example of how to create a Multidimensional Array:

```
int[][] arra=new int[4][4];//4 row and 4
column
```

In Java, an example of how to initialize a Multidimensional Array:

```
arr[0][0]=2;
arr[0][1]=3;
arr[0][2]=4;
arr[1][0]=6;
arr[1][1]=7;
arr[1][2]=3;
arr[2][0]=8;
arr[2][1]=9;
arr[2][2]=3;
```

Example:

```
public class arrayTest
{
public static void main(String args[])
{
//2D array declaring and initializing
int arra[][]={{10,21,23},{12,42,51},{4
,44,65}};
//printing
for(int c=0;c<3;c++)
{
```

```
 for(int d=0;d<3;d++){
   System.out.print(arra[c][d]+" ");
 }
 System.out.println();
}
}
}
```

Output:

```
10 21 23
12 42 51
 4 44 65
```

Java's Jagged Array

A jagged array has an odd number of columns in a 2D array. In other words, it is a collection of arrays with varying numbers of columns.

Example:

```
public class JaggedArrayTest
{
    public static void main(String[] args)
{
          // with odd columns declaring 2D
array
          int arra[][] = new int[3][];
          arra[0] = new int[3];
          arra[1] = new int[4];
          arra[2] = new int[2];
          //jagged array initializing
          int counts = 0;
         for (int c=0; c<arra.length; c++)
```

```
                for(int d=0; d<arra[c].
length; d++)
                        arra[c][d] = counts++;

        //printing
        for (int c=0; c<arra.length; c++)
{
                for (int d=0; d<arra[c].
length; d++)
{
                        System.out.print(arra[c]
[d]+" ");
                }
                System.out.println();
        }
    }
}
```

Output:

```
0 1 2
3 4 5 6
7 8
```

What Is the Name of the Java Array Class?

An array is a kind of object in Java. A proxy class is generated for array objects whose name may be retrieved by calling the getClass().getName() method on the object.

Example:

```
public class arrayTest
{
public static void main(String args[])
```

```
{
//array declaration and initialization
int arra[]={41,34,25};
//getting the class name
Class cs=arra.getClass();
String names=cs.getName();
//printing
System.out.println(names);
}
}
```

Output:

```
[I
```

Creating a Java Array Copy

Using the arraycopy() function of the System class, we may copy one array to another.

Syntax:

```
public static void arraycopy
(
Object src, int srcPos,Object dest,
int destPos, int length
)
```

Example:

```
public class ArrayCopyDemoTest
{
    public static void main(String[]
args)
{
```

```
        // source array declaring
        char[] copyFrom = { 'e', 'd',
'c', 'a', 'f', 'f', 'e',
                'i', 'n', 'b', 'c', 'a',
't' };
        // destination array
declaring
        char[] copyTo = new char[7];
        //copying array
        System.arraycopy(copyFrom, 2,
copyTo, 0, 7);
        //printing
        System.out.println(String.
valueOf(copyTo));
    }
}
```

Output:

```
caffeine
```

In Java, Clone an Array

We can build a clone of the Java array since it implements the Cloneable interface. When we clone a single-dimensional array, we get a deep duplicate of the Java array. That is, it will duplicate the actual value. However, cloning a multidimensional array makes a shallow duplicate of the Java array, implying it replicates the references.

Example:

```
public class arrayTest
{
public static void main(String args[])
```

```
{
int arra[]={23,33,41,59};
System.out.println("Printing array
original:");
for(int c:arra)
System.out.println(c);

System.out.println("Printing clone
array:");
int carra[]=arra.clone();
for(int c:carra)
System.out.println(c);

System.out.println("Are both
equal??");
System.out.println(arra==carra);

}
}
```

Output:

```
 Printing array original:
23
33
41
59
Printing clone array:
23
33
41
59
Are both equal??
false
```

In Java, Add Two Matrices

Example:

```
public class arrayTest
{
public static void main(String args[])
{
// two matrices creating
int x[][]={{10,35,42},{13,34,55}};
int y[][]={{11,32,49},{23,74,65}};
//to store the sum of two matrices
creating another matrix
int a[][]=new int[2][3];
//adding and printing addition of 2
matrices
for(int c=0;c<2;c++){
for(int d=0;d<3;d++){
a[c][d]=x[c][d]+y[c][d];
System.out.print(a[c][d]+" ");
}
System.out.println();//new line
}
}
}
```

Output:

```
21 67 91
36 108 120
```

In Java, Multiply Two Matrices

Matrix multiplication involves multiplying a one-row element of the first matrix by all the columns of the second matrix.

Example:

```
public class
ExampleMatrixMultiplication
{
public static void main(String
args[])
{
// two matrices creating
int x[][]={{11,11,11},{22,22,22},{33,3
3,33}};
int y[][]={{11,11,11},{22,22,22},{33,3
3,33}};

//creating another matrix
int a[][]=new int[3][3]; //3 rows 3
columns


//multiplying
for(int c=0;c<3;c++)
{
for(int d=0;d<3;d++)
{
a[c][d]=0;
for(int e=0;e<3;e++)
{
a[c][d]+=x[c][e]*y[e][d];
}//end of e loop
System.out.print(a[c][d]+" "); //
printing
}//end j loop
System.out.println(); //new line
}
}}
```

Output:

```
726 726 726
1452 1452 1452
2178 2178 2178
```

JAVA SETS

The set interface is included in java.util package. The set interface is an extension of the Collection interface. A collection interface is an unordered collection or list in which duplicates are not permitted. To build the mathematical set, the set interface is utilized. To avoid the insertion of the identical components, the set interface takes advantage of the collection interface's methods. The interfaces SortedSet and NavigableSet enhance the set implementation.

Example:

```
import java.util.*;
public class Exampleset
{
    public static void main(String[] args)
    {
        // using the Set  creating
LinkedHashSet
        Set<String> datas = new
LinkedHashSet<String>();

        datas.add("JavaPro");
        datas.add("Set");
        datas.add("Example");
        datas.add("Check");

        System.out.println(datas);
    }
}
```

Output:

```
[JavaPro, Set, Example, Check]
```

The Set Interface's Operations

We can do all basic mathematical operations on the Set, such as intersection, union, and difference.

Consider the following two sets: set1 = [77, 45, 33, 22, 66, 55, 34] and set2 = [83, 33, 2, 55, 45, 3, 12]. On the Set, we may execute the following operation:

- **Intersection:** The intersection operation returns all elements that lappear in both sets. Set1 and set2 will cross at [33, 45, 55].
- **Union:** The union operation returns all of the elements of sets 1 and 2 in a single set, which might be set1 or set2. The sum of setsl1 and 2 is [2, 3, 12, 22, 33, 34, 45, 55, 66, 77, 83].
- **Difference:** The difference operation removes from the set any values that are also present in another set. The difference between sets 1 and 2 is [66, 34, 22, 77].

In set, the union is performed using the addAll() method, the intersection is performed using the retainAll() method, and the difference is performed using the removeAll() method: an example to see how these techniques execute intersection, union, and difference operations.

Example:

```
import java.util.*;
public class OperationSet
```

```
{
    public static void main(String args[])
    {
        Integer[] X = {33, 55,38, 86,
22, 33, 72};
        Integer[] Y = {55, 24, 83, 51,
63, 12, 33};
        Set<Integer> sets1 = new
HashSet<Integer>();
        sets1.addAll(Arrays.asList(X));
        Set<Integer> sets2 = new
HashSet<Integer>();
        sets2.addAll(Arrays.asList(Y));

        // Union of set1 and set2 Finding
        Set<Integer> union_datas = new
HashSet<Integer>(sets1);
        union_datas.addAll(sets2);
        System.out.print("Union is:");
        System.out.
println(union_datas);

        // Intersection of set1 and
set2 Finding
        Set<Integer> intersection_datas =
new HashSet<Integer>(sets1);
        intersection_datas.
retainAll(sets2);
        System.out.print("Intersection
is:");
        System.out.
println(intersection_datas);

        // Difference of set1 and set2
Finding
```

```
        Set<Integer> difference_datas
= new HashSet<Integer>(sets1);
        difference_datas.
removeAll(sets2);
        System.out.print("Difference
is:");
        System.out.println(difference_
datas);
    }
}
```

Output:

```
Union is: [33, 83, 51, 38, 86, 22, 55,
72, 24, 12, 63]
Difference is: [38, 86, 22, 72]
Intersection is: [33, 55]
```

In the above code, we first construct two arrays of type integer, X and Y. Following that, we build two sets of type integer, sets1, and sets2. We convert both arrays to lists and add the items of array A to sets1 and the elements of array B to sets2.

We build a new set of union data with the same element as sets1 to execute the union. The sets2 is then passed as an input to the addAll() function of the set. This function will add all missing pieces to the union data and return the union of the two sets.

We build a new set of intersection data with the same element as set1 to execute the intersection. The sets2 is then passed as an input to the retainAll() function of the set. This function will get all intersection_datas items present in set2 and save them in the intersection data. The intersection_datas now contains the intersection value of both sets.

We make a new set difference_datas with the same element as setl to conduct the difference. The sets2 is then sent as an input to the removeAll() function of the set.

Methods of Set

In the set interface, there are various methods that we may utilize to execute a particular operation on our sets. These techniques are as follows:[2]

1. **add():** The add() function adds a new value to the collection. Depending on the existence of the insertion element, the method returns true or false. If the element exists already in the set, it returns false; otherwise, it returns true.

   Syntax:

   ```
   boolean add(type_element)
   ```

   Example:

   ```
   import java.io.*;
   import java.util.*;
   public class Methodadd
   {
       public static void main(String
   args[])
       {
   ```

[2] https://www.javatpoint.com/set-in-java, javaTpoint

```
        Set<Integer> datas = new
LinkedHashSet<Integer>();
        datas.add(33);
        datas.add(25);
        datas.add(47);
        datas.add(11);
        datas.add(63);
        datas.add(58);
        System.out.println("data: "
+ datas);
    }
}
```

Output:

```
data: [33, 25, 47, 11, 63, 58]
```

2. **addAll():** The addAll() function appends to the set all the elements of the given collection.

Syntax:

```
boolean addAll(Collection_data)
```

Example:

```
import java.io.*;
import java.util.*;
public class MethodaddAll
{
    public static void main(String
args[])
    {
        Set<Integer> datas = new
LinkedHashSet<Integer>();
```

```
        datas.add(31);
        datas.add(21);
        datas.add(41);
        System.out.println("Set: " +
datas);
        ArrayList<Integer> newData =
new ArrayList<Integer>();
        newData.add(99);
        newData.add(17);
        newData.add(89);
        datas.addAll(newData);
        System.out.println("Set: " +
datas);
    }
}
```

Output:

```
Set: [31, 21, 41]
Set: [31, 21, 41, 99, 17, 89]
```

3. **clear():** The method discards all of the elements in the set. It does not remove the set's reference. It just deletes the set's items.

Syntax:

```
void clear()
```

Example:

```
import java.io.*;
import java.util.*;
public class Methodclear
{
```

```
    public static void main(String
args[])
    {
        Set<Integer> datas = new
LinkedHashSet<Integer>();
        datas.add(34);
        datas.add(22);
        datas.add(40);
        System.out.println("Set: " +
datas);
        datas.clear();
        System.out.println("The final
set: " + datas);
    }
}
```

Output:

```
Set: [34, 22, 40]
The final set: []
```

4. **contains():** The contains() function determines the existence of an element in a set. Its return value is either true or false, depending on whether the component is present.

Syntax:

```
boolean contains(Object_element)
```

Example:

```
import java.io.*;
import java.util.*;
public class Methodcontains
{
```

```
    public static void main(String
args[])
    {
        Set<Integer> datas = new
LinkedHashSet<Integer>();
        datas.add(38);
        datas.add(29);
        datas.add(34);
        datas.add(57);
        datas.add(19);
        datas.add(82);
        System.out.println("Set: " +
datas);
        System.out.println("Does the
Set contains 93?" + datas.
contains(93));
        System.out.println("Does the
Set contains javaTpoint? " + datas.
contains("44"));
        System.out.println("Does the
Set contains 15? " + datas.
contains(15));
    }
}
```

Output:

```
Set: [38, 29, 34, 57, 19, 82]
Does the Set contains 93?false
Does the Set contains javaTpoint?
false
Does the Set contains 15? false
```

5. **containsAll():** The technique is used to determine whether or not all of the collection components are

present in the existing set. It returns true if all of the collection's items are present and false if one of the elements is missing from the current set.

Syntax:

```
public boolean
containsAll(Collection_data)
```

Example:

```
import java.io.*;
import java.util.*;
public class MethodcontainsAll
{
    public static void main(String
args[])
    {
        Set<Integer> datas = new
LinkedHashSet<Integer>();
        datas.add(31);
        datas.add(21);
        datas.add(41);
        datas.add(51);
        datas.add(11);
        datas.add(81);

        System.out.println("data: " +
datas);

        Set<Integer> newData = new
LinkedHashSet<Integer>();
        newData.add(37);
        newData.add(29);
        newData.add(42);
```

```
        System.out.println("\nDoes data
contains newdata?: "+ datas.
containsAll(newData));

    }
}
```

Output:

```
data: [31, 21, 41, 51, 11, 81]

Does data contains newdata?: false
```

6. **hashCode():** The method returns the hash code value for the set's current instance. It returns an integer hash code value.

Syntax:

```
public int hashCode()
```

Example:

```
import java.io.*;
import java.util.*;
class MethodhashCode
{
    public static void main(String
args[])
    {
        Set<Integer> datas = new
LinkedHashSet<Integer>();
        datas.add(31);
        datas.add(21);
        datas.add(41);
        datas.add(51);
        datas.add(11);
```

```
        datas.add(81);
        System.out.println("data: "
+ datas);
        System.out.println("\nHash
code value of set:"+ datas.
hashCode());
    }
}
```

Output:

```
data: [31, 21, 41, 51, 11, 81]
Hash code value of set: 236
```

7. **isEmpty():** isEmpty() function is used to determine whether the set is empty. If the set is empty, it returns true; otherwise, it returns false.

Syntax:

```
boolean isEmpty()
```

Example:

```
import java.io.*;
import java.util.*;
public class MethodisEmpty
{
    public static void main(String
args[])
    {
        Set<Integer> datas = new
LinkedHashSet<Integer>();
        datas.add(31);
        datas.add(21);
```

```
            datas.add(41);
            datas.add(51);
            datas.add(11);
            datas.add(81);
            System.out.println("data: "
+ datas);
           System.out.println("\nIs Data
empty: "+ datas.isEmpty());
    }
}
```

Output:

```
data: [31, 21, 41, 51, 11, 81]

Is Data empty: false
```

8. **iterator():** The iterator() function is used to locate the set's iterator. The iterator is used to get the elements one at a time.

Syntax:

```
Iterator iterate_value = set1.
iterator();
```

Example:

```
import java.io.*;
import java.util.*;
public class Methoditerator
{
    public static void main(String
args[])
    {
        Set<Integer> datas = new
LinkedHashSet<Integer>();
```

```
        datas.add(38);
        datas.add(12);
        datas.add(48);
        datas.add(55);
        datas.add(31);
        datas.add(89);
        System.out.println("data: "
+ datas);

        Iterator new_Data = datas.
iterator();
        System.out.println("The
NewData values: ");
        while (new_Data.hasNext()) {
            System.out.println(new_
Data.next());
        }
    }
}
```

Output:

```
data: [38, 12, 48, 55, 31, 89]
The NewData values:
38
12
48
55
31
89
```

9. **remove():** The technique is used to delete an element from the Set. The element's availability determines its return value. If the component is available in the set, it returns true; otherwise, it returns false.

Syntax:

```
boolean remove(Object O)
```

Example:

```
import java.io.*;
import java.util.*;
public class Methodremove
{
    public static void main(String args[])
    {
        Set<Integer> datas = new
LinkedHashSet<Integer>();
        datas.add(38);
        datas.add(23);
        datas.add(49);
        datas.add(53);
        datas.add(21);
        datas.add(89);
        System.out.println("data: "
+ datas);

        datas.remove(89);
        datas.remove(21);
        datas.remove(38);
        System.out.println("data
after removing elements: " + datas);
    }
}
```

Output:

```
data: [38, 23, 49, 53, 21, 89]
data after removing elements: [23,
49, 53]
```

10. **removeAll():** The method removes all of the existing set's elements from the provided collection.

Syntax:

```
public boolean
removeAll(Collection_data)
```

Example:

```
import java.io.*;
import java.util.*;
public class MethodremoveAll
{
    public static void main(String
args[])
    {
        Set<Integer> datas = new
LinkedHashSet<Integer>();
        datas.add(31);
        datas.add(21);
        datas.add(41);
        datas.add(91);
        datas.add(71);
        datas.add(81);
        System.out.println("data: "
+ datas);

        ArrayList<Integer> newDatas
= new ArrayList<Integer>();
        newDatas.add(99);
        newDatas.add(72);
        newDatas.add(83);
        System.out.println("NewData:
" + newDatas);
```

```
            datas.removeAll(newDatas);
            System.out.println("after
removing Newdata element : " + datas);
     }
}
```

Output:

```
data: [31, 21, 41, 91, 71, 81]
NewData: [99, 72, 83]
after removing Newdata element: [31,
21, 41, 91, 71, 81]
```

11. **retainAll():** The method keeps all elements from the provided set in the supplied collection.

Syntax:

```
public boolean
retainAll(Collection_data)
```

Example:

```
import java.io.*;
import java.util.*;
public class MethodretainAll
{
    public static void main(String
args[])
     {
          Set<Integer> datas = new
LinkedHashSet<Integer>();
          datas.add(31);
          datas.add(21);
```

```
        datas.add(41);
        datas.add(91);
        datas.add(71);
        datas.add(81);
        System.out.println("data: "
+ datas);

        ArrayList<Integer> newDatas
= new ArrayList<Integer>();
        newDatas.add(91);
        newDatas.add(71);
        newDatas.add(81);
        System.out.println("newData
is: " + newDatas);

        datas.retainAll(newDatas);
        System.out.println("data
after retaining newdatas elements :
" + datas);
    }
}
```

Output:

```
data: [31, 21, 41, 91, 71, 81]
newData is: [91, 71, 81]
data after retaining newdatas
elements: [91, 71, 81]
```

12. **size():** The method returns the set's size.

Syntax:

```
int size()
```

Example:

```
import java.io.*;
import java.util.*;
public class Methodsize
{
    public static void main(String
args[])
    {
        Set<Integer> datas = new
LinkedHashSet<Integer>();
        datas.add(31);
        datas.add(29);
        datas.add(40);
        datas.add(92);
        datas.add(72);
        datas.add(83);
        System.out.println("data is:
" + datas);

        System.out.println("size is
: " + datas.size());
    }
}
```

Output:

```
data is: [31, 29, 40, 92, 72, 83]
size is: 6
```

13. **removeAll():** The technique is used to generate an array that contains the same elements as the set.

Syntax:

```
Object[] toArray()
```

Example:

```
import java.io.*;
import java.util.*;
public class MethodtoArray
{
    public static void main(String
args[])
    {
        Set<Integer> datas = new
LinkedHashSet<Integer>();
        datas.add(31);
        datas.add(21);
        datas.add(41);
        datas.add(91);
        datas.add(71);
        datas.add(81);
        System.out.println("data is:
" + datas);

        Object[] array_datas = datas.
toArray();
        System.out.println("Array:");
        for (int c = 0; c < array_datas.
length; c++)
            System.out.
println(array_datas[c]);
    }
}
```

Output:

```
data is: [31, 21, 41, 91, 71, 81]
Array:
31
21
41
```

```
91
71
81
```

LIST IN JAVA

In Java, a list allows you to keep an ordered collection. It includes index-based techniques for inserting, updating, deleting, and searching items. It may also include redundant components. The null entries can also be stored in the list.

The Collection interface is inherited by the List interface, which is available in java.util package. It is a ListIterator interface factory. We can iterate the list in both forward and backward directions using the ListIterator. The List interface's implementation classes include ArrayList, LinkedList, Stack, and Vector. In Java programming, the ArrayList and LinkedList are extensively utilized. Since Java 5, the Vector class has been deprecated.

Syntax:

```
public interface List<E> extends
Collection<E>
```

List Methods in Java

Method	Description
void add(int index, E element)	It is used to insert the supplied element into a list at the specified location.
boolean add(E e)	It appends the supplied element to the end of a list.
boolean addAll(Collection<? extends E> c)	It is used to add to the end of all of the entries in the given collection.
boolean addAll(int indexs, Collection<? extends E> c)	It is used to add all of the entries in the provided collection, beginning at the point indicated in the list.

(*Continued*)

(Continued) List Methods in Java

Method	Description
void clear()	It is used to delete every entry from this list.
boolean equals(Object o)	It compares the supplied item to the elements in a list.
int hashcode()	It is used to return a list's hash code value.
E get(int index)	It is used to retrieve an element from a certain place in the list.
boolean isEmpty()	If the list is empty, it returns true; otherwise, it returns false.
int lastIndexOf(Object o)	It return index of the last occurrence of the provided element in this list, or -1 if it is not found.
Object[] toArray()	It's used to return an array with all of the entries in this list in the right order.
<T> T[] toArray(T[] a)	It return an array with all of the elements in this list in the correct order.
boolean contains(Object o)	If the list includes the supplied element, it returns true.
boolean containsAll(Collection<?> c)	If the list contains all of the provided elements, it returns true.
int indexOf(Object o)	It return the index of the first occurrence of the supplied element in this list, or -1 if the List does not include this element.
E remove(int index)	It is used to delete the entry from the list at the specified location.
boolean remove(Object o)	It's used to get rid of the first instance of the supplied element.
boolean removeAll(Collection<?> c)	It is used to delete all of the list's items.
void replaceAll(UnaryOperator<E> operator)	It is used to replace all of the list's elements with the supplied element.

(*Continued*)

(Continued) List Methods in Java

Method	Description
void retainAll(Collection<?> c)	It is used to keep all of the list's elements that are present in the given collection.
E set(int index, E element)	It replaces the specified element in the list, which is currently present at the specified position.
void sort(Comparator<? super E> c)	It is used to order the list's elements based on the given comparator.
Spliterator<E> spliterator()	It's used to make a spliterator out of the elements of a list.
List<E> subList(int fromIndex, int toIndex)	It is used to get all items that fall inside the specified range.
int size()	Its purpose is to return the number of elements in the list.

ArrayList vs. Java List

The list is an interface, and ArrayList is its implementation class.

How to Make a List

List interface is implemented by the ArrayList and LinkedList classes. Let's look at few instances of how to make a List:

```
// ArrayList is used to create a String List.
List<String> lists=new ArrayList<String>();

// ArrayList is used to create an Integer List
List<Integer> lists=new ArrayList<Integer>();

// ArrayList is used to create a list of type
Books
List<Book> lists=new ArrayList<Book>();

// LinkedList is used to create a String
List.
List<String> lists=new LinkedList<String>();
```

Example:

```
import java.util.*;
public class ListsExample
{
public static void main(String args[])
{
 //Creating List
 List<String> lists=new
ArrayList<String>();
 //Adding elements
 lists.add("Kiwi");
 lists.add("Banana");
 lists.add("Apple ");
 lists.add("Oranges");
 // using for-each loop Iterating the
List element
 for(String fruit:lists)
  System.out.println(fruit);

}
}
```

Output:

```
Kiwi
Banana
Apple
Oranges
```

Converting an Array to a List

We may convert an array to a list by traversing the array and adding each element to the list one at a time with the list.add() function. Let's look at a basic example of converting array items to List.

Example:

```
import java.util.*;
public class ExampleArrayToList
{
public static void main(String args[])
{
// Array Creation
String[] arra={"C#","AdvPython","Java",
"C++"};
System.out.println("Printing Array is:
"+Arrays.toString(arra));
//Converting Array to List
List<String> lists=new ArrayList<String>();
for(String lang:arra)
{
lists.add(lang);
}
System.out.println("Printing List is:
"+lists);
}
}
```

Output:

```
Printing Array is: [C#, AdvPython, Java,
C++]
Printing List is: [C#, AdvPython, Java,
C++]
```

How to Convert a List to an Array

By using the list.toArray() function, we can convert the List to an Array. Let's look at a basic example of converting list elements to array elements.

Example:

```
import java.util.*;
public class ExampleListToArray
{
public static void main(String args[])
{
 List<String> fruitLists = new
ArrayList<>();
 fruitLists.add("Kiwi");
 fruitLists.add("Grapes");
 fruitLists.add("Oranges");
 fruitLists.add("Strawberry");
 //Converting ArrayList to Array
 String[] array = fruitLists.
toArray(new String[fruitLists.size()]);
 System.out.println("Printing Array
is: "+Arrays.toString(array));
 System.out.println("Printing List is:
"+fruitLists);
}
}
```

Output:

```
Printing Array is: [Kiwi, Grapes,
Oranges, Strawberry]
Printing List is: [Kiwi, Grapes,
Oranges, Strawberry]
```

Get and Set an Element in a List

The element at the specified index is returned by the get() function, whereas the component is changed or replaced by the set() method.

Example:

```
import java.util.*;
public class ExampleList
{
 public static void main(String args[])
{
 //Creation of List
 List<String> lists=new
ArrayList<String>();
 //Adding elements in the List
 lists.add("Mango");
 lists.add("Apple");
 lists.add("Banana");
 lists.add("Grapes");
 //accessing the element
 System.out.println("Returning element:
"+lists.get(1)); //it return the 2nd
element
// element changing
 list.set(1,"Dates");
 //Iterating the List
 for(String fruit:lists)
  System.out.println(fruits);

 }
}
```

Output:

```
Returning element: Apple
Mango
Dates
Banana
Grapes
```

Sorting a List

There are other methods for sorting a List; in this case, we will utilize the Collections.sort() function to sort the list element. Collections is a utility class in java.util package has the static method sort (). We may simply sort any List using the Collections.sort() function.

Example:

```
import java.util.*;
public class ListSortArray
{
 public static void main(String args[])
{
  //Creating list
  List<String> lists1=new
ArrayList<String>();
  lists1.add("Kiwi");
  lists1.add("Mango ");
  lists1.add("Oranges");
  lists1.add("Grapes");

  //Sorting list
  Collections.sort(lists1);

   //Traversing list
  for(String fruit:lists1)
  System.out.println(fruit);
  System.out.println("Sorting
numbers");

//Creating a list
  List<Integer> lists2=new
ArrayList<Integer>();
```

```
    lists2.add(24);
    lists2.add(17);
    lists2.add(58);
    lists2.add(10);
    //Sorting the list
    Collections.sort(lists2);
     //Traversing list through the for-
  each loop
    for(Integer number:lists2)
      System.out.println(number);
   }

  }
```

Output:

```
Grapes
Kiwi
Mango
Oranges
Sorting numbers
10
17
24
58
```

Interface for Java ListIterator

To traverse the element backward and forth, the ListIterator interface is utilized.

Syntax:

```
public interface ListIterator<E>
extends Iterator<E>
```

Java ListIterator Interface Methods

Method	Description
void add(E e)	This function adds the provided item to the list.
boolean hasNext()	When traversing the list in the forward mode, this method returns true if the list iterator has more entries.
E next()	This function returns the next element in the list and moves the cursor to the next place in the list.
int nextIndex()	This function returns the index of the element that would be returned by the following method call to next()
boolean has Previous()	If this list iterator contains more elements while traversing the list in the other way, this function returns true.
E previous()	This function returns the previous item in the list and shifts the cursor backward.
E previousIndex()	This function returns the element index returned by the preceding call to the previous().
void remove()	This function deletes the final member of the list returned by the next() or previous() methods.
void set(E e)	This function replaces the supplied element with the latest element returned by the next() or previous() methods.

Example:

```
import java.util.*;
public class ExampleListIterator
{
public static void main(String args[])
{
List<String> adl=new ArrayList<String>();
        adl.add("Anita");
        adl.add("Vicky");
        adl.add("Karan");
```

```
            adl.add(1,"Sneha");
            ListIterator<String> itrr=adl.
listIterator();
            System.out.println("Traversing
elements in forward:");
            while(itrr.hasNext())
{
            System.out.println("index:"+
itrr.nextIndex()+" value:"+itrr.
next());
            }
            System.out.println("Traversing
elements in backward");
            while(itrr.hasPrevious())
{
            System.out.println("index:"+itrr.
previousIndex()+" value:"+itrr.
previous());
            }
}
}
```

Output:

```
Traversing elements in forward:
index:0 value:Anita
index:1 value:Sneha
index:2 value:Vicky
index:3 value:Karan
Traversing elements in backward direction
index:3 value:Karan
index:2 value:Vicky
index:1 value:Sneha
index:0 value:Anita
```

MAP INTERFACE IN JAVA

A map includes values based on the key, i.e., a key and value pair. Each key-value pair is referred to as an entry. A Map has distinct keys.[3]

A Map is essential when searching, updating, or deleting items based on a key.

Hierarchy of Java Map

Map in Java has two interfaces: Map and SortedMap, as well as three classes: HashMap, LinkedHashMap, and TreeMap. The Java Map hierarchy is as follows:

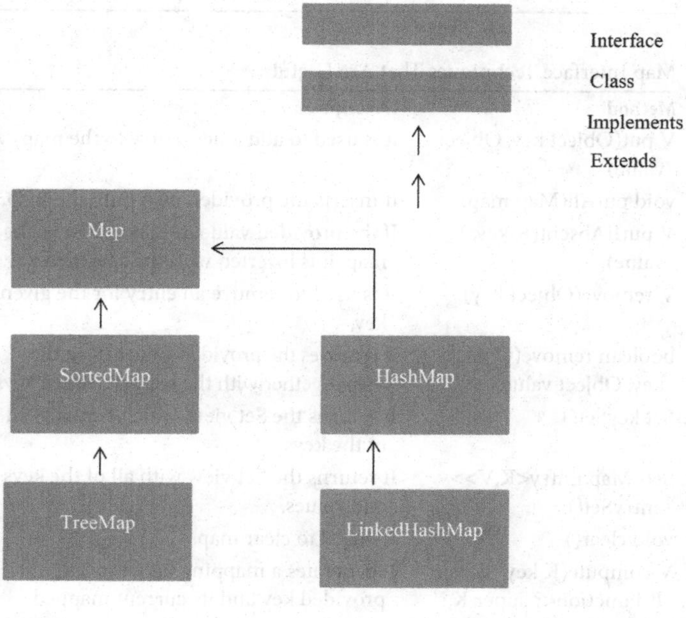

[3] https://docs.oracle.com/javase/tutorial/collections/interfaces/map.html, Oracle

Duplicate keys are not permitted in a Map, although duplicate values are allowed. TreeMap does not support null keys or values, but HashMap and LinkedHashMap do.

Because a Map cannot be browsed, you must convert it to a Set using the keySet() or entrySet() methods.

Class	Description
HashMap	HashMap is a Map implementation; however, it does not keep track of the order.
LinkedHashMap	LinkedHashMap is the implementation of Map. It inherits the HashMap class. It maintains insertion order.
TreeMap	TreeMap is a Map and SortedMap implementation. It keeps ascending order.

Map Interface Techniques That Are Useful

Method	Description
V put(Object key, Object value)	It is used to add a new entry to the map.
void putAll(Map map)	It inserts the provided map onto the map.
V putIfAbsent(K key, V value)	If the provided value does not exist in the map, it is inserted with the specified key.
V remove(Object key)	It is used to remove an entry for the given key.
boolean remove(Object key, Object value)	It removes the provided values from the map together with the related defined keys.
Set keySet()	It returns the Set view, which contains all of the keys.
Set<Map.Entry<K,V>> entrySet()	It returns the Set view with all of the keys and values.
void clear()	It's used to clear map.
V compute(K key, BiFunction<? super K,? super V,? extends V> remappingFunction)	It generates a mapping between the provided key and its current mapped value.

(*Continued*)

(Continued) Map Interface Techniques That Are Useful

Method	Description
V computeIfAbsent(K key, Function<? super K,? extends V> mappingFunction)	If the supplied key is not already associated with a value, It computes its value using the supplied mapping function and adds it into this map unless null.
V computeIfPresent(K key, BiFunction<? super K,? super V,? extends V> remappingFunction)	If the value for the supplied key is present and non-null, it is utilized to generate a new mapping given the key and its existing mapped value.
boolean containsValue(Object value)	If a value equal to the value exists in the map, this function returns true; otherwise, it returns false.
boolean containsKey(Object key)	If key with the same name as the key exists in the map, this function returns true; otherwise, it returns false.
boolean equals(Object o)	Its purpose is to compare the provided Object to the Map.
void forEach(BiConsumer<? super K,? super V> action)	It executes the specified action for each entry in the map until all entries are processed, or the action produces an exception.
V get(Object key)	This function returns the object containing the key's related value.
V getOrDefault(Object key, V defaultValue)	It returns the value to which the provided key is mapped or defaultValue if no mapping for the key exists in the map.
int hashCode()	It returns the Map's hash code value.
boolean isEmpty()	If the map is empty, this function returns true; otherwise, it returns false.
V merge(K key, V value, BiFunction<? super V,? super V,? extends V> remappingFunction)	Associates the specified key with the provided non-null value if it is not already associated with a value or is associated with null.
V replace(K key, V value)	It replaces the specified value for the specified key.

(*Continued*)

(Continued) Map Interface Techniques That Are Useful

Method	Description
boolean replace(K key, V oldValue, V newValue)	For a given key, it replaces the previous value with the new value.
void replaceAll(BiFunction<? super K,? super V,? extends V> function)	It changes the value of each item with the result of executing the provided function on that entry until all entries are processed, or the method produces an exception.
Collection values()	It gives you a collection view of the values on the map.
int size()	This function returns the number of entries on the map.

The interface of Map.Entry

Map's subinterface is Entry. As a result, we will use Map to go there. Name of the entry. It returns a map collection-view with components of this type. It provides ways for obtaining keys and value.

Map.Entry Interface Methods

Method	Description
K getKey()	It's used to get a key.
V getValue()	It is utilized to acquire value.
int hashCode()	It is used to obtain hashCode.
V setValue(V value)	It is used to overwrite the value associated with this item with the supplied value.
boolean equals(Object o)	It is used to compare the provided item to other things that already exist.
static <K extends Comparable<? super K>,V> Comparator<Map.Entry<K,V>> comparingByKey()	It returns a comparator that compares the items on key in natural order.

(Continued)

(Continued) Map.Entry Interface Methods

Method	Description
static <K,V> Comparator<Map.Entry<K,V>> comparingByKey(Comparator<? super K> cmp)	It return a comparator that uses the provided Comparator to compare the objects by key.
static <K,V extends Comparable<? super V>> Comparator<Map.Entry<K,V>> comparingByValue()	It return a comparator that compares the objects on value in natural order.
static <K,V> Comparator<Map.Entry<K,V>> comparingByValue(Comparator<? super V> cmp)	It return a comparator that uses the provided Comparator to compare the objects by value.

Examplel: Non generic method

```
import java.util.*;
public class ExampleMap
{
public static void main(String[] args)
{
    Map maps=new HashMap();
    //Adding elements
    maps.put(11,"Anita");
    maps.put(4,"Ridhi");
    maps.put(1,"Jatin");
    maps.put(3,"Alex");
    //Traversing Map
    Set sets=maps.entrySet(); //
Converting to Set
    Iterator itrr=sets.iterator();
    while(itrr.hasNext())
{
        Map.Entry entr=(Map.Entry)
itrr.next();
```

```
        System.out.println(entr.
getKey()+" "+entr.getValue());
     }
}
}
```

Output:

```
1 Jatin
3 Alex
4 Ridhi
11 Anita
```

Example2: Generic method

```
import java.util.*;
public class ExampleMap
{
 public static void main(String args[])
{
  Map<Integer,String> maps=new
HashMap<Integer,String>();
  maps.put(101,"Anita");
  maps.put(103,"Vicky");
  maps.put(108,"Riti");
  // in any order  elements can
traverse
  for(Map.Entry mp:maps.entrySet())
{
   System.out.println(mp.getKey()+"
"+mp.getValue());
   }
 }
}
```

Output:

```
101 Anita
103 Vicky
108 Riti
```

Example: comparingByValue()

```
import java.util.*;
public class ExampleMap
{
 public static void main(String
args[])
{
Map<Integer,String> maps=new
HashMap<Integer,String>();
      maps.put(100,"Amit");
      maps.put(101,"Vijay");
      maps.put(102,"Rahul");
      // Returns a Set representation
of the mappings included in this
map.
      maps.entrySet()
      // This collection is used as
the source for a sequential Stream
      .stream()
      // Sorted based on the supplied
Comparator
      .sorted(Map.Entry.
comparingByValue())
      //This procedure is performed on
each element of this stream
      .forEach(System.out::println);
 }
}
```

Output:

```
100=Amit
102=Rahul
101=Vijay
```

IN JAVA, ITERATING COLLECTIONS

The Four Java Collection Iteration Methods

Iteration is one of the most fundamental operations performed on a collection. Iterations essentially extract components from a collection one after the other, from the first to the last.

For example, you could want to browse through all of the students in a class to print their names or see who got good marks on the most recent exam. Alternatively, you might iterate through a list of integers to compute the total and average. Such procedures are pretty prevalent in programming.[4]

For loops, iterator, and forEach are the four methods the Java programming language provides for iterating through collections.

Assume we have the following List collection before proceeding to each type of iteration:

```
List<String> listname = new ArrayList<>();

listname.add("Tomi");
listname.add("Mari");
listname.add("Peti");
listname.add("Johi");
listname.add("Kimi");
```

4 https://www.codejava.net/java-core/collections/the-4-methods-for-iterating-collections-in-java, CodeJava

This list includes the names of all pupils in a class. Take note of the diamond operator <> used in the assignment's right side:

```
ArrayList<>();
```

From Java 7, we may use this syntax to declare generics collections more compactly because the compiler can infer the parameter type on the right side from the left side.

1. **The Classic for Loop:** This iteration approach is fairly known in programming, and it involves running a counter variable from the first entry in the collection to the final one. Here is the code that iterates across the listNames collection:

```
for (int c = 0; c < listNames.size();
c++)
{
    String nName = listNames.get(c);
    System.out.println(nName);
}
```

2. **The Iterator Method:** Because of the standard for loop restrictions, the Iterator function was designed to allow us to iterate across any type of collection. As you can see, the Collection interface requires all collections to implement the iterator() function.

   The following example exemplifies the iterator concept:

```
Iterator<String> iterators = listNames.
iterator();
while (iterators.hasNext()) {
```

```
        String nName = iterators.next();
        System.out.println(nName);
    }
```

3. **The Enhanced for Loop:** Since Java 5, programmers may iterate over a collection using a more concise syntax, improving a loop.

   For example, the following iterates through the listNames collection using the extended for loop:

```
for (String nName : listNames)
{
    System.out.println(nName);
}
```

4. **The forEach Method with Lambda Expressions:** The forEach method, introduced in Java 8 with Lambda expressions, is a whole new approach of iterating through collections.

   What is the primary distinction between the forEach technique and the preceding ones?

   In the primary ways, the programmers control how the collection is iterated(traditional for loop, iterator, and improved for-loop). The iteration code is not included in the collection and is created by programmers, thus the external name iteration.

   On the other hand, the new approach wraps the iteration logic in the collection itself, removing the need for programmers to create code for iterating collections. On the other hand, the programmers describe what to do in each iteration – this is a significant distinction! As a result, the phrase "internal iteration" was coined: the collections manage the iteration, whilst the programmers pass the action – what has to be done in each iteration.

Following example will help you grasp the concepts:

```
listNames.forEach(names -> System.out.
println(names));
```

Method of Java Collection iterator()

The iterator() function of the Java Collection Interface returns an iterator through the collection's items.

Syntax:

```
public Iterator <E> iterator()
```

Parameters:

NA

Return:

The iterator () function iterates across the members of this collection.

Example 1:

```
import java.util.Collection;
import java.util.Iterator;
import java.util.concurrent.
ConcurrentLinkedQueue;
public class ExampleJavaCollectionIterator
{
    static int c = 1;
    public static void main(String[] args)
{
```

```
        Collection<String> collections
= new ConcurrentLinkedQueue<String>();
        collections.add("Raman");
        collections.add("Shiv");
        collections.add("Murat");
        collections.add("Rakesh");
        Iterator<String> iterators =
collections.iterator();
        // over the elements returns
an iterator
        while (iterators.hasNext())
{
              System.out.println(c++ +
"." + iterators.next());
        }
    }
}
```

Output:

```
1.Raman
2.Shiv
3.Murat
4.Rakesh
```

Example 2:

```
import java.util.Collection;
import java.util.Collections;
import java.util.Iterator;
import java.util.concurrent.
ConcurrentLinkedQueue;
public class ExampleJavaCollectionIterator
{
    public static void main(String[] args)
```

```
{
        Integer[] vals = new Integer[2];
        Collection<Integer> collections
= new ConcurrentLinkedQueue<Integer>();
        collections.add(71098);
        collections.add(8090);
        collections.add(1278);
        collections.add(1490);
        // over the elements returns
an iterator
        Iterator<Integer> iterators =
collections.iterator();
        while(iterators.hasNext()){
            System.out.
println(iterators.next());
            vals[0] = Collections.
max(collections);
            vals[1] = Collections.
min(collections);
        }
        System.out.println("Maxi number
= "+ vals[0]);
        System.out.println("Mini number
= "+ vals[1]);
    }
}
```

Output:

```
71098
8090
1278
1490
Maxi number = 71098
Mini number = 1278
```

This chapter defined arrays and discussed their benefits, drawbacks, and array kinds. We also learned about sets in Java and its interface operations, list, list methods in Java, how to build a list, and how to convert an array to a list or a list to an array. In addition, we spoke about the Map Interface in Java and its hierarchy. What is Iterating with Collections, and what are the many forms of it?

CHAPTER 6

Libraries, Packages, and Modules

IN THIS CHAPTER

- ➢ Introduction
- ➢ Organizing Code into Packages
- ➢ Maven and Grandle
- ➢ Access Modifiers
- ➢ Encapsulation
- ➢ Cloning Objects

In the previous chapter, we covered arrays and their different types of array. We also studied sets in Java. Moreover, we learned about lists and maps as well as iterating with collections. This chapter will learn about the introduction

DOI: 10.1201/9781003229063-6

of Libraries, Packages, and Modules and Organizing Code into Packages also Maven and Grandle.

WHAT IS THE LIBRARY IN JAVA?

As of now, we've depended on Java's standard classes, which we can learn about in the Java Application Programming Interface (API). These classes were created by the same people that made Java, and they may be used on any machine that has Java installed.[1]

We are not, however, confined to utilizing only those classes. You've previously seen how to make classes that interact with one another. We may also use classes created by others.

Java library is a collection of classes that have previously been developed by someone else. You download those classes, inform your computer about them, and then utilize them in your code. This allows you to extend what Java can accomplish and depend on code others have tested rather than doing everything yourself.

Locating a Library

Before we can utilize a library, we must first pick which library we wish to use. How do we know which library to use when there are so many available?

The answer, like most things in programming, is Google. A search for the "Java ABC library," where ABC is what we want to perform, will often provide a plethora of results. Assume we wish to write Java software that

[1] https://happycoding.io/tutorials/java/libraries, Happy Coding

displays graphs. We'd start by Googling the "Java graph library," which yielded a plethora of options.

We'd next go through the results until we discovered one that helped us achieve our aim. When deciding on a library, don't be scared to try them all! Create basic programs with each and see which one works best for us.

The JFreeChart library, which allows us to add interactive charts and graphs to Swing applications, will be used for the rest of the course.

.jar Files Downloading

We've probably come across.zip files, which are archive files or files that contain other files. Similarly, .jar files are a type of archive file that typically contains.class files. Java libraries are often packaged in.jar files. (In reality, they're generally in.zip files that contain.jar files that contain.class files)

Anyway, now that we've settled on a library, the next step is to get it. JFreeChart's download page may be found on the library's website: https://www.jfree.org/jfreechart/download.html

Download zip file and unzip it wherever you wish. This produces a directory containing a slew of .jar files.

Documentation in the Library

We should be pretty comfortable with looking at the Java API, tutorials, and conducting Google searches by this point. Using a library is no different: going through its documentation to understand what it can accomplish is one of the first stages in working with it.

JFreeChart API documentation can be found at https://www.jfree.org/jfreechart/api/javadoc/index.html. It includes a list of all the classes in the library and the variables and functions they contain. That may seem like a lot, but our objective isn't to read it all. Simply browse the classes to get a broad sense of your possibilities, and then start focusing on anything that sounds like it could be what we're looking for.

Classpath

When we build and run Java files, Java looks for them in the current directory by default.

As an example:

```
javac MyJavaProgram.java
```

When we run this command, the Java compiler searches the current directory for classes. So, if MyProgram.java refers to another class called MyDependency, it explores the current directory for MyDependency.class or MyDependency.java. This is how you can build several classes using just the main file.

However, our library files are contained within the. jar file rather than in the current directory! If we wish to use the library classes, we must tell Java where to find them.

To put it another way, we must specify the classpath, which is a list of places where Java will look for class files. We do this by supplying a list of paths as the -cp option to a Java command.

As an example:

```
javac -cp. ;path/to/first/jarFile.
jar;path/to/second/jarFile.jar
MyFirstProgram.java
```

This command starts the Java compiler and sends it a -cp parameter containing three entries:

1. '.' This adds the current directory to the classpath since we probably want Java to keep looking in that location.
2. path/to/first/jarFile.jar a.jar file is added to the classpath as a result of this. Any .class files included within that.jar file can now be used in our software.
3. path/to/second/jarFile.jar A second .jar file is added to the classpath as a result.

What Exactly Is a Java Class Library?

Because Java is not reliant on any particular operating system, Java programs cannot rely on platform-specific native libraries; instead, Java offers a collection of dynamically loaded libraries common to current operating systems.

These libraries offer:

- Regular Expressions and container classes
- Interfaces for activities that rely on the Operating System's (OS) hardware, such as network and file access.
- If the underlying platform does not support a specific Java feature, these libraries will override that feature if necessary.

Java Library classes are a collection of predefined classes in packages that are made available to programmers as part of the Java installation process. Library classes make it easier for programmers to do their jobs by providing built-in methods for ordinary and non-trivial activities like accepting input from the user, presenting output to the user, and so on. For example, the System class provides the print() and println() methods in java.lang package of Java Library classes for presenting output to the user.

Library Classes in Java

This lesson will go through the package java.lang, which contains classes essential to the Java programming language design. The most critical classes are Object (the base of the class hierarchy) and Class (which represent classes at run time).

The following list of the classes in java.lang package. These classes are critical for any Java programmer to understand. To learn more about a particular class, click on its link. We can turn to standard Java manuals for more practice.

Sr. No	Methods with Explanations
1	Boolean Boolean
2	Byte The Byte class creates an object out of a primitive type byte value.
3	Character A value of the primitive type char is wrapped in an object by the Character class.
4	Class In a running Java application, instances of the class. The class represents classes and interfaces.
5	ClassLoader A class loader is an entity that is in charge of class loading.

(*Continued*)

Sr. No	Methods with Explanations
6	Compiler The Compiler class is given to aid in the development of Java-to-native-code compilers and related services.
7	Double The Double class is an object that encapsulates a value of the basic type double.
8	Float The Float class is an object that contains a value of the basic type float.
9	Integer The Integer class is an object that encapsulates a value of the primitive type int.
10	Long A value of the primitive type long is wrapped in an object by the Long class.
11	Math Math class includes fundamental mathematical operations such as trigonometric, square root, logarithmic, and exponential functions.
12	Number The number is the abstract superclass of BigDecimal, BigInteger, Byte, Double, Float, Integer, Long, and Short.
13	Object The root of the class hierarchy is Class Object.
14	Package Package objects include info of versions about a Java package's implementation and specification.
15	Process The Runtime.exec techniques produce a native process and return an instance of a subclass of Process that may be used to control and query the process.
16	Runtime Every Java program has a single instance of the class Runtime, which allows the application to communicate with the environment it is executing.
17	RuntimePermission This class is used to manage runtime permissions.

(*Continued*)

Sr. No	Methods with Explanations
18	SecurityManager A security manager is a class that enables applications to apply security policies.
19	Short The Short class wraps an object around a value of the primitive type short.
20	StackTraceElement In a stack trace an element, as returned by Throwable.getStackTrace().
21	StrictMath Methods in the StrictMath class execute fundamental mathematical operations such as the elementary exponential, trigonometric, logarithm, and square root functions.
22	String The String class represents character strings.
23	StringBuffer A string buffer is a character sequence that may be changed.
24	System The System class has several essential class fields and methods.
25	Thread A thread is an execution thread in a program.
26	ThreadGroup Thread group is a group of threads.
27	ThreadLocal This class provides Thread-local variables.
28	Throwable It is the superclass of all Java errors and exceptions.
29	Void The Void class is an uninstantiable placeholder class that references the Java keyword void's Class object.

Making Use of Java Libraries

While there are still a few essential basic programming principles to learn, we'd like to use existing libraries in the

Java Software Development Kit (SDK) as soon as feasible. To that end, this outline will give "just enough" information to demonstrate the actual core usage of current Java class libraries.

User vs. Builder

Two points of view should always be addressed while developing any reusable programming construct:

1. The builder is responsible for declaring and defining how some module works.
2. The caller (i.e., some code, often another module) uses an existing module to perform a task.

It is critical to remember that, for this session (Using Java Libraries), we are looking at things from the user's point of view. In other words, what we need to know to use a pre-existing Java library from the SDK and its many predefined features.

What Is Included in the Java SDK?

- There are several types of library constructions to examine, such as:
    - Classes and interfaces with generic type arguments are packaged as classes and interfaces.
    - Packages are groups of classes and interfaces.
- The dot operator is used to divide packages into categories and subcategories. Packages include java.lang, java.util, java.util.concurrent, and methods.

- If a class is included within a package, we may refer to the entire name by using the package name, dot-operator, and class name.
  Examples: java.lang.String, java.util.Scanner.

- Fields can be included in classes and interfaces, techniques.

WHAT ARE THE PACKAGES IN JAVA?

A Java package is a gathering of comparable sorts of classes, interfaces, and sub-bundles.

Bundle in java can be classified into two structures, inherent bundle and client characterized bundle. There are many inherent bundles like Java, lang, awt, javax, swing, net, io, util, sql, etc. Here, we will have the itemized learning of making and utilizing client characterized bundles.

The benefit of Java Package

1. The Java package is utilized to arrange the classes and interfaces to be handily kept up with.

2. Java package gives access assurance.

3. Java package eliminates the naming impact.

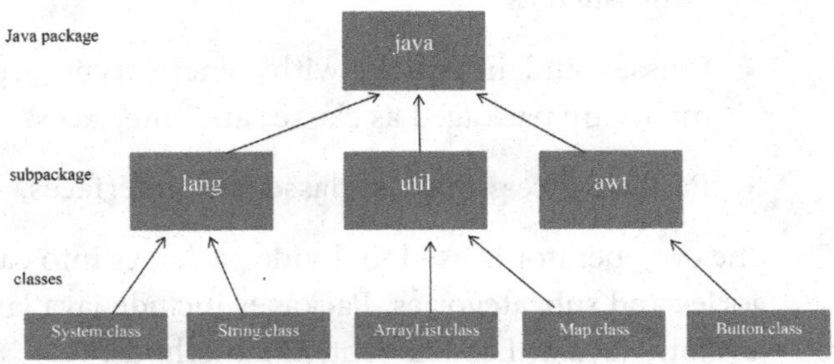

Example:

```
package pack;
public class simplepack
{
 public static void main(String
args[])
{
    System.out.println("package welcome
");
   }
}
```

To Compile a Java Package, Follow These Steps

If we are not using an IDE, we must use the following syntax:

```
javac -d directory namejavafile
```

Example:

```
javac -d. Simplepro.java
```

The -d switch specifies the location of the produced class file. You can use any directory name, such as /home (in Linux), d:/abc (in Windows), and so on. You can use it if you wish to keep the package in the same directory (dot).

To Launch a Java Package Application, Follow These Steps

We must use a fully qualified name, such as mypack. Simplepro. To execute the class, use simple, etc.

How Do I Go to a Package from Another Package?

There are three ways to get inside the package from outside of it.

1. Import package.*;
2. Import package.class_name;
3. qualified name

- **Using Packagename.*:** If you use package.*, all of this package's classes and interfaces will be available, but not sub-packages.

  The import keyword is used to create another package's classes and interface available to the current package.

  Example:

```
//save by X.java

package packg;
public class X
{
  public void msg()
{
System.out.println("Hello Everyone");
}
}

//save by Y.java

package mypackg;
import packg.*;
```

```
class Y
{
  public static void main(String
args[])
{
   X objt = new X();
   objt.msg();
  }
}
```

- **Using packagename.classname:** Only the defined classes of this package will be accessible if you import package.classname.

Example:

```
//save by X.java

package packg;
public class X
{
  public void msg()
{
System.out.println("Hello Everyone");
}
}

//save by Y.java

package mypackg;
import packg.X;

class Y
{
 public static void main(String args[])
```

```
{
    X objt = new X();
    objt.msg();
  }
}
```

- **Using the Fully Qualified Name:** Only the stated classes of this package will be available if you use a suitably qualified name. Importing is no longer necessary. However, when accessing the class or interface, you must always use the fully qualified name.

  It is typically used when two packages include the same class name, such as when the java.util and java.sql packages both contain the Date class.

  Example:

```
//save by X.java

package packg;
public class X
{
  public void msg()
{
System.out.println("Hello everyone");
}
}


//save by Y.java

package mypackg;
class Y
{
  public static void main(String args[])
```

```
{
   pack.X objt = new pack.X(); //fully
qualified name using
   objt.msg();
  }
}
```

JAVA SUBPACKAGE

The package within the package is referred to as the sub-package. It should be developed to classify the package further.

For example, Sun Microsystems' java package comprises various classes such as System, String, Reader, Writer, Socket, and so on. These classes represent a particular group; for example, Reader and Writer classes represent Input/Output operations, Socket and ServerSocket classes represent networking, etc. As a result, Sun has divided the java package into sub-packages such as lang, net, io, and so on, and placed Input/Output related classes in the io package, Server and ServerSocket classes in the net packages, etc.

Example:

```
package com.javatpoint.core;
class Simple
{
  public static void main(String
args[])
{
   System.out.println("Hello everyone
subpackage");
  }
}
```

How Do I Transfer the Class File to a Different Directory or Drive?

There is a case; I want to place the class file of X.java source file in the c: drive class file. As an example:

Example:

```
//save as Simplepro.java
package mypackg;
public class Simplepro
{
 public static void main(String args[])
{
    System.out.println("Welcome to the
package");
   }
}
```

To Compile:

```
e:\sources> javac -d c:\classes
Simplepro.java
```

To Execute:

To run this program from the e:\source directory, specify the classpath to the directory containing the class file.

```
e:\sources> set classpath=c:\classes;.;
e:\sources> java mypackg.Simplepro
```

Another Approach to Execute this Program Is to Use the Java -Classpath Switch

The -classpath option is supported by both javac and the java tool.

To execute this program from the e: source directory, use the java -classpath switch, which instructs the program to look for class files. As an example:

```
e:\sources> java -classpath c:\classes
mypackg.Simplepro
```

Methods for Loading Class Files or Jar Files Include

The class files can be loaded in two ways: temporarily and permanently.

Temporary:

- In the command prompt, set the classpath
- Using the -classpath switch

Permanent:

- Set the classpath in the environment variables
- By generating a Java Archive (JAR) file that contains all of the class files and placing them in the jre/lib/ext folder

How Do You Combine Two Public Classes into a Single Package?

If you want to include two public classes in a package, create two java source files, each with one public class, but keep the package name the same. For instance:

```
//save as X.java

package javatpoints;
```

```
public class X
{
}


//save as Y.java

package javatpoints;
public class Y
{
}
```

JAVA ACCESS MODIFIERS

In Java, there are two kinds of modifiers: access modifiers and non-access modifiers.

In Java, access modifiers define the accessibility or scope of a field, method, or class. Using the access modifier may modify the access level of fields, constructors, methods, and classes.

Java access modifiers are classified into four types:

1. **Private:** A private modifier's access level is restricted to the class. It cannot be retrieved from outside the class.
2. **Default:** A default modifier's access level is limited to the package. It cannot be retrieved from outside the package. If no access level is specified, the default will be used.
3. **Protected:** A protected modifier's access level is within and outside the package through a child class. If the child class is not created, it cannot be accessed from outside the package.

4. **Public:** A public modifier's access level is present everywhere. It is accessible from within the class, outside the class, within the package, and from outside the package.

Non-access modifiers include static, abstract, synchronized, native, volatile, transitory, and so on. We will just cover access modifiers in this section.

Using a basic table, let's look at how access modifiers work in Java.

Java Access Modifiers Explained

Access Modifier	Within class	Within package	Outside package by subclass only	Outside package
Private	Ys	No	No	No
Default	Ys	Ys	No	No
Protected	Ys	Ys	Ys	No
Public	Ys	Ys	Ys	Ys

- **Private:** The private access modifier is only available within the class.

  A basic example of a private access modifier

  We've generated two classes in this example: A and Simple. A private data member and a private method are both found in a class. There is a compile-time issue since we are accessing these secret members from outside the class.

  Example:

```
class X
{
private int data=30;
private void msg(){System.out.
println("Hello java program");
```

```
}
}
public class Simple
{
 public static void main(String
args[])
{
   X objt=new X();
   System.out.println(objt.data); //
Compile Error
   objt.msg(); //Compile Error
   }
}
```

Private Constructor's Role

If you make a class constructor private, you will be unable to create a class object outside the class. As an example:

```
class X
{
private X(){} //private_constructor
void msg()
{
System.out.println("Hello java program");
}
}
public class Simplepro
{
 public static void main(String args[])
{
   X objt=new X(); //Compile Error
 }
}
```

- **Default:** If no modifier is used, it is considered as default by default. The default modifier is only available within the package. It cannot be retrieved from outside the package. It is more accessible than a private residence. However, it is more restricted than protected and open.

  As an example of a default access modifier, consider the following:

  We've built two packages in this example: packg and mypackg. We're accessing the A class from outside its package since it's not public and can't be accessed from outside the package.

Example:

```
//save by X.java

package pack;
class X
{
  void msg()
{
System.out.println("Hello Java
program");
}
}


//save by Y.java

package mypackg;
import packg.*;
class Y
{
```

```
public static void main(String args[])
{
  Y objt = new Y(); //Compile Error
  objt.msg(); //Compile Error
  }
}
```

- **Protected:** The protected access modifier is accessible both within and outside of the package, but only through inheritance.

  The protected access modifier applies to data members, methods, and constructors. It cannot be used in class.

  It's more accessible than the default modifier.

Example:

In this example, we've made two packages: packg and mypackg. Because the pack package's A class is public, it may be accessed from outside the package. However, the message method of this package is marked as protected; thus, it can only be accessed from outside the class via inheritance.

```
//save by X.java

package packg;
public class X
{
protected void msg()
{
System.out.println("Hello Java");
}
}
```

```
//save by Y.java

package mypackg;
import packg.*;

class Y extends X
{
  public static void main(String args[])
{
  Y objt = new Y();
  objt.msg();
  }
}
```

- **Public:** The public access modifier can be accessed from anywhere. It has the broadest reach of any modifier.

Example:

```
//save by X.java

package packg;
public class X
{
public void msg()
{
System.out.println("Hello java");
}
}


//save by Y.java

package mypackg;
import packg.*;
```

```
class Y
{
  public static void main(String args[])
{
   X objt = new X();
   objt.msg();
  }
}
```

Access Modifiers with Method Overriding in Java

If we override a method, the overridden method (defined in a subclass) cannot be more restricted.

Example:

```
class X
{
protected void msg()
{
System.out.println("Hello java program");
}
}

public class Simplepro extends X
{
void msg()
{
System.out.println("Hello java
program");} //compile.error
 public static void main(String args[])
{
   Simplepro objt=new Simplepro();
   objt.msg();
   }
}
```

The protected modifier is more restricted than the default modifier. As a result, there is a compile-time error.

ENCAPSULATION

Encapsulation in Java combines code and data into a single unit, such as a capsule containing numerous medications.

In Java, we may construct a fully enclosed class by keeping all of the class's data members private. We can now use setter and getter methods to set and get data from it.

A completely enclosed class is an example of a Java Bean class.

The Benefits of Encapsulation in Java

- You may make the class read-only or write-only by simply giving a setter or getter method. In other words, you don't have to use the getter or setter procedures.
- It gives you control over the data. If you want to set the value of id to be larger than 100 alone, you may do it within the setter method. You may implement logic to prevent negative values from being stored in the setter methods.
- It is a method of achieving data concealing in Java since other classes will not access the data through private data members.
- The encapsulate class is simple to put to the test. As a result, it is preferable for unit testing.
- Typical IDEs provide the ability to produce getters and setters. As a result, creating an enclosed class in Java is simple and quick.

Example:

File save: Students.java

```
// A Java class that is entirely
encapsulated
// It includes a private data member as
well as getter and setter methods

package com.javatpoints;
public class Students
{
//data member private
private String names;
// for name getter method
public String getName()
{
return names;
}
//setter method for name
public void setName(String names)
{
this.names=names
}
}
```

File save: Testpro.java

```
//Java class to test

package com.javatpoints;
class Testpro
{
public static void main(String[] args)
{
//creating instance
```

```
Students st=new Students();
//setting value
st.setName("vicky");
//getting value
System.out.println(st.getName());
}
}
```

Class Read-Only

```
// A Java class that solely contains getter
methods.

public class Students
{
// data member private
private String colleges="XYZ";
//for college getter method
public String getCollege()
{
return colleges;
}
}
```

You can no longer modify the value of the college data member “XYZ.”

```
st.setCollege("INFD"); //compile time error
will render
```

Class Write-Only

```
// A Java class that solely contains setter
methods.

public class Students
{
```

```
//data member private
private String colleges;
// for college getter method
public void setCollege(String colleges)
{
this.colleges=colleges;
}
}
```

You can no longer obtain the value of the college; instead, you can only alter the value of the college data component.

```
System.out.println(st.getCollege()); //
Compile Time Error, since no such method
exists.
System.out.println(st.colleges); // Because
the college data member is private, there
is a compile time error.
//As a result, it cannot be accessible from
outside the class.
```

CLONING OBJECTS IN JAVA

Item cloning is a method of creating an identical duplicate of an object. The Object class's clone() function is used to duplicate an object.[2]

java.lang.Cloneable interface must implemented by the class whose clone object we wish to generate. If we do not implement the Cloneable interface, the clone() function throws a CloneNotSupportedException.

The clone() function is defined in the Object class.

The clone() method's syntax is as follows:

```
protected Object clone() throws
CloneNotSupportedException
```

2 https://www.javatpoint.com/object-cloning, javaTpoint

Why Should You Use the Clone() Method?

The Clone() method avoids the need for subsequent processing to generate a duplicate of an object. If we do it using the new keyword, it will take a long time to process, so we utilize object cloning.

The Benefit of Object Cloning

Although Object.clone() has several design flaws, it is a standard and straightforward method of copying objects. Some of the advantages of using the clone() function are as follows:

There is no need to create lengthy and repeated code. Simply use an abstract class with a clone() function that is 4 or 5 lines long.

It is the simplest and efficient method for copying items, mainly when used to an already established or old project. Simply build a parent class, implement Cloneable, then define the clone() function and complete the work.

Clone() is the quickest way to duplicate an array.

Object Copying Has the Following Disadvantages

The following are some drawbacks of the clone() method:

- To utilize the Object.clone() method, we must alter several syntaxes in our code, such as implementing a Cloneable interface, defining the clone() function, and handling CloneNotSupportedException, and ultimately using Object.clone(), among other things.
- We must implement a cloneable interface even though it has no methods. We just utilize it to inform the JVM that we may execute clone() on our object.

- Because Object.clone() is protected, we must supply our own clone() and call Object.clone() indirectly from it.
- Because Object.clone() does not execute any function, we do not influence object formation.
- If you wish to write a clone method in a child class, all superclasses must declare it or inherit it from another parent class. The super.clone() chain will fail otherwise.
- Object.clone() only allows shallow copying; we must override it if we require deep cloning.

Example:

```
class Students18 implements Cloneable
{
int roll_no;
String names;

Students18(int roll_no,String names)
{
this.roll_no=roll_no;
this.names=names;
}

public Object clone()throws
CloneNotSupportedException
{
return super.clone();
}

public static void main(String args[])
{
```

```
Try
{
Students18 st1=new
Students18(101,"anita");

Students18 st2=(Students18)st1.
clone();

System.out.println(st1.roll_no+"
"+st1.names);
System.out.println(st2.roll_no+"
"+st2.names);

}
catch(CloneNotSupportedException c)
{}

}
}
```

MODULES IN JAVA

A Java module is a technique for packaging a Java application or Java API as a distinct Java module. A modular JAR file contains a Java module. A Java module can define which Java packages it contains and which should be visible to other Java modules that utilize it. A Java module must additionally describe which other Java modules are required to complete its task.

Java modules are a new feature introduced in Java 9 through the Java Platform Module System (JPMS). Depending on where you read, the Java Platform Module System is sometimes known as Java Jigsaw or Project Jigsaw. During development, the internal project name was

Jigsaw. The jigsaw was later renamed Java Platform Module System.

Benefits of Java Modules

The Java Platform Module System provides numerous advantages to Java developers. We'll mention the essential benefits below.

Modular Java Platform for Smaller Application Distribution

All of the Java Platform APIs have been separated into distinct modules as part of Project Jigsaw. The advantage of breaking up all of the Java APIs into modules is that you can now define which modules of the Java platform your application needs. Knowing which Java Platform modules your application requires, Java can package your program such that it only includes the Java Platform modules that your application utilizes.

Because there were no official means of accurately validating which classes your Java program utilized before Java 9 and the Java Platform Module System, you would have had to bundle all of the Java Platform APIs with your Java application. Because the Java Platform APIs have become fairly extensive over the years, your application would receive many Java classes in its deployment, many of which we would probably not need.

Because of the unneeded classes, our applications distributable are more significant than it needs to be. This can be an issue for tiny devices such as mobile phones, Raspberry Pis, etc. You may now package your application with only the modules of the Java Platform APIs that your application uses, thanks to the Java Platform Module System. As a result, application distributable will be smaller.

Internal Package Encapsulation

A Java module must specify which Java packages within the module are to be exported to other Java modules that use the module. A Java module may include Java packages that are not exported. Classes in not exported packages are inaccessible to other Java modules. Such packages are only usable within the Java module that includes them.

Packages that are not exported are often known as hidden or encapsulated packages.

Start Detection of Absent Modules

Beginning with Java 9, Java programs must also be bundled as Java modules. As a result, an application module defines the other modules (Java API modules or third-party modules) that it employs. As a result, when the Java VM starts up, it may examine the whole module dependency chain from the application module onward. If any needed modules are not discovered when the Java VM boots up, it reports the absent module and closes down.

Before Java 9, missing classes (for example, from a missing JAR file) were not identified until the program attempted to utilize the missing class. This might occur at some point during runtime, depending on when the program attempted to utilize the missing class.

Having absent modules notified at program startup time is a significant benefit to having the missing module/JAR/class reported at runtime when attempting to utilize the absent module/JAR/class.

Module Basics in Java

Now that you know what a Java module is and the merits of Java modules let's look at the fundamentals of Java modules.

Modules Consist One or More Packages: A Java module collects one or even more Java packages. A module might be a whole Java program, a Java-based API, or a third-party API.

Naming a Java Module

A Java module must have a different name. A valid module name, for example.

```
com.jenkov.mymodules
```

A Java module's name follows the same naming conventions as a Java package's name. However, from Java 9 and beyond, you should not use underscores (_) in module names (or package names, class names, method names, variable names, and so on) because Java intends to utilize underscore as a reserved identifier in the future.

If feasible, it is suggested to name a Java module the same as the name of the root Java package included in the module.

Module's Root Directory

Before Java 9, all Java classes for an application or API were nested immediately within a root class directory (added to the classpath) or directly inside a JAR file. For example, the directory structure for com.jenkov.mymodules built packages might look like this:

```
com/jenkov/mymodules
```

Module System

The Java Module System is a significant change in the Java 9 version. Java introduced this functionality to group Java packages and code into a single unit known as a module.

There was no notion of modules in previous versions of Java; therefore, it was challenging to construct modular Java programs, which increased the size of the application and made it harder to move about. Even the JDK was too large; in Java 8, the rt.jar file size is about 64MB.

Java 9 reorganized JDK into a series of modules to deal with the problem, allowing us to utilize just the components we needed for our project.

Aside from the JDK, Java also allows us to construct our modules, developing module-based applications.

The module system comes with a variety of tools and choices, which are listed below:

- Includes several options for the Java tools javac, jlink, and java where we may define module paths that point to the module's location.
- The modular JAR file format is introduced. The module-info.class file is located in the root folder of this JAR.
- The JMOD format, which is a packaging format similar to JAR but may incorporate native code and configuration files, is introduced.
- Both the JDK and Java Runtime Environment (JRE) have been rebuilt to allow modules. It boosts performance, security, and maintenance.

- For naming modules, classes, and resources, Java introduces a new Uniform Resource Identifier (URI) system.

Modularized Java 9 JDK

Module for Java 9

A module is a grouping of Java applications or software. A Java file module-info.java is required to describe a module. This file, often known as a module descriptor, contains the following information:

- Name of the module.
- What exactly does it export?
- What are the requirements?

Module Name

This module name should follow the reverse-domain-pattern as we name packages, for example, com.javapoint.

How to Make a Java Module

The following steps were necessary to create a Java module:

- Construct a directory structure
- Make a module declarator
- Source code for Java

Construct a Directory Structure

Constructing modules using the given directory structure is suggested, similar to how we create packages and project structures in Java utilizing the reverse-domain-pattern.

Make a file called module-info.java and declare a module inside it by using the module identifier and providing the same name as the directory that contains it. In our example, the directory is called com.javapoint.

```
module com.javapoint
{

}
```

If the module does not have module dependencies, leave the module body empty. Save this file as module-info.java under src/com.javapoint.

Source Code for Java

Create a Java file to compile and run the module. In our case, we have a Helloeveryone.java file with the following code.

```
class Helloeveryone
{
    public static void main(String[] args)
{
        System.out.println("Hello from the
everyone");
    }
}
```

Compile Java Module

To compile the module, use the following command:

```
javac -d mods --module-source-path src/
--module com.javapoint
```

It will generate a new directory with the following structure after building.

We now have a built module that can simply be executed.

Module Execution

Use the following command to run the built module:

```
java --module-path mods/ --module com
.javapoint/com.javapoint.Hello
```

WHAT EXACTLY IS MAVEN?

Maven is a sophisticated project management tool based on the POM paradigm (project object model). It is used for project development, dependency management, and documentation. It, like ANT, streamlines the construction process. However, it is far more sophisticated than ANT.

In a nutshell, a maven is a tool that can be used to create and manage any Java-based project. Maven simplifies the day-to-day work of Java developers and aids in the understanding of any Java-based project.

What Does Maven Do?

Maven does a variety of useful tasks, such as:

- We can easily create a project with maven.
- We can simply add jars and other project dependencies with the assistance of maven.
- Maven gives project details (a log document, a dependency list, unit test results, and so on).

- Maven is quite helpful for a project when it comes to upgrading the central repository of JARs and other dependencies.
- We can use Maven to build any number of projects into output formats such as JAR, Web Application Resources (WAR), and so on without performing any programming.
- We can simply connect our project with a source controller by using Maven.

Maven's Core Ideas

- **Project Object Model Files:** POM Files are XML files that include project and configuration information such as dependencies, source directory, plugin, objectives, and so on. Maven utilizes them to create the project. When you want to run a maven command, you provide it a POM file to work with. Maven reads the pom.xml file to configure and run its activities.
- **Dependencies and Repository:** Dependencies are external Java libraries required by the project, whereas repositories are folders containing bundled JAR files. The local repository is simply a directory on your computer's hard drive. If the dependencies aren't discovered in your local Maven repository, Maven gets them from a central Maven repository and stores them in your local repository.
- **Build Life Cycles, Phases, and Objectives:** A build life cycle comprises a series of build phases, and each build phase is made up of a series of goals. The

name of a Maven command refers to a build lifecycle, phase, or objective. When a lifecycle is asked to be run using the maven command, all build steps in that life cycle are likewise executed. When a build phase is requested to be conducted, the build phases in the given order are also performed.

- **Build Profiles:** A build profile is a collection of configuration settings that allows you to build your project with various configurations. For example, you may need to compile your project for development and testing on your local computer. To allow multiple builds, use the profile components in your POM files to add different build profiles triggered in several ways.

- **Build Plugins:** Build plugins are used to do specific tasks. A plugin may be added to the POM file. You can use Maven's standard plugins, or you can write your own in Java.

Maven Installation Procedure

- Check to see if your machine has Java installed. If not, download and install Java.

- Check to see if the Environmental java variable is set. If this is not the case, then set the java environmental variable.

- Install Maven (https://maven.apache.org/download.cgi).

- Unzip your maven zip file anywhere on your system.

- Add the bin directory of the newly formed directory apache-maven-3.5.3 (depending on your installation version) to the PATH environment variable and the system variable.
- Run the mvn -v command in cmd. If it prints the lines of code below, the installation is complete.

pom.xml Maven File

POM, which stands for Project Object Model, is essential for Maven to function. Maven reads the pom.xml file to configure and run its activities. It is an Extensible Markup Language (XML) file that provides project-related and configuration information such as dependencies, source directory, plugin, objectives, etc. It is utilized by Maven to create the project.[3]

```
<project xmlns="http://maven.apache.org/
POM/4.0.0"
xmlns:xsi="http://www.w3.org/2001/
XMLSchema-instance"
xsi:schemaLocation="http://maven.apache.
org/POM/4.0.0
http://maven.apache.org/xsd/
maven-4.0.0.xsd">

<modelVersion>4.0.0</modelVersion>
<groupId> com.project.loggerapi
</groupId>
```

[3] https://www.geeksforgeeks.org/introduction-apache-maven-build-automation-tool-java-projects/, greeksforgeeks

```
<artifactId>LoggerApi</artifactId>
<version>0.0.1-SNAPSHOT</version>

<!-- Add typical dependencies for a web
application -->
<dependencies>
<dependency>
<groupId>org.apache.logging.log4j</groupId>
<artifactId>log4j-api</artifactId>
<version>2.11.0</version></dependency>
</dependencies>

</project>
```

Elements Utilized in Creating the pom.xml File

- **project:** The root element of the pom.xml file is the project.
- **modelVersion:** It refers to the version of the POM model that you are utilizing. For Maven 2 and Maven 3, use version 4.0.0.
- **groupId:** The project group's id is represented by groupId. It is unique, and you will most likely choose a group ID close to the root Java package name of the project as we did with the groupId com.project.loggerapi.
- **artifactId:** It is used to specify the name of the project you are constructing. LoggerApi is the name of our project in this example.
- **version:** The version element includes the project's version number. If your project has been released in many versions, it is essential to provide the version of your project.

Other Pom.xml File Elements

- **Dependencies:** The dependencies element is used to describe a list of project dependencies.
- **Dependency:** It specifies a dependence and is used within the dependencies tag. Each dependency is identified by a groupId, an artifactId, and a version.
- **Name:** This element is utilized to give our maven project a name.
- **Scope:** This element is used to describe the scope of this maven project, which may be compile, runtime, test, supplied system, and so on.
- **Packaging:** The packaging element is utilized for packaging our project into output kinds such as JAR, WAR, etc.

The Benefits and Drawbacks of Using Maven

Benefits

- By scanning the pom file, Maven can automatically add all of the project's dependencies.
- Using Maven, one may quickly compile their project to the jar, war, and other formats as needed.
- Maven makes it simple to start projects in multiple settings and eliminates the need to handle dependency injection, builds, processing, and so on.
- It is quite simple to add a new dependent. Simply write the dependent code in the pom file.

Drawbacks

- Maven requires a maven installation on the system and a maven plugin for the IDE to function.
- If the maven code for an existing dependent is not accessible, maven cannot be used to add that dependency.

When Should Maven be Used?

- When the project has many dependents, then, using maven, you can easily manage those dependencies.
- When the dependent version is regularly updated, simply update the version ID in the pom file to update dependencies.
- Maven makes it simple to handle continuous builds, integration, and testing.
- When there is a requirement for a simple approach to generate documentation from source code, Compiling source code, and then packaging it into JAR or ZIP files.

Maven in Practical Application

When working on a java project that has a lot of dependencies, builds, and requirements, handling all of those things manually is quite tedious and monotonous. Thus, having a tool that can perform these tasks is quite beneficial.

It is a build management tool that can handle everything from adding dependencies to managing a project's classpath to automatically creating war and jar files.

Maven Repository

Maven repositories are folders that contain packaged JAR files along with some information. The metadata are POM files that provide information on the projects to which each packaged JAR file belongs and what external dependencies each packaged JAR has.

This information instructs Maven to download dependents of your dependencies recursively until all dependencies have been downloaded and installed on your local computer.

Maven offers three different types of repositories:

1. Local repository
2. Central repository
3. Remote repository

WHAT EXACTLY IS GRADLE?

Gradle is an open-source build automation platform that is intended to be versatile enough to create nearly any sort of software. The following are some of its features:

High Performance

Gradle eliminates redundant work by only performing tasks required to run because their inputs or outputs have changed. A build cache can also be used to reuse task results from earlier runs or even from a separate computer.

Gradle incorporates several more improvements, and the development team is always working to enhance Gradle's speed.

The JVM Foundation

Gradle operates on the JVM, and you must have a Java Development Kit (JDK) installed to use it. This is advantageous for Java platform users since you may utilize normal

Java APIs in your build logic, such as custom task types and plugins. It also makes it simple to run Gradle on many platforms.

It's worth noting that Gradle isn't just for generating JVM applications; it also has support for building native projects.

Conventions

Gradle takes a page from Maven's book and implements standards to make common sorts of projects, such as Java projects, easier to create. With the right plugins, you can quickly create compact build scripts for a variety of projects. These conventions, however, do not limit you: Gradle allows you to override them, add your jobs, and customize your convention-based builds in a variety of ways.

Flexibility

Gradle's flexibility allows you to add your task types easily or even build models. For example, consider Android build support, introducing numerous additional build concepts such as flavors and build types.

Gradle: Five Things You Should Know

Gradle is a versatile and powerful build tool that might be frightening when you first start using it. Understanding the following fundamental concepts, on the other hand, will make Gradle much more approachable, and you will be an expert with the tool before you realize it.

- Gradle is a build tool that may be used for a variety of purposes
- The basic model is task-based

- Gradle features several fixed build stages
- Gradle may be extended in a variety of ways
- Build scripts interact with an API

What Is the Difference between Gradle and Maven?

A program and group of programs containing instructions that deliver the intended functionality are referred to as software. Engineering is the process of creating and producing anything to suit a specific function while also finding a cost-effective solution to issues. Gradle and Maven are two software development technologies. The contrasts between these two tools are explained.

1. **Gradle:** Gradle is an open-source technology that allows us to automate the creation of software. Because of its excellent performance, this tool is extensively utilized to develop various types of software. It creates the project structure using Java and a Groovy-based Domain-Specific Language (DSL). Gradle facilitates the development of mobile and online apps and their testing and deployment across many platforms. It is considered an official tool for creating Android applications because of its capabilities.
2. **Maven:** Maven is an open-source program management tool that assists us in creating various applications throughout the lifespan of this tool. This tool focuses on standardization (i.e., developing software in a standard layout in a short amount of time). We can use this to construct Java projects, but it can also be used for other languages. Maven structures the application using Extensible Markup Language.

	Gradle	Maven
Based on	Gradle is a framework for creating domain-specific language applications.	Maven is a framework for creating pure Java language-based applications.
Configuration	It creates project structure using a Groovy-based Domain-specific language.	It uses Extensible Markup Language for creating project structure.
Focuses on	Adding additional features to existing apps to make them more useful.	Creating applications within a specific time frame.
Performance	It outperforms Maven since it is geared for tracking only the currently executing task.	Because it does not create a local temp folder during software creation, it takes a long time.
Java Compilation	It does not require compilation.	Compilation is required.
Usability	It is a new tool that will take some time for people to become used to.	This tool is well-known among many users and is easily accessible.
Customization	Because it supports several IDEs, this application is very configurable.	This program only supports a small number of developers and is not very configurable.
Languages supported	It supports Java, C, C++, and Groovy program development.	It supports Scala, C#, and Ruby program development.

In this chapter, we discussed libraries, packages, and modules and access modifiers and Access Modifiers with Method Overriding in Java. In addition, we learned about encapsulation and object cloning in Java. We also learned about Maven and Grandle.

CHAPTER 7

Java Database Connectivity

IN THIS CHAPTER

- ➢ What is JDBC?
- ➢ Relational Databases
- ➢ Relational Database Management Systems
- ➢ Learning SQL

We discussed Libraries, Packages, and Modules in the previous chapter and how to arrange packages. We also discussed access modifiers, encapsulation, and cloning objects. In Java, we also discussed Maven and Grandle. We will learn about Java Database Connectivity (JDBC), as well as relational databases and Structured Query Language (SQL).

DOI: 10.1201/9781003229063-7

WHAT IS JDBC IN JAVA?

JDBC is an acronym for Java Database Connectivity. JDBC is a Java Application Programming Interface (API) that connects to databases and runs queries against them. It is a part of JavaSE. JDBC API connects to the database using JDBC drivers. JDBC drivers are classified into four types:

- JDBC-ODBC Bridge Driver
- Native Driver
- Network Protocol Driver
- Thin Driver

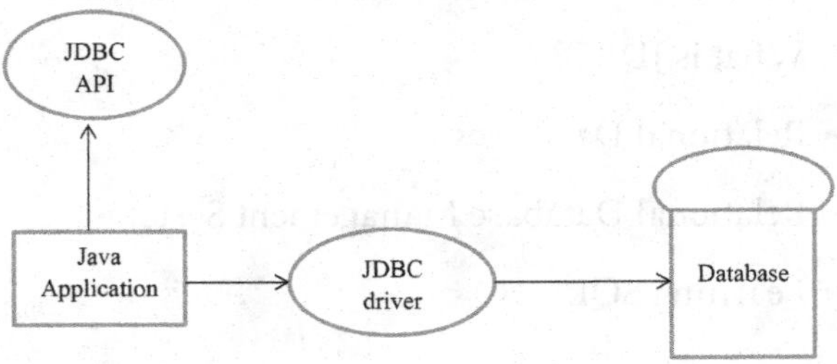

JDBC API may be used to retrieve tabular data contained in any relational database. We may store, edit, remove, and retrieve data from the database using the JDBC API. It is similar to Microsoft's Open Database Connectivity (ODBC). JDBC 4.3 is the most recent version. It has been steady since September 21, 2017. Its foundation is the X/Open SQL Call Level Interface. The java.sql package contains JDBC API classes and interfaces. The following is a list of standard JDBC API interfaces:

- Driver
- Connection
- Statement
- PreparedStatement
- CallableStatement
- ResultSet
- ResultSetMetaData
- DatabaseMetaData
- RowSet

The Following Is a Collection of Popular Jdbc Api Classes:

- DriverManager
- Blob
- Clob
- Types

What Are the Benefits of Using JDBC?

Prior to JDBC, the database API to connect to and run queries with the database was ODBC API. However, the ODBC API uses an ODBC driver written in C. (i.e., platform-dependent and unsecured). As a result, Java has created its API (JDBC API) that employs JDBC drivers.

We may use JDBC API to manage databases in Java programs and do the following tasks:

- Connect to database
- Run queries and update statements against the database.
- Obtain the outcome of the database query.

What Exactly Is API?

An API is a document that describes all of the characteristics of a product or software. It depicts the classes and interfaces that software applications can use to interact with one another. APIs can be written for programs, libraries, operating systems, and so on.

DRIVER FOR JDBC

JDBC Driver is a piece of software that enables Java programs to connect with databases. JDBC drivers are classified into four types:

1. Driver for JDBC-ODBC Bridge
2. Driver for native API
3. Driver for the Network Protocol
4. Thin driver

- **Driver for JDBC-ODBC Bridge:** The JDBC-ODBC bridge driver connects to the database using the ODBC driver. The JDBC-ODBC bridge driver converts JDBC method calls to ODBC function calls. Because of the thin driver, this is now discouraged.

Oracle does not support the Java 8 JDBC-ODBC Bridge. Instead of using the JDBC-ODBC Bridge, Oracle advises that you utilize JDBC drivers provided by your database vendor.

- Benefits:
  - Simple to use.
  - It is simple to connect to any database.
- Disadvantages:
  - Performance suffers since JDBC method calls are translated into ODBC function calls.
  - The client machine must have the ODBC driver installed.

- **Driver for Native API:** The Native API driver takes advantage of the client-side libraries provided by the database. The driver transforms JDBC method calls into database API native calls. It is not entirely written in Java.
  - Advantage:
    - Superior performance than the JDBC-ODBC bridge driver.
  - Disadvantage:
    - Each client system must have the Native driver installed.
    - On the client system, the Vendor client library must be installed.

- **Driver for the Network Protocol:** The Network Protocol driver uses middleware (application servers) to transform JDBC calls actively or passively into supplier database protocols. It's entirely written in Java.
  - Advantage:
    - There is no need for a client-side library because the application server can do various activities like auditing, load balancing, logging, etc.
  - Disadvantages:
    - The client machine must have network capability.
    - Database-specific coding must be done at the middle tier.
    - Servicing Internet Protocol drivers is expensive since it necessitates data system coding in the intermediate tier.
- **Thin Driver:** The thin driver immediately transforms JDBC calls into the vendor-specific database protocol. That is why it is referred to as a thin driver. It is entirely written in Java.
  - Advantage:
    - Outperforms all other drivers in terms of performance.
    - There is no software required on either the client or server-side.

- Disadvantage:
    - Drivers are dependent on the database.

5 Steps to Connecting a Java Database

To connect any Java program to a database using JDBC, follow these five steps. These are the actions to take:

1. Register for the Driver class
2. Make a connection
3. Make a statement
4. Perform out inquiries
5. Close connection

- **Register for the Driver class:** The Class class's forName() function is used to register the driver class. This technique is used to load the driver class dynamically.

  forName() method syntax:

  ```
  public static void forName(String
  class_Name)throws
  ClassNotFoundException
  ```

  The following is an example of how to register the OracleDriver class:

  In this case, the Java program is loading the Oracle driver to establish a database connection.

  ```
  Class.forName("oracle.jdbc.driver.
  OracleDriver");
  ```

- **Make a Connection:** The DriverManager class's getConnection() function is used to connect to the database.

  getConnection() method syntax:

  ```
  public static Connection
  getConnection(String_url)throws
  SQLException
  public static Connection
  getConnection(String url,String_
  name,String_password) throws
  SQLException
  ```

  Example:

  ```
  Connection con=DriverManager.
  getConnection(
  "jdbc:oracle:thin:@localhost:1521:xe",
  "root1","passwords");
  ```

- **Make a Statement:** To construct a statement, utilize the Connection interface's createStatement() function. The statement's object is in charge of doing queries to the database.

  Syntax of the method createStatement():

  ```
  public Statement create-Statement()
  throws SQLException
  ```

  Example:

  ```
  Statement stmt=con.create-Statement();
  ```

- **Perform Out Inquiries:** The executeQuery() function of the Statement interface is used to execute database queries. This function provides a ResultSet object that may retrieve all of the records in a table.

  ExecuteQuery() method syntax:

  ```
  public ResultSet executeQuery(String
  sql)throws SQLException
  ```

  Example:

  ```
  ResultSet rts=stmt.
  executeQuery("select * from empy");
  while(rts.next())
  {
  System.out.println(rts.
  getInt(1)+" "+rts.getString(2));
  }
  ```

- **Close Connection:** By closing the connection object statement, the ResultSet will be immediately closed. The Connection interface's close() function is used to end the connection.

  Close() method syntax:

  ```
  public void close()throws
  SQLException
  ```

  Example:

  ```
  con.close();
  ```

ORACLE DATABASE CONNECTIVITY IN JAVA

To connect a Java program to an Oracle database, we must first complete the five procedures listed below. The database used in this sample is Oracle 10g. As a result, the following information is required for the Oracle database:

- **Driver class:** Oracle.jdbc.driver.OracleDriver is the driver class for the Oracle database.
- **URL for the connection:** The Oracle10G database connection URL is jdbc: oracle:thin:@localhost:1521:xe where jdbc is the API, oracle is the database, thin is the driver, localhost is the server name (or IP address), 1521 is the port number, and XE is the Oracle service name All of this information is available in the tnsnames.ora file.
- **Username:** System is the default username for the Oracle database.
- **Password:** This is the password entered by the user while installing the Oracle database.

Creating a Table

Before we connect, let's first create a table in the Oracle database. The SQL statement to create a table is shown below.

```
create table empy(id number(20),name
varchar2(30),age number(5));
```

Example

In this instance, we connect to an Oracle database and retrieve data from the emp table. Here, the system and oracle are the Oracle database's login and password.

```
import java.sql.*;
class OracleConnc
{
public static void main(String args[])
{
try
{
// load the driver class step1
Class.forName("oracle.jdbc.driver.
OracleDriver");

// create the connection object step2
Connection connc=DriverManager.
getConnection(
"jdbc:oracle:thin:@localhost:1521:xe","root",
"password");

// create the statement object step3
Statement stmt=connc.createStatement();

// execute query step4
ResultSet rts=stmt.executeQuery("select *
from empy");
while(rts.next())
System.out.println(rts.getInt(1)+"  "+rts.
getString(2)+"  "+rts.getString(3));
```

```
// close the connection object step5
connc.close();

}catch(Exception e)
{
 System.out.println(e);
}

}
}
```

There are two methods for loading the jar file:

1. **Paste the ojdbc14.jar file into the jre/lib/ext folder:** To begin, look for the ojdbc14.jar file, then navigate to the JRE/lib/ext folder and paste the jar file there.
2. **Set the Classpath:** The classpath may be established in two ways: temporary and permanent.

How to Configure the Temporary Classpath

To begin, look for the ojdbc14.jar file, then open a command line and type:

```
C:>set class-path=c:\folder\ojdbc14.jar;.;
```

How to Configure the Permanent Classpath

Navigate to an environment variable and then to a new tab. In variable name, write classpath, and in variable value, attach ojdbc14.jar to the path to ojdbc14.jar;.; as C:oraclexeapporacleproduct10.2.0serverjdbclibojdbc14.jar;.

MySQL Database Connectivity in Java

To connect a Java program to a MySQL database, we must first go through the five steps below.

In this example, MySql is used as the database. As a result, we must know these facts about the mysql database:

```
com.mysql.jdbc. Driver is the mysql
database driver class.
```

URL for the connection: The connection URL for the mysql database is jdbc:mysql:/localhost:2306/root, where jdbc is the API mysql is the database, localhost is the server name, 2306 is the port number, and root is the database name. We may use any database; in that case, we must change the root with the name of our database.

- **Username:** The mysql database's default username is root.
- **Password:** This is the password entered by the user while installing the mysql database. In this example, we'll use root as the password.

Let's begin by creating a table in the mysql database, but first, we must build the database:

```
create database example;
use example;
create table empy(id int(20),name
varchar(50),age int(4));
```

Example:

```
import java.sql.*;
class MysqlConn
{
public static void main(String args[]){
try{
Class.forName("com.mysql.jdbc.Driver");
Connection con=DriverManager.getConnection(
"jdbc:mysql://localhost:3306/
example","root","ABC");
//here example is database name, root is
username and password
Statement stmt=conn.createStatement();
ResultSet rts=stmt.executeQuery("select
* from empy");
while(rts.next())
System.out.println(rs.getInt(1)+"  "+rts.
getString(2)+"  "+rts.getString(3));
conn.close();
}catch(Exception e)
{
 System.out.println(e);
}
}
}
```

CONNECTIVITY WITH ACCESS WITHOUT DATA SOURCE NAME (DSN)

There are two methods for connecting a Java program to an Access database.

1. Without Data Source Name

2. With Data Source Name

Example of Connecting a Java Application without a DSN

In this example, we will link the java program to the access database. In this example, we set up the login table in the access database. In the table, there is just one column called name. Let's retrieve the login table's full name.

```
import java.sql.*;
class Test1
{
public static void main(String ar[])
{
 try{
   String database1="student.mdb"; // In
this case, the database exists in the
current directory.

   String url="jdbc:odbc:Driver={Microsoft
Access Driver (*.mdb)};
                    DBQ=" + database1 +
";DriverID=22;READONLY=true";

   Class.forName("sun.jdbc.odbc.
JdbcOdbcDriver");
   Connection c1=DriverManager.
getConnection(url);
   Statement sts=c1.createStatement();
   ResultSet rts=sts.executeQuery("select
* from login");

   while(rts.next()){
    System.out.println(rts.getString(1));
   }
```

```
}catch(Exception ee){System.out.
println(ee);}

}}
```

Example of Connecting a Java Application to a DSN

Connectivity with a type 1 driver is regarded as poor. To connect a Java application to a type 1 driver, first, construct a DSN; in this example, we'll assume your DSN name is mydsn.

```
import java.sql.*;
class Test1
{
public static void main(String ar[])
{
 try{
   String url="jdbc:odbc:mydsn";
   Class.forName("sun.jdbc.odbc.
JdbcOdbcDriver");
   Connection c1=DriverManager.
getConnection(url);
   Statement sts=c1.createStatement();
   ResultSet rts=sts.executeQuery("select
* from login");

   while(rts.next()){
    System.out.println(rts.getString(1));
   }

 }catch(Exception ee){System.out.
println(ee);}

 }}
```

DRIVERMANAGER CLASS

The DriverManager class serves as a bridge between the user and the drivers. It maintains track of the available drivers and facilitates the establishment of a link between a database and the right driver. The DriverManager class keeps track of all Driver classes that have registered themselves by invoking the DriverManager.registerDriver function ().

DriverManager Class Methods That Are Useful

Method	**Description**
public static void registerDriver(Driver driver):	It is used to add the specified driver to DriverManager.
public static void deregisterDriver(Driver driver):	It is used to deregister the specified driver with DriverManager (to remove the driver from the list).
public static Connection getConnection(String url):	It is used to make a connection to the provided url.
public static Connection getConnection(String url,String_userName,String_password):	It is used to connect with the provided url, username, and password.

Interface of Connection

A Connection is a session that exists between a Java program and a database. The Connection interface is a factory for Statement, PreparedStatement, and DatabaseMetaData, which means that the Connection object may be used to get the Statement and DatabaseMetaData objects. The Connection interface provides several transaction management methods such as commit(), rollback(), etc.

Methods of the Connection interface that are often used:

- **public Statement createStatement():** This function generates a statement object that may be used to perform SQL queries.
- **public Statement createStatement(int resultSetType,int resultSetConcurrency):** This method creates a Statement object that will generate ResultSet objects of the specified type and concurrency.
- **public void setAutoCommit(boolean status):** This function is used to set the commit status.
  - It is true by default.
- **public void commit():** Permanently saves the modifications made since the last commit/rollback.
- **public void rollback():** Removes any modifications made since the previous commit/rollback.
- **public void close():** instantly ends the connection and releases any JDBC resources.

Statement Interface

The Statement interface offers ways for querying the database. The statement interface is a ResultSet factory, which means it provides a factory method for obtaining a ResultSet object.

Statement interface techniques that are often used:

The following are the essential Statement interface methods:

- **public ResultSet executeQuery(String sql):** this method is used to run a SELECT query. It returns the ResultSet object.
- **public int executeUpdate(String sql):** is used to execute the provided query, which might be create, drop, insert, update, delete, and so on.
- **public boolean executes (String sql):** this method is used to run searches that may yield numerous results.
- **public int[] executeBatch():** is used to run a series of instructions in a row.

Example:

```
import java.sql.*;
class FetchRecords
{
public static void main(String args[])
throws Exception{
Class.forName("oracle.jdbc.driver.
OracleDriver");
Connection conn=DriverManager.getConne
ction("jdbc:oracle:thin:@localhost:152
1:xe","system","root");
Statement stmts=cons.createStatement();

int result=stmts.executeUpdate("delete
from emp765 where id=43");
```

```
System.out.println(result+" records
affected");
con.close();
}}
```

DATABASE MANAGEMENT SYSTEM

DBMS Tutorial teaches fundamental and advanced database topics. Our DBMS Tutorial is intended for both beginners and experienced users.

A database management system (DBMS) is software that is used to manage databases.

Our DBMS Tutorial covers all DBMS subjects: introduction, ER model, keys, relational model, join operation, SQL, functional dependence, transaction, concurrency control, etc.

What Exactly Is a Database?

The database is a collection of meaningful connections used to retrieve, insert, and delete items efficiently. It is also used to arrange data into tables, schema, views, and reports, among other things.[1]

For example, the college database organizes data on the administration, staff, students, and professors, among other things.

You can quickly access, insert, and delete information using the database.

Database Management System

A DBMS is a piece of software used to manage databases. For example, MySQL, Oracle, and other commercial databases are often used in a wide range of applications.

[1] https://www.geeksforgeeks.org/introduction-of-dbms-database-management-system-set-1/, geeksforgreeks

DBMS offers an interface for performing different activities such as database creation, data storage, data updating, table creation in the database, and much more.

It ensures the database's safety and security. It also ensures data consistency in the case of numerous users.

DBMS allows users to do the following tasks:

- **Data Definition:** It is used to create, modify, and remove definitions that describe the arrangement of data in a database.
- **Data Updation:** It is used for inserting, modifying, and deleting actual data from the database.
- **Data Retrieval:** It is used to retrieve data from a database so that programs may utilize it for various reasons.
- **User Administration:** It is used for enrolling and monitoring users, maintaining data integrity, enforcing data security, dealing with concurrency control, monitoring performance, and restoring information damaged by unexpected failure.

DBMS Features Include the Usage of a Digital Repository Built on a Server to Store and Manage Information

- It can give a clear and logical perspective of the data manipulation process.
- Automatic backup and recovery processes are built into DBMS.

- It has ACID characteristics that keep data in a healthy condition in the event of a failure.
- It has the potential to simplify the complicated connection between data.
- It is used to help in data manipulation and processing.
- It is used to ensure data security.
- It may see the database from several perspectives based on the user's needs.

Benefits of DBMS

- **Controls database redundancy:** It can manage data redundancy since it keeps all of the data in a single database file and that recorded data is stored in the database.
- **Data sharing:** In DBMS, an organization's authorized users can exchange data among numerous users.
- **Easily Maintenance:** Because of the centralized structure of the database system, it is readily maintenance.
- **Reduce development and maintenance time:** It decreases development and maintenance time.
- **Backup:** It includes backup and recovery subsystems that generate automatic backups of data in the event of hardware or software failures and restore the data if necessary.
- **Multiple user interfaces:** It offers a variety of user interfaces, including graphical user interfaces and application program interfaces.

DBMS Disadvantages

- **Cost of Hardware and Software:** A high-speed data processor and a big memory capacity are required to execute DBMS software.
- **Size:** To operate them efficiently, it requires a vast amount of storage space and RAM.
- **Complexity:** A database system adds complexity and needs.
- **Higher impact of failure:** Failure has a more significant effect on the database since, in most organizations, all data is kept in a single database, and if the database is destroyed due to an electric failure or database corruption, the data may be lost permanently.

DATABASE

What Exactly Is Data?

A collection of unique tiny units of information is referred to as data. It can take several forms, including text, numbers, media, bytes, and so on. It can be saved on paper or in electronic memory, for example.

The term "data" is derived from the Latin word "datum," which signifies a "single item of information?" It is the plural form of the word data.

Data is information in computing that can be converted into a form that allows for efficient transportation and processing. Data can be interchanged.

What Exactly Is a Database?

A database is a structured collection of data that can be accessed and handled simply.

To make it simpler to discover important information, you may arrange data into tables, rows, and columns and index it.

Database handlers design databases so that just one set of software programs gives data access to all users.

The database's primary function is to run a vast quantity of information by storing, retrieving, and managing data.

Nowadays, there are numerous dynamic websites on the World Wide Web that are managed by databases. For example, consider a model that checks the availability of hotel rooms. It is an example of a database-driven dynamic webpage.

MySQL, Sybase, Oracle, MongoDB, Informix, PostgreSQL, SQL Server, and more databases are available.

The DBMS manages modern databases.

Structured Query Language(SQL), is a programming language used to manipulate data contained in a database. SQL(Structured Query Language) is predicated on relational algebra and tuple relational calculus.

The image of a database is displayed using a circular shape.

DATABASE EVOLUTION

The database has evolved over more than 50 years, from flat-file systems to relational and object-relational systems. It has been passed down for too many generations.

File-Based

File-Based databases were first presented in 1968. Data was stored as a flat file in file-based databases. Although files offer numerous benefits, they do have certain limits.

One of the significant benefits is that the file system supports a variety of access techniques, such as sequential, indexed, and random.

It necessitates considerable programming in a third-generation language like COBOL or BASIC.

Hierarchical Data Model

The Hierarchical Database reigned supreme from 1968 until 1980. IBM's initial DBMS used a prominent hierarchical database model. It was known as IMS (Information Management System).

Files are connected in this paradigm in a parent/child relationship.

The figure below depicts a hierarchical data model. Objects are represented by little circles.

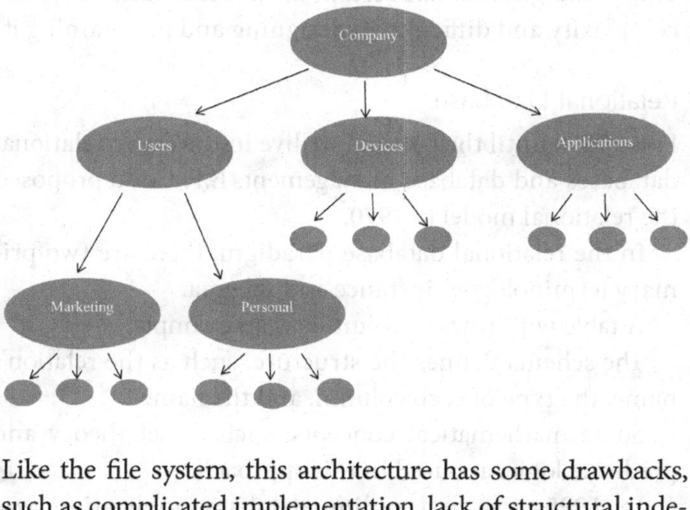

Like the file system, this architecture has some drawbacks, such as complicated implementation, lack of structural independence, inability to manage a many-many connection, etc.

Network Data Model

At Honeywell, Charles Bachman created the first DBMS, named Integrated Data Store (IDS). It was built in the early 1960s, but the CODASYL group standardized it in 1971.

Files in this architecture are connected as owners and members, similar to the standard network model.

The following components were discovered using the network data model:

- Network schema
- Sub-schema
- Data management language

This paradigm also has certain drawbacks, such as system complexity and difficulty in designing and maintaining it.

Relational Database

From 1970 until the present, we live in the era of relational databases and database management. E.F. Codd proposed the relational model in 1970.

In the relational database paradigm, there are two primary terminologies: instance and schema.

A table with rows or columns is an example.

The schema defines the structure, such as the relation's name, the type of each column, and the name.

Some mathematical concepts, such as set theory and predicate logic, are used in this approach.

In 1995, the first online database application was developed.

Many additional models were introduced throughout the relational database era, such as the object-oriented model, the object-relational model, etc.

Cloud Database

A cloud database allows you to store, manage, and retrieve structured and unstructured data over a cloud platform. This information is available over the Internet. Because they are provided as a managed service, cloud databases are also known as databases as a service.

The following are some of the significant cloud options:

- Amazon Web Services
- Snowflake Computing
- Oracle Database Cloud Services
- Microsoft SQL server
- Google cloud spanner

Benefits of a Cloud Database

- **Reduced costs:** In general, a firm provider is not required to invest in databases. It is capable of running and supporting one or more data centers.
- **Automated:** A range of automatic procedures, such as recovery, failover, and auto-scaling, are added to cloud databases.
- **Improved accessibility:** You may access your cloud-based database at any time and from any location. All you require is an Internet connection.

NoSQL DATABASE

A NoSQL database is a database architecture method that can support a wide range of data structures. NoSQL is an abbreviation for "not only SQL." It is an alternative to typical relational databases in which data is stored in tables, and the data structure is meticulously developed before the database is constructed.

NoSQL databases are beneficial for vast amounts of dispersed data.

The following are some examples of NoSQL database systems and their categories:

- MongoDB, CouchDB, Cloudant
- Memcached, Redis, Coherence
- HBase, Big Table, Accumulo

The Benefit of NoSQL Is Its Scalability

- **Excellent scalability:** Because of its scalability, NoSQL can manage a large quantity of data. If the amount of data increases, the NoSQL database scales to manage it efficiently.
- **Availability is high:** Auto replication is supported by NoSQL. Because data replicates itself to the prior consistent state in the event of a failure, it is highly accessible.

The Disadvantage of NoSQL Is That It Is Open Source

- **Open-source:** Because NoSQL is an open-source database, there is currently no credible standard for NoSQL.

- **Management difficulty:** Data administration in NoSQL is far more difficult than in traditional databases. It isn't easy to install and considerably more challenging to handle regularly.
- **No graphical user interface:** There aren't many GUI tools for NoSQL databases on the market.
- **Backup:** Backup is a significant weakness for NoSQL databases. Some databases, such as MongoDB, lack robust data backup solutions.

OBJECT-ORIENTED DATABASES

Object-oriented databases (OODs) store data as objects and classes. Things are real-world entities, while types are groups of objects. An OOD combines aspects of the relational model with object-oriented principles. It is a different implementation than the relational model.

OODs adhere to object-oriented programming principles. A hybrid application is an object-oriented DBMS.

The OOD model has the following characteristics.

- Object-Oriented Programming (OOP) Characteristics
  - Objects
  - Classes
  - Inheritance
  - Polymorphism
  - Encapsulation

- Properties of a Relational Database
    - Atomicity
    - Consistency
    - Integrity
    - Durability
    - Concurrency
    - Query processing

WHAT EXACTLY IS RELATIONAL DATABASE MANAGEMENT?

RDBMS is an abbreviation for Relational Database Management Systems.

RDBMS is the foundation of all current DBMSs such as SQL, MS SQL Server, IBM DB2, ORACLE, My-SQL, and Microsoft Access.[2]

It is known as the RDBMS since it is based on E.F. Codd's relational paradigm.

How Does It Work?

In RDBMS, data is represented as tuples (rows).

The most popular type of database is a relational database. It comprises a number of tables, each with its own primary key.

Data in RDBMS may be retrieved simply due to a collection of structured tables.

[2] https://www.javatpoint.com/what-is-rdbms, javaTpoint

RDBMS History

From 1970 to 1972, E.F. Codd released a study proposing the usage of the relational database model.

RDBMS is based on E.F. Codd's development of the relational model.

What Actually Is a Table?

Tables are used to hold data in the RDBMS database. A table is a collection of connected data items that uses rows and columns to hold information.

A table is the most basic type of data storage in an RDBMS. Let's look at an example of a student table.

ID	Name	AGE	COURSE
1	Anita	23	MSC
2	Arnav	20	Commerce
3	Mayank	22	B-Tech
4	Rita	21	Maths
5	Vicky	22	IT

What Exactly Is a Field?

A field is a subset of a table that provides particular information about each entry in the table. The fields in the student table in the above example are id, name, age, and course.

What Is Row or Record?

A table row is also known as a record. It gives information about each individual entry in the table. In the table, it is a horizontal object. As an example: There are five records in the table above.

Let's take a look at one record/row in the table.

1	Anita	23	MSC

What Basically Is a Column?

A column is a vertical object in a table that includes all information connected with a given field. For example, in the following table, "name" is a column that provides all information on the student's name.

Anita
Arnav
Mayank
Rita
Vicky

- **NULL Values:** A NULL value in a table indicates that a field was left blank during record creation. It is not the same as a value of zero or a field containing space.
- **Data Integrity:** Each RDBMS has the following categories of data integrity:
- **Entity integrity:** Entity integrity requires that there be no duplicate rows in a table.
- **Domain integrity:** It ensures that valid entries for a particular column are entered by limiting the type, format, or range of values.
- **Referential integrity:** This indicates that rows that are utilized by other records cannot be removed.
- **User-defined integrity:** It enforces some specific business rules that users set. These rules are distinct from those governing entity, domain, or referential integrity.

What Is the Distinction between DBMS and RDBMS?

Although both DBMS and RDBMS store data in physical databases, there are significant distinctions between them.

The following are the primary distinctions between DBMS and RDBMS.

No.	DBMS	RDBMS
1	Data is stored as a file in DBMS applications.	RDBMS applications use tabular data to store information.
2	Data in DBMS is often stored in either a hierarchical or a navigational format.	Tables in RDBMS contain a unique identifier known as the primary key, and data values are kept in the form of tables.
3	DBMS does not support normalization.	RDBMS supports normalization.
4	DBMS does not apply any security with regard to data manipulation.	RDBMS(Relational database management system) defines the integrity constraint for the purpose of the ACID (Atomicity, Consistency, Isolation, and Durability) characteristic.
5	DBMS(database management system) uses a file system to store data, so there will be no relation between the tables.	Because data values in RDBMS are kept in the form of tables, a connection between these data values will also be recorded in the form of a table.
6	DBMS has to provide some uniform methods to access the stored information.	The RDBMS system offers a tabular data structure and a link between them to retrieve the stored information.
7	DBMS does not support distributed databases.	RDBMS allows for distributed databases.
8	DBMS is designed for tiny organizations for dealing with minor amounts of data. It only supports a single user.	RDBMS is built to manage massive amounts of data. It allows for numerous users.
9	File systems, XML, and other DBMS are examples.	RDBMS examples include mysql, postgre, sql server, and oracle.

After examining the distinctions between DBMS and RDBMS, you can conclude that RDBMS is a subset of DBMS. There are numerous software solutions on the market today that are DBMS and RDBMS compatible. That is, an RDBMS application is now a DBMS application and vice versa.

File System vs. DBMS

The following distinctions exist between DBMS and file systems:

DBMS	File System
A DBMS is a collection of data. The user is not necessary to write procedures in DBMS.	The file system is a collection of data, and the user must create the methods for maintaining the database in this system.
Database management system offers an abstract representation of data that hides the details.	The file system specifies the details of data representation and storage.
DBMS offers a crash recovery mechanism, which protects the user in the event of a system failure.	The file system lacks a crash mechanism, which means that if the machine fails while inputting data, the file's information is lost.
A decent protection method is provided by DBMS.	It is extremely difficult to secure a file in the file system.
DBMS contains a wide variety of sophisticated techniques to store and retrieve the data.	The file system is incapable of storing and retrieving data effectively.
Concurrent data access is handled by DBMS employing some type of locking.	Concurrent access poses numerous difficulties in the file system, such as forwarding the file while another person deletes or updates data.

ARCHITECTURE OF DBMS

A DBMS's architecture has an impact on its design. The primary client/server design is used to cope with a large number of network-connected PCs, web servers, database servers, and other components.

The client/server architecture is made up of numerous PCs and a workstation that are linked together via a network.

DBMS design is determined by how users connect to the database to complete their requests.

DBMS Architecture Types

Database architecture can be single-tiered or multi-tiered. However, conceptually, database architecture is divided into two types: 2-tier architecture and 3-tier architecture.

1st-Tier Architecture

The database is immediately accessible to the user in this architecture. It means that the user may sit right on the DBMS and utilize it.

Any modifications made here will have an immediate impact on the database. It does not offer end consumers with a helpful tool.

The 1-tier design is utilized for local application development, where programmers may directly connect with the database for rapid response.

2-Tier Architecture

The 2-tier architecture is the same as the basic client-server design. In a two-tier design, client-side apps can connect directly with the database on the server-side. APIs like ODBC and JDBC are utilized for this interaction.

On the client-side, user interfaces and application programs are executed.

The server side is in charge of providing functions such as query processing and transaction management.

To communicate with the DBMS, the client-side application connects to the server-side.

3-Tier Architecture

Another layer exists between the client and the server in the 3-Tier architecture. The client cannot connect directly with the server under this design.

The client-side application talks with an application server, which then communicates with the database system.

Beyond the application server, the end-user is unaware of the presence of the database. Aside from the program, the database does not know about any other users.

In the event of an extensive online application, the 3-Tier design is employed.

The Architecture Consists of Three Schema

Three schema architecture is sometimes referred to as ANSI/SPARC architecture or three-level architecture.

This framework describes the structure of a particular database system.

The three schema architecture is often used to differentiate between user applications and actual databases.

There are three levels in the three schema architecture. It categorizes the database into three distinct sections.

1. **Internal Level:** The internal level has an internal schema that specifies the database's actual storage structure. The internal schema is sometimes referred

to as the physical schema. It takes advantage of the physical data model. It is used to specify how data will be stored in a block. The physical level is used to explain complete complicated low-level data structures.

2. **Conceptual Level:** At the conceptual level, the conceptual schema explains the architecture of a database. The conceptual level is sometimes referred to as the logical level. The conceptual schema defines the overall organization of the database. The conceptual level specifies what data will be kept in the database and the relationships that exist between those data. Internal specifics, such as the implementation of the data structure, are buried at the conceptual level. At this level, programmers and database administrators work.
3. **External Level:** A database has many schemas at the external level, which are frequently referred to as subschema. The subschema is used to specify the many database views. An external schema is sometimes referred to as a view schema. Each view schema defines the database component in which a specific user group is interested while hiding the remainder of the database from that user group. The view schema specifies how the database system interacts with the end-user.

MODELS OF DATA

The modeling of the data semantics, data description, and consistency requirements is known as a data model. It gives conceptual tools for specifying a database's design at each level of data abstraction. As a result, the following four data models are used to explain the structure of the database:

1. **Relational Data Model:** This model organizes data into rows and columns within a table. As a result, a relational model employs tables to describe data and in-between connections. Tables are sometimes referred to as relations. Edgar F. Codd first described this concept in 1969. The relational data model is the most frequently used model, with commercial data processing systems mainly using it.
2. **Entity-Relationship Data Model (ER Model):** An ER model is a logical representation of data as objects with relationships between them. These things are referred to as entities, and a relationship is a connection between them. Peter Chen created this model, which was published in 1976 publications. It was commonly utilized in database design. A collection of characteristics describes the entities. For example, the "student" object is represented by student name and student id. An "entity set" is a collection of the same kind of entities, while a "relationship set" is a collection of the same type of relationships.
3. **Object-Based Data Model:** An expansion of the ER model that includes concepts like functions, encapsulation, and object identification. This model provides a comprehensive type system with structured and collection types. As a result, numerous database systems based on the object-oriented paradigm were created in the 1980s. Objects in this context are nothing more than data with attributes.

4. **Semistructured Data Model:** Unlike the other three data models, this one is semistructured (explained above). The semistructured data model supports data specifications at points where specific data items of the same type may have varying attribute sets. The Extensible Markup Language (XML), often known as a markup language, is commonly used to describe semistructured data. Although XML was initially intended to add markup information to text documents, it has grown in popularity due to its usage in data sharing.

SCHEMA AND INSTANCE OF A DATA MODEL

- An instance of the database is the data saved in the database at a specific point in time.
- Schema refers to a database's general design.
- A database schema is the database's skeletal structure. It reflects the database's logical structure.
- A schema includes schema objects like tables, foreign keys, primary keys, views, columns, data types, stored procedures, etc.
- A visual diagram can be used to depict a database schema. This diagram depicts the database items and their relationships.
- Database designers create a database schema to assist programmers whose software will interface with the database. The process of constructing a database is referred to as data modeling.

A schema diagram can only show some schema features, such as the name of the record type, data type, and constraints. The schema diagram does not allow for the specification of other aspects. The presented image, for example, does not display the data type of each data item or the link between multiple files.

INDEPENDENCE OF DATA

- The three-schema architecture may be used to explain data independence.
- Data independence refers to changing the schema at one level of a database system without affecting the schema at the next higher level.

Data independence is classified into two types:

1. **Independence of Logical Data**
   - Logical data independence refers to the capacity to change the conceptual schema without affecting the external schema.
   - To separate the external level from the conceptual perspective, logical data independence is utilized.
   - If we modify the conceptual perspective of the data, it will not affect the user's view of the data.
   - At the user interface level, logical data independence arises.

2. **Independence of Physical Data**

- The ability to modify the internal schema without changing the conceptual schema is referred to as physical data independence.
- If we alter the storage amount of the database system server, the conceptual structure of the database will remain unchanged.
- To distinguish conceptual levels from internal levels, physical data independence is employed.
- The logical interface level is when physical data independence occurs.

Language of Database

A DBMS contains appropriate languages and interfaces for expressing database queries and changes.

To read, save, and update data in a database, database languages can be utilized.

Database Language Varieties

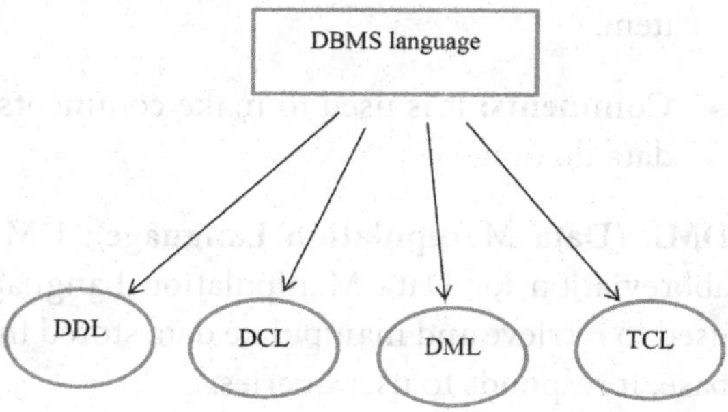

1. **DDL (Data Definition Language):** DDL is an abbreviation for Data Definition Language. It is used to define the structure or pattern of a database.

   It is used in the database to build schema, tables, indexes, constraints, etc.

   The backbone of the database may be created using DDL statements.

   The data definition language is used to record metadata like the number of tables and schemas, their names, indexes, columns in each table, constraints, and so on.

   DDL encompasses the following tasks:

   - **Create:** It is used to create database objects.
   - **Alter:** It is used to change the database's structure.
   - **Drop:** This method is used to remove objects from the database.
   - **Truncate:** This function is used to delete all records from a table.
   - **Rename:** This command is used to rename an item.
   - **Comments:** It is used to make comments on the data dictionary.

2. **DML (Data Manipulation Language):** DML is an abbreviation for Data Manipulation Language. It is used to retrieve and manipulate data stored in a database. It responds to user queries.

DML encompasses the following tasks:

- **Select:** It is used to obtain information from a database.
- **Insert:** This function is used to insert data into a table.
- **Update:** This function is used to update existing data in a table.
- **Delete:** This command is used to remove all records from a table.
- **Merge:** It executes UPSERT actions, such as insert or update operations.
- **Call:** It is used to invoke a structured query language or a Java subprogram.
- **Explain Plan:** It has a parameter for describing data.
- **Lock Table:** Lock It manages concurrency through a table.

3. **DCL (Data Control Language)**

- DCL is an abbreviation for Data Control Language. It is used to retrieve data that has been saved or stored.
- The execution of the DCL is transactional. It also offers rollback options.

(However, with Oracle databases, the execution of data control language does not provide rolling back.)

Here are some examples of DCL tasks:

- **Grant:** It is used to grant a user access to a database.
- **Revoke:** This command is used to revoke a user's permissions.

Revoke permission is granted for the following operations:

- CONNECT, INSERT, USAGE, EXECUTE, DELETE, UPDATE, and SELECT are all commands.

4. **Transaction Control Language:** TCL is used to execute the DML statement's modifications. TCL can be combined to form a logical transaction.

   TCL encompasses the following tasks:

   - **Commit:** This command is used to save the transaction to the database.
   - **Rollback:** It is used to restore the database to its original state after the most recent Commit.

In this chapter, we discussed Java Database connection, its benefits, and JDBC drivers. Steps for Connecting a Java Database to a Different Server were also covered. We learned about DBMSs, RDBMSs, and NoSQL databases and their benefits and drawbacks. We also discussed DBMS architecture and database language.

CHAPTER 8

Java I/O

IN THIS CHAPTER

- ➤ Console I/O in Java
- ➤ Reading from a File
- ➤ Creating and Writing to a File
- ➤ Reading a Properties File

In the previous chapter, we discussed Java database Connectivity (JDBC), Relational Databases and Structured Query Language (SQL), and various JDBC with different servers. In this chapter, we will cover the input-output console in Java, how to read, write, and create files in Java, and their many properties.

WHAT IS INPUT/OUTPUT IN JAVA?

Java I/O is used to process input and output results. Java employs the idea of a stream to speed up I/O operations.

DOI: 10.1201/9781003229063-8

All of the classes necessary for input and output operations are included in the java.io package. The java.io package provides virtually every class required for input and output in Java. Each of these streams serves as both an input source and an output destination. The stream in the java.io package supports a wide range of data types, including primitives, objects, and localized characters.

The Java I/O API allows us to do file handling in Java.

Stream

A stream is a data sequence. A stream in Java is made up of bytes. It's called a stream because it resembles a flowing stream of water. Three streams are automatically established for us in Java. All of these streams are linked to the console.

- System.out is a generic output stream.
- System.in is the standard input stream.
- System.err is a standard error stream.

Let's have a look at the code for printing output and an error message to the console:

```
System.out.println("simple -message in
java");
System.err.println("error-message in java");
```

Let's look at the code for getting input from the console:

```
int a=System.in.read(); //returns 1st
character ASCII code
System.out.println((char)a); //print
character
```

OutputStream versus InputStream

The following is a description of the OutputStream and InputStream classes:

OutputStream

A Java program employs an output stream to publish data to a destination, which might be a file, array, peripheral device, or socket.

InputStream

An input stream is used by a Java program to read data from a source, which might be a file, an array, a peripheral device, or a socket.

Class OutputStream

The OutputStream class is abstract. It is the superclass of all classes that represent a bytes output stream. An output stream receives output bytes and routes them to a sink.

Useful OutputStream Methods

Method	Description
public void write(int)throws IOException	It is used to add a byte to the currently active output stream.
public void write(byte[])throws IOException	It is used to write a byte array to the currently active output stream.
public void flush()throws IOException	The current output stream is flushed.
public void close()throws IOException	This function closes the current output stream.

Class InputStream Class

The InputStream class is abstract. It is the superclass of all classes that represent a bytes input stream.

InputStream Techniques That Are Useful

Method	Description
public abstract int read()throws IOException	The following byte from the input stream is read. After the file, it returns -1.
public int available()throws IOException	It provides a rough estimate of how many bytes can be read from the current input stream.
public void close()throws IOException	This function closes the current input stream.

FileOutputStream Class in Java

The Java FileOutputStream is an output stream that is used to write data to a file.

Use the FileOutputStream class to write basic values to a file. The FileOutputStream class allows you to write both byte-oriented and character-oriented data. However, for character-oriented data, FileWriter is preferable than FileOutputStream.

Declaration of the FileOutputStream Class

Example:

```
public class FileOutputStreams1 extends
OutputStreams
```

Methods of the FileOutputStream Class

Method	Description
protected void finalize()	Its purpose is to close the connection with the file output stream.
void write(byte[] ary)	It is used to write the byte array's ary.length bytes to the file output stream.
void write(byte[] ary, int off, int leng)	It is used to write leng bytes to the file output stream from the byte array beginning at offset off.
void write(int b)	It writes the provided byte to the file output stream.
FileChannel getChannel()	It's used to get the file channel object that's connected with the file output stream.
FileDescriptor getFD()	It is used to return the stream's file descriptor.
void close()	Its purpose is to close the file output stream.

Example: write byte

```
import java.io.FileOutputStream;
public class FileOutputStreamExample1
{
    public static void main(String
args[])
{
           try{
             FileOutputStream fouts=new
FileOutputStream("D:\\testout.txt");
```

```
                fouts.write(85);
                fouts.close();
                System.out.
println("success is here ");
               }catch(Exception e)
{
System.out.println(e);
}
        }
}
```

Example: write string

```
import java.io.FileOutputStream;
public class FileOutputStreamExample1
{
    public static void main(String
args[])
{
            try{
                FileOutputStream fouts=new
FileOutputStream("D:\\testout.txt");
                String st="Welcome to
javaTpoint.";
                byte b[]=st.getBytes();
//converting string into byte array
                fouts.write(b);
                fouts.close();
                System.out.
println("success is here");
               }catch(Exception e){System.
out.println(e);}
        }
}
```

FileInputStream Class in Java

The Java FileInputStream class reads bytes from a file. It is used to read byte-oriented data (raw bytes streams) such as picture data, audio, video, etc. You may also read data from a character stream. However, when reading character streams, it is best to utilize the FileReader class.

Declaration of the Java FileInputStream Class

```
public class FileInputStream1 extends
InputStream
```

Methods of the Java FileInputStream Class

Method	Description
int available()	It is used to return an approximation of how many bytes can be read from the input stream.
int read()	It is used to read a single byte from the input stream.
int read(byte[] b)	It is used to read data from the input stream up to a length of b.length bytes.
int read(byte[] b, int off, int leng)	It reads up to leng bytes of data from the input stream.
long skip(long xx)	It skips over and discards xx bytes of data from the input stream.
FileChannel getChannel()	It's used to get the return FileChannel object that's connected with the file input stream.
FileDescriptor getFD()	It's used to get the FileDescriptor object back.
protected void finalize()	It is used to guarantee that the closure method is called when the file input stream is no longer referenced.
void close()	It is used to stop the flow of the stream.

Example: read a single character

```
import java.io.FileInputStream;
public class DataStreamExample1
{
    public static void main(String
args[])
{
        try{
            FileInputStream fint=new
FileInputStream("D:\\testout.txt");
            int c=fint.read();
            System.out.print((char)c);

            fint.close();
        }catch(Exception e){System
.out.println(e);}
        }
      }
```

Example: read all character

```
package com.javapoint;

import java.io.FileInputStream;
public class DataStreamExample1
{
    public static void main(String
args[])
{
        try{
            FileInputStream fint=new
FileInputStream("D:\\testout.txt");
```

```
            int c=0;
            while((c=fint.read())!=-1)
    {
             System.out.print((char)c);
            }
            fint.close();
          }catch(Exception e){System.
 out.println(e);}
          }

       }
```

BufferedOutputStream Class in Java

The BufferedOutputStream class in Java is used to buffer an output stream. It stores data internally in a buffer. It is more efficient than just writing data into a stream. As a result, the performance is quick.

Use the BufferedOutputStream class to add a buffer to an OutputStream. Let's look at the syntax for inserting a buffer into an OutputStream:

```
OutputStream ots= new
BufferedOutputStream(new
FileOutputStream("D:\\IO Package\\testout.
txt"));
```

Declaration of the Java BufferedOutputStream Class

```
public class BufferedOutputStreamexample
extends FilterOutputStream
```

Constructors of the Java BufferedOutputStream Class

Constructor	Description
BufferedOutputStream(OutputStream os)	It generates a new buffered output stream for writing data to the given output stream.
BufferedOutputStream(OutputStream os, int size)	It generates a new buffered output stream for writing data to the given output stream with the provided buffer size.

Methods of the Java BufferedOutputStream Class

Method	Description
void write(int b)	It inserts the provided byte into the buffered output stream.
void write(byte[] b, int off, int leng)	It writes the bytes from the provided byte-input stream into the specified byte array, beginning at the specified offset.
void flush()	The buffered output stream is flushed.

BufferedOutputStream Class Example

In this example, we are writing text into the Buffered-OutputStream object linked to the FileOutputStream object. The flush() method flushes data from one stream and sends it to another. It's necessary if you've linked one stream to another.

```
package com.javatpoint;
import java.io.*;
public class BufferedOutputStreamExample1
{
public static void main(String args[])
```

```
throws Exception{
     FileOutputStream fouts=new
FileOutputStream("D:\\testout.txt");
     BufferedOutputStream bouts=new
BufferedOutputStream(fout);
     String st="Welcome to javaTpoint.";
     byte bt[]=st.getBytes();
     bouts.write(bt);
     bouts.flush();
     bouts.close();
     fouts.close();
     System.out.println("success is
here");
}
}
```

BufferedInputStream Class in Java

To read data from a stream, use the Java BufferedInputStream class. To increase performance, it utilizes a buffer method inside.

The following are the essential aspects of BufferedInputStream:

When bytes from the stream are skipped or read, the internal buffer is automatically replenished, several bytes at a time, from the enclosed input stream.

An internal buffer array is produced when a BufferedInputStream is established.

Declaration of the Java BufferedInputStream Class

```
public class BufferedInputStreams extends
FilterInputStream
```

Constructors of the Java BufferedInputStream Class

Constructor	Description
BufferedInputStream(InputStream IS)	It constructs the BufferedInputStream and stores its parameter, the input stream IS, for subsequent use.
BufferedInputStream(InputStream IS, int size)	It constructs the BufferedInputStream with the specified buffer size and stores the input stream IS as an argument for subsequent usage.

Methods of the Java BufferedInputStream Class

Method	Description
int available()	It returns an estimate of the amount of bytes that can be read from the input stream without causing the next invocation method for the input stream to block.
int read()	It took the next byte of data from the input stream and read it.
int read(byte[] b, int off, int lng)	It reads bytes from the provided byte-input stream into a specified byte array, beginning at the offset indicated.
void close()	It closes the input stream and frees any system resources connected with it.
void reset()	It repositions the stream at the point where the mark method on this input stream was last invoked.
void mark(int readlimit)	It sees the mark method's general contract for the input stream.
long skip(long x)	It skips x bytes of data from the input stream and discards it.
boolean markSupported()	It checks to see if the input stream supports the mark and reset methods.

Example:

```
package com.javapoint;

import java.io.*;
public class BufferedInputStreamExample1
{
 public static void main(String args[])
{
  try{
    FileInputStream fins=new
FileInputStream("D:\\testout.txt");
    BufferedInputStream bins=new
BufferedInputStream(fin);
    int i;
    while((c=bins.read())!=-1)
{
     System.out.print((char)c);
    }
    bins.close();
    fins.close();
  }catch(Exception e){System.out.
println(e);}
 }
}
```

SequenceInputStream Class in Java

The SequenceInputStream class in Java is used to read data from many streams at once. It reads data sequentially (one by one).

Declaration of the Java SequenceInputStream class

```
public class SequenceInputStreams extends
InputStream
```

SequenceInputStream Class Constructors

Constructor	Description
SequenceInputStream(InputStream s1, InputStream s2)	It generates a new input stream by sequentially reading the data from two input streams, s1 and s2.
SequenceInputStream(Enumeration e)	It reads the contents of an enumeration whose type is InputStream to build a new input stream

Method	Description
int read()	It takes the next byte of data from the input stream and reads it.
int read(byte[] ary, int off, int leng)	It reads leng bytes of data from the input stream into the bytes array.
int available()	It is used to return the most bytes that can be read from an input stream.
void close()	Its purpose is to shut the input stream.

SequenceInputStream Class Methods

Example:

```
package com.javapoint;

import java.io.*;
class InputStreamExample1
{
  public static void main(String
args[])
throws Exception
```

```
  {
     FileInputStream inputs1=new
  FileInputStream("D:\\testin.txt");
     FileInputStream inputs2=new
  FileInputStream("D:\\testout.txt");
     SequenceInputStream insta=new
  SequenceInputStream(inputs1, inputs2);
     int k;
     while((k=insts.read())!=-1)
  {
      System.out.print((char)k);
     }
     insts.close();
     inputs1.close();
     inputs2.close();
    }
  }
```

Example of a program that reads data from two files and writes it to another

```
package com.javapoint;

import java.io.*;
class Inputs1
{
  public static void main(String args[])
throws Exception{
   FileInputStream fins1=new
FileInputStream("D:\\testin1.txt");
   FileInputStream fins2=new
FileInputStream("D:\\testin2.txt");
   FileOutputStream fouts=new
FileOutputStream("D:\\testout.txt");
```

```
    SequenceInputStream sist=new SequenceIn
putStream(fin1,fin2);
    int c;
    while((c=sist.read())!=-1)
    {
      fout.write(c);
    }
    sist.close();
    fouts.close();
    fins1.close();
    fins2.close();
    System.out.println("Success is here");
   }
}
```

An example of a SequenceInputStream that reads data via enumeration

Enumeration is required if we need to read data from more than two files. The Vector class's elements() function may be used to obtain an enumeration object. Let's look at a basic example in which we read data from four files: d.txt, e.txt, f.txt, and g.txt.

```
package com.javatpoint;
import java.io.*;
import java.util.*;
class Inputs2
{
public static void main(String args[])
throws IOException{
// creating FileInputStream objects for
all files
FileInputStream fins=new
FileInputStream("D:\\d.txt");
```

```
FileInputStream fins2=new
FileInputStream("D:\\e.txt");
FileInputStream fins3=new
FileInputStream("D:\\f.txt");
FileInputStream fins4=new
FileInputStream("D:\\g.txt");
// to all the stream creating Vector object
Vector v1=new Vector();
v1.add(fins);
v1.add(fins2);
v1.add(fins3);
v1.add(fins4);
// using the elements method to create an
enumeration object
Enumeration e=v1.elements();
//passing the enumeration object in the
constructor
SequenceInputStream bin=new
SequenceInputStream(e);
int c=0;
while((c=bin.read())!=-1){
System.out.print((char)c);
}
bins.close();
fins.close();
fins2.close();
}
}
```

Class Java ByteArrayOutputStream

The Java ByteArrayOutputStream class is used to write data into many files at once. The data in this stream is stored into a byte array, which can later be sent to other streams.

The ByteArrayOutputStream keeps a copy of the data and sends it to various streams.

ByteArrayOutputStream's buffer expands automatically in response to data.

Declaration of the Java ByteArrayOutputStream Class

```
public class ByteArrayOutputStreams extends
OutputStream
```

Constructors of the Java ByteArrayOutputStream Class

Constructor	Description
ByteArrayOutputStream()	It create new byte array output stream with a default size of 32 bytes that can be extended if needed.
ByteArrayOutputStream(int size)	It create new byte array output stream with the specified buffer capacity in bytes.

Methods of the Java ByteArrayOutputStream Class

Method	Description
int size()	It is used to return the current buffer size.
byte[] toByteArray()	It is used to allocate a new byte array.
String toString()	It converts the content into a string decoding bytes using the platform's default character set.
String toString(String charsetName)	It is used to transform the content into string decoding bytes using the charsetName supplied.
void write(int b)	It is used to write the given byte to the byte array output stream.
void write(byte[] b, int off, int leng	It writes len bytes from the supplied byte array to the byte array output stream starting at offset off.

(Continued)

(Continued) Methods of the Java ByteArrayOutputStream Class

Method	Description
void writeTo(OutputStream out)	It writes the whole contents of a byte array output stream to the chosen output stream.
void reset()	It is used to clear the count field of a byte array output stream.
void close()	It's used to shut off the ByteArrayOutputStream.

Example:

```
package com.javatpoint;
import java.io.*;
public class DataStreamExample1
{
public static void main(String args[])
throws Exception{
      FileOutputStream fouts1=new
FileOutputStream("D:\\fs1.txt");
      FileOutputStream fouts2=new
FileOutputStream("D:\\fs2.txt");

      ByteArrayOutputStream bouts=new
ByteArrayOutputStream();
      bouts.write(85);
      bouts.writeTo(fouts1);
      bouts.writeTo(fouts2);

      bouts.flush();
      bouts.close();
      System.out.println("Success is
here");
    }
  }
```

Class Java ByteArrayInputStream

ByteArrayInputStream is made up of two words: ByteArray and InputStream. It may be used to read byte arrays as input streams, as the name implies.

The Java ByteArrayInputStream class has an internal buffer for reading byte arrays as streams. The data in this stream is read from a byte array.

ByteArrayInputStream's buffer expands automatically in response to data.

Declaration of the Java ByteArrayInputStream Class

```
public class ByteArrayInputStreams extends
InputStream
```

Constructors of the Java ByteArrayInputStream Class

Constructor	Description
ByteArrayInputStream(byte[] ary)	Creates a new byte array input stream using the buffer array ary.
ByteArrayInputStream(byte[] ary, int offset, int leng)	Creates a new byte array input stream using ary as its buffer array and the ability to read up to leng bytes of data from an array.

Methods of the Java ByteArrayInputStream Class

Methods	Description
int available()	It returns the number of bytes that can still be read from the input stream.
int read()	Returns the number of bytes written to the data output stream.
int read(byte[] ary, int off, int leng)	It is used to read up to leng bytes of data from the input stream's array of bytes.

(Continued)

(*Continued*) Methods of the Java ByteArrayInputStream Class

Methods	Description
boolean markSupported()	It is used to validate the input stream for the mark and reset methods.
long skip(long xx)	It is used to skip the xx bytes of the input stream.
void mark(int readAheadLimit)	It is used to identify the current location in the stream.
void reset()	It is used to reset a byte array's buffer.
void close()	It's used to end a ByteArrayInputStream.

Example:

```
package com.javatpoint;
import java.io.*;
public class ReadExample1
{
  public static void main(String[] args)
throws IOException {
    byte[] bufs = { 95, 26, 39, 31 };
    // new byte array input stream
Create
    ByteArrayInputStream byts = new
ByteArrayInputStream(bufs);
    int h = 0;
    while ((h = byts.read()) != -1) {
      //Conversion byte into character
      char chr = (char) h;
      System.out.println("ASCII value
of Character is:" + h + "; Special
character is: " + chr);
    }
  }
}
```

DataOutputStream Class in Java

The Java DataOutputStream class allows an application to write machine-independent primitive Java data types to the output stream.

The data output stream is typically used by Java applications to write data that a data input stream may subsequently read.

Declaration of the Java DataOutputStream Class

```
public class DataOutputStreams extends
FilterOutputStream implements DataOutput
```

Methods of the Java DataOutputStream Class

Method	**Description**
int size()	It returns the number of bytes written to the data output stream.
void write(int b)	It writes the supplied byte to the underlying output stream.
void write(byte[] b, int off, int leng)	It writes leng bytes of data to the output stream.
void writeBoolean(boolean v)	It is used to write a 1-byte Boolean value to the output stream.
void writeChar(int v)	It is used to write char as a 2-byte value to the output stream.
void writeChars(String s)	It is used to write a string as a sequence of characters to the output stream.
void writeByte(int v)	It is used to write a byte as a 1-byte value to the output stream.
void writeBytes(String s)	It is used to write a string as a sequence of bytes to the output stream.

(Continued)

(Continued) Methods of the Java DataOutputStream Class

Method	Description
void writeInt(int v)	Its purpose is to write an integer to the output stream.
void writeShort(int v)	It's used to send a brief message to the output stream.
void writeShort(int v)	It writes a short to the output stream.
void writeLong(long v)	Its purpose is to write a long to the output stream.
void writeUTF(String str)	It is used to write a string to the output stream in a portable manner using UTF-8 encoding.
void flush()	Its purpose is to flush the data output stream.

Example:

```
package com.javapoint;

import java.io.*;
public class OutputExample1
{
    public static void main(String[] args)
throws IOException {
        FileOutputStream file1 = new
FileOutputStream(D:\\testsout.txt);
        DataOutputStream data1 = new
DataOutputStream(file1);
        data1.writeInt(85);
        data1.flush();
        data1.close();
        System.out.println("Succcess
is here");
    }
}
```

DataInputStream Class in Java

The Java DataInputStream class enables applications to read primitive data from an input stream in a machine-independent manner.

The data output stream is typically used by Java applications to write data that a data input stream may subsequently read.

Declaration of the Java DataInputStream Class

```
public class DataInputStreams extends
FilterInputStream implements DataInput
```

Methods of the Java DataInputStream Class

Method	Description
int read(byte[] b)	It reads the number of bytes from the input stream.
int read(byte[] b, int off, int leng)	It reads leng bytes of data from the input stream.
int readInt()	It reads input bytes and returns an int value.
byte readByte()	It reads and returns the single input byte.
char readChar()	It takes two bytes as input and returns a char value.
double readDouble()	It takes eight input bytes and returns a double value.
boolean readBoolean()	It reads one input byte and returns true if the byte is not zero and false if the byte is zero.
int skipBytes(int x)	It skips over x bytes of data from the input stream.
String readUTF()	It is used to read a string that has been encoded in UTF-8.

(Continued)

(Continued) Methods of the Java DataInputStream Class

Method	Description
void readFully(byte[] b)	It is responsible for reading bytes from the input stream and storing them in the buffer array.
void readFully(byte[] b, int off, int leng)	It reads len bytes from the input stream.

Example:

```
package com.javatpoint;
import java.io.*;
public class DataStreamExample1
{
  public static void main(String[] args)
throws IOException {
    InputStream input1 = new
FileInputStream("D:\\testsout.txt");
    DataInputStream inst1 = new
DataInputStream(input1);
    int counts = input1.available();
    byte[] arry = new byte[counts];
    inst1.read(arry);
    for (byte bt : arry) {
      char c = (char) bt;
      System.out.print(c+"-");
    }
  }
}
```

FilterOutputStream Class in Java

The Java FilterOutputStream class implements the OutputStream class. To offer extra functionality, it supports subclasses such as BufferedOutputStream and DataOutputStream. As a result, it is utilized less frequently on an individual basis.

Declaration of the Java FilterOutputStream Class

```
public class FilterOutputStreams extends
OutputStream
```

Methods of the Java FilterOutputStream Class

Method	Description
void write(int b)	It writes the provided byte to the output stream.
void write(byte[] ary)	It writes an ary.length byte to the output stream.
void write(byte[] b, int off, int leng)	It is used to write len bytes to the output stream starting at offset off.
void flush()	Its purpose is to flush the output stream.
void close()	Its purpose is to shut the output stream.

Example:

```
import java.io.*;
public class FilterExample1
{
    public static void main(String[]
args)
 throws IOException {
        File data1 = new File("D:\\
testsout.txt");
        FileOutputStream file1 = new
FileOutputStream(data1);
        FilterOutputStream filter1 =
new FilterOutputStream(file1);
        String s1="Welcome to
javaTpoint.";
        byte b1[]=s.getBytes();
        filter1.write(b1);
        filter1.flush();
```

```
            filter1.close();
            file1.close();
            System.out.println("Success is
  here");
        }
  }
```

FilterInputStream Java Class

The Java FilterInputStream class implements the InputStream. It has other subclasses, such as BufferedInputStream and DataInputStream, that provide extra capabilities. As a result, it is utilized less frequently on an individual basis.

Declaration of the Java FilterInputStream Class

```
public class FilterInputStreams extends
InputStream
```

Methods of the Java FilterInputStream Class

Method	Description
int available()	It gives an estimate of how many bytes can be read from the input stream.
int read()	It takes the next byte of data from the input stream and reads it.
int read(byte[] b)	It reads data from the input stream up to the byte.length is measured in bytes.
long skip(long nn)	It skips over and discards nn bytes of data from the input stream.
boolean markSupported()	It is used to determine if the input stream supports the mark and reset methods.
void mark(int readlimit)	It is used to indicate the current location in the input stream.
void reset()	Its purpose is to reset the input stream.
void close()	Its purpose is to shut the input stream.

Example:

```
import java.io.*;
public class FilterExample1
{
    public static void main(String[]
args)
throws IOException {
        File data1 = new File("D:\\
testsout.txt");
        FileInputStream  file1 = new
FileInputStream(data1);
        FilterInputStream filter1 =
new BufferedInputStream(file1);
        int c =0;
        while((c=filter1.read())!=-1){
            System.out.print((char)c);
        }
        file1.close();
        filter1.close();
    }
}
```

Console Class in Java

To receive input from the console, the Java Console class is utilized. It includes methods for reading text and passwords.

If you use the Console class to read a password, it will not be displayed to the user.[1]

Internally, the java.io.Console class is linked to the system console. Since version 1.5, the Console class has been available.

[1] https://www.javatpoint.com/java-console-class, javaTpoint

Example of reading text from the console:

```
String text1=System.console().readLine();
System.out.println("Text is: "+text1);
```

Declaration of the Java Console Class

```
public final class Console1 extends
Object implements Flushable
```

Methods of the Java Console Class

Method	Description
Reader reader()	It is used to get the reader object that is connected with the console.
String readLine()	It reads a single line of text from the console.
String readLine(String fmt, Object... args)	It displays a prepared prompt before reading a single line of text from the console.
char[] readPassword()	It is used to read passwords that are not visible on the terminal.
char[] readPassword(String fmt, Object... args)	It displays a formatted prompt before reading the password that is not visible on the console.
Console format(String fmt, Object... args)	It writes a prepared string to the console output stream.
Console printf(String format, Object... args)	It is used to write a string to the console output stream.
PrintWriter writer()	It is used to get the PrintWriter object that is connected with the console.
void flush()	It's used to clear the console.

How to Get the Console Object

The System class has a static function console() that returns a singleton instance of the Console class:

```
public static Console console(){}
```

Let's look at the code to get an instance of the Console class:

```
Console c1=System.console();
```

Example:

```
import java.io.Console;
class ReadStringTest1
{
public static void main(String args[])
{
Console c1=System.console();
System.out.println("Enter name: ");
String n1=c1.readLine();
System.out.println("Welcome "+n1);
}
}
```

Example of a Java Console Command to Read a Password

```
import java.io.Console;
class ReadPasswordTest1
{
public static void main(String args[]){
Console c1=System.console();
System.out.println("Enter password ");
char[] ch1=c1.readPassword();
String passw=String.valueOf(ch1);//
converting char array into string
System.out.println("Password is: "+passw);
}
}
```

FilePermissions Class in Java

The FilePermission class holds the permissions for a directory or file. All permissions are linked to a route. There are two sorts of paths:

- **D:\\IO\\-:** This indicates that the permission is connected with all subdirectories and files in a recursive manner.
- **D:\\IO*:** This specifies that the permission applies to all directories and files in this directory, excluding subdirectories.

Declaration of the Java FilePermission Class

```
public final class FilePermissions extends
Permission implements Serializable
```

FilePermission Class Methods

Method	Description
ByteArrayOutputStream()	It create new byte array output stream with a default size of 32 bytes that can be expanded if necessary.
ByteArrayOutputStream(int size)	It create new byte array output stream with the specified buffer capacity in bytes.

Methods of the Java FilePermission Class

Method	Description
int hashCode()	It is used to return an object's hash code value.
String getActions()	It is used to return an action's "canonical string representation."
boolean equals(Object obj)	It is used to compare the equivalence of two FilePermission objects.

(Continued)

(Continued) Methods of the Java FilePermission Class

Method	Description
boolean implies(Permission p)	It is used to look for the provided permission in the FilePermission object.
PermissionCollection newPermissionCollection()	It is used to return a new PermissonCollection object that will be used to store the FilePermission object.

Example:

```
package com.javatpoint;

import java.io.*;
import java.security.
PermissionCollection;
public class FilePermissionExample1
{
        public static void main(String[]
args)
throws IOException {
         String srrg = "D:\\IO Package\\
java.txt";
         FilePermission files1 = new
FilePermission("D:\\IO Package\\-",
"read");
         PermissionCollection permission
= files1.newPermissionCollection();
         permission.add(files1);
              FilePermission files2 = new
FilePermission(srrg, "write");
              permission.add(files2);
              if(permission.implies(new
FilePermission(srrg, "read,write"))) {
```

```
                System.out.println("Read,
Write permission is granted for the path
"+srrg );
                }else {
                System.out.println("No
Read, Write permission is granted for
the path "+srrg);               }
            }
}
```

Writer in Java

It is a general-purpose class for writing to character streams. A subclass must implement the following methods: write(char[], int, int), flush(), and close (). Most subclasses will override some of the methods specified here to improve efficiency, functionality, or both.

Fields

Modifier and Type	Field	Description
protected Object	lock	This is the object that is used to synchronize operations on this stream.

Constructor

Modifier	Constructor	Description
Protected	Writer()	It generates a new character-stream writer, whose crucial portions will synchronize with the writer.
Protected	Writer(Object lock)	It generates a new character-stream writer, the crucial parts of which will synchronize with the supplied object.

Methods

Modifier and Type	Method	Description
Writer	append(char c)	It adds the specified character to this writer's name.
Writer	append(CharSequence csq)	This writer has the given character sequence appended to it.
Writer	append(CharSequence csq, int start, int end)	It appends to this writer a subsequence of the supplied character sequence.
abstract void	close()	It flushes the stream before closing it.
abstract void	flush()	It cleans the stream.
Void	write(char[] cbuf)	It writes a string array of characters.
abstract void	write(char[] cbuf, int off, int leng)	It writes a subset of a character array.
Void	write(int c)	It just writes one character.
Void	write(String str)	It generates a string.
Void	write(String str, int off, int leng)	It writes a segment of a string.

Example:

```
import java.io.*;
public class WriterExample1
{
    public static void main(String[] args)
{
        try {
            Writer wr = new
FileWriter("output.txt");
            String content1 = "I love
India";
```

```
                wr.write(content1);
                wr.close();
                System.out.println("Done..");
            } catch (IOException e)
{
                e.printStackTrace();
            }
        }
}
```

Reader in Java

The Java Reader class is used to read character streams. The only methods that a subclass must implement are read(char[], int, int) and close (). On the other hand, most subclasses will override some of the methods to improve efficiency, expand functionality, or both.

BufferedReader, CharArrayReader, FilterReader, InputStreamReader, PipedReader, and StringReader are some of the implementation classes.

Fields

Modifier and Type	Field	Description
protected Object	lock	This object is used to synchronize operations on this stream.

Constructor

Modifier	Constructor	Description
Protected	Reader()	It creates a new character-stream reader, with crucial portions that synchronize with the reader itself.
Protected	Reader(Object lock)	It creates a new character-stream reader, the crucial parts of which will synchronize with the given object.

Methods

Modifier and Type	Method	Description
abstract void	close()	It shuts the stream and releases any related system resources.
Void	mark(int readAheadLimit)	It denotes the current location in the stream.
Boolean	markSupported()	It tells whether this stream supports the mark() operation.
Int	read()	It just reads one character.
Int	read(char[] cbuf)	It reads characters into an array.
abstract int	read(char[] cbuf, int off, int leng)	It reads characters into a section of an array.
Int	read(CharBuffer target)	It tries to read characters into the character buffer given.
Boolean	ready()	It indicates whether or not this stream is ready to be read.
Void	reset()	Resets stream.
Long	skip(long n)	Skips characters.

Example:

```
import java.io.*;
public class ReaderExample1
  {
     public static void main(String[] args)
{
           try {
                Reader reader1 = new
FileReader("file.txt");
                int data1 = reader1.read();
                while (data1!= -1) {
                     System.out.print((char)
data1);
                     data1 = reader1.read();
                }
                reader1.close();
```

```
            } catch (Exception ex) {
                System.out.println(ex.
    getMessage());
            }
        }
    }
```

FileWriter Class in Java

The FileWriter class in Java is used to save character-oriented data to a file. It is a character-oriented class that is used in Java for file management.

Unlike the FileOutputStream class, it does not need you to transform a string to a byte array because it includes a method for writing a string directly.

Declaration of the Java FileWriter Class

```
public class FileWriter1 extends
OutputStreamWriter
```

FileWriter Class Constructors

Constructor	Description
FileWriter(String file)	Makes a new file. It receives the file name as a string.
FileWriter(File file)	Creates a new file. It obtains the file name from the File object.

FileWriter Class Methods

Method	Description
void write(String text)	It's used to write the string to FileWriter.
void write(char c)	It is used to write the character in FileWriter.
void write(char[] c)	It is used to write a char array to a file using FileWriter.
void flush()	It is used to flush FileWriter's data.
void close()	It is used to shut down the FileWriter.

Example:

```
package com.javatpoint;
import java.io.FileWriter;
public class FileWriterExample1
{
    public static void main(String args[])
{
         try{
           FileWriter fwr=new
FileWriter("D:\\testsout.txt");
           fwr.write("Welcome to java");
           fwr.close();
          }catch(Exception e)
{
System.out.println(e);
}
          System.out.println("Success is
here");
     }
}
```

FileReader Class in Java

To read data from a file, the Java FileReader class is utilized. It, like the FileInputStream class, returns data in byte format.

In Java, it is a character-oriented class that is used for file management.

Declaration of the Java FileReader Class

```
public class FileReader1 extends
InputStreamReader
```

FileReader Class Constructors

Constructor	Description
FileReader(String file)	It gets the filename as a string. It opens the specified file in read-only mode. If a file does not exist, the FileNotFoundException is thrown.
FileReader(File file)	It gets the filename from the file instance. It opens the specified file in read-only mode. If the file does not exist, the FileNotFoundException is thrown.

FileReader Class Methods

Method	Description
int read()	It is used to return an ASCII character. At the conclusion of the file, it returns -1.
void close()	It's used to close the FileReader class.

Example:

```
package com.javatpoint;

import java.io.FileReader;
public class FileReaderExample1
{
    public static void main(String args[])
throws Exception{
        FileReader frr=new
FileReader("D:\\testsout.txt");
        int c;
        while((c=frr.read())!=-1)
        System.out.print((char)c);
        frr.close();
    }
}
```

Java's Properties Class

The properties object includes both a key and a value pair as strings. The java.util.Properties class is a Hashtable subclass.

It may be used to determine the value of a property depending on its key. The Properties class offers methods for reading data from and writing data to the properties file. It may also be used to obtain the characteristics of a system.

The properties file has the following advantages:

An advantage of the properties file is that recompilation is not necessary if the information in the properties file is changed: If any information in the properties file is updated, you do not need to recompile the java class. It is used to store information that is regularly updated.

Properties Class Constructors

Method	Description
Properties()	It creates a property list that is empty and has no default values.
Properties(Properties defaults)	It creates an empty property list with the default values given.

Properties Class Methods

Method	Description
public void load(Reader r)	It reads data from the Reader object.
public void load(InputStream is)	It reads data from the InputStream object.
public void loadFromXML(InputStream in)	It is used to load into this properties table all of the properties provided by the XML document on the given input stream.
public String getProperty(String key)	Based on the key, it returns a value.

(Continued)

(continued) Properties Class Methods

Method	Description
public String getProperty(String key, String defaultValue)	It searches for the property with the given key.
public void setProperty(String key, String value)	It invokes Hashtable's insert function.
public void list(PrintStream out)	It prints the property list to the given output stream.
public void list(PrintWriter out))	It is used to print the property list to the chosen output stream.
public Enumeration<?> propertyNames())	It gives an enumeration of all the keys in the property list.
public Set<String> stringPropertyNames()	It returns a collection of keys from the property list, where the key and its associated value are both strings.
public void store(Writer w, String comment)	It saves the writer object's properties.
public void store(OutputStream os, String comment)	The properties are written to the OutputStream object.
public void storeToXML(OutputStream os, String comment)	It writes the properties in the writer object to generate an XML document.
public void storeToXML(Writer w, String comment, String encoding)	It writes the properties in the writer object to generate an XML document with the given encoding.

Example:

An example of a Properties class that retrieves information from a properties file:

To obtain information from the properties file, you must first create it.

```
dtb.properties
user =systems
password =root
```

Let's now create the java class that will read the data from the properties file.

```
import java.util.*;
import java.io.*;
public class Test1
{
public static void main(String[] args)
throws Exception{
    FileReader reader1=new FileReader("dtb.
properties");

    Properties p1=new Properties();
    p1.load(reader);

    System.out.println(p1.
getProperty("user"));
    System.out.println(p1.
getProperty("password"));
}
}
```

The following is an example of a Properties class that can be used to retrieve all of the system properties:

We can retrieve all of the system's properties using the System.getProperties() function. Let's make the class that retrieves data from the system properties.

```
import java.util.*;
import java.io.*;
public class Test1
{
public static void main(String[] args)
throws Exception{
```

```
Properties p1=System.getProperties();
Set set=p1.entrySet();

Iterator itrr=set.iterator();
while(itrr.hasNext()){
Map.Entry entry=(Map.Entry)itrr.next();
System.out.println(entry.getKey()+" =
"+entry.getValue());
}

}
}
```

An example of a Properties class used to create a properties file

```
import java.util.*;
import java.io.*;
public class Test1
 {
public static void main(String[] args)
throws Exception{

Properties p1=new Properties();
p1.setProperty("Name","Simran Jaitin");
p1.setProperty("e-mail","simran@java.com");

p1.store(new FileWriter("info.
properties"),"Java Properties Example");

}
}
```

We covered java input output using Console I/O in Java, how to read from a file, how to create and write to a file in this chapter. We also learned about the Java properties class. We also talked about FileInputStream and OutputStream.

CHAPTER 9

Java Streams

IN THIS CHAPTER

- ➤ Creating Streams
- ➤ Processing Data with Streams
- ➤ Steam Filter
- ➤ Bas64 Encode Decode
- ➤ Using Collectors

In the previous chapter, we covered console input-output (I/O) in Java and how to read and write the file. We also covered properties class in Java. In this chapter, we will learn Java streams in which we covered how to create streams and how to Processing Data with Streams and how to use collectors in Java.

DOI: 10.1201/9781003229063-9

STREAMING IN JAVA 8

In Java 8, there is a special additional package named java.util.stream. This package contains classes, interfaces, and enumerations that enable operational functions on the items. By importing the java.util.stream package, you may utilize stream.

Stream Has the Following Features

- Elements are not stored in a stream. It simply transports components from a source, such as a data structure, array, or I/O channel, through a pipeline of computational processes.
- The stream serves a purpose in nature. The actions done on a stream do not affect its origin. Filtering a Stream received from a collection, for example, creates a new Stream devoid of the filtered items rather than deleting elements from the original collection.
- Stream is lazy and only evaluates code when it is needed.
- During a stream's existence, the elements are only visited once. A fresh stream, similar to an Iterator, must be produced to revisit the same components of the source.

The stream can be used to filter, gather, print, and convert from one data structure to another, among other things. In the following examples, we've used streams to perform a variety of activities.

STREAM PIPELINE IN JAVA

A stream pipeline comprises three parts: a source, intermediate operations, and terminal operation. Because intermediate operations yield a new modified stream, several intermediate operations can be chained together. Terminal operations, on the other hand, return a value or void. It is no longer feasible to operate with the stream after a terminal procedure. When a terminal action is short-circuited, the stream may end before all values have been processed. If the stream is limitless, this is beneficial.

Intermediate processes are time-consuming. They will not be called until the terminal operation has been completed. This improves performance while dealing with more significant data streams.

Methods of the Java Stream Interface

Methods	Description
boolean allMatch(Predicate<? super T> predicate)	It returns all components of this stream that satisfy the given criteria. If the stream is empty, the predicate is not evaluated, and the true is returned.
boolean anyMatch(Predicate<? super T> predicate)	It returns any component of this stream that matches the criteria supplied. If the stream is empty, the predicate is not evaluated and returns false.
static <T> Stream.Builder<T> builder()	It returns a Stream builder.

(Continued)

Methods	Description
<D,A> D collect(Collector<? super T,A,D> collector)	Using a Collector, it performs a mutable reduction operation on the elements of this stream. A Collector encapsulates the functions used as inputs to collect (Supplier, BiConsumer, BiConsumer), allowing for collection strategy reuse and the composition of collect operations such as multiple-level grouping or splitting.
<D> D collect(Supplier<D> supplier, BiConsumer<D,? super T> accumulator, BiConsumer<D,D> combiner)	On the elements of this stream, it performs a mutable reduction operation. A mutable reduction is when the reduced value is a changeable result container, as in an ArrayList, and items are integrated rather than replaced by changing the state of the result.
static <C> Stream<C> concat(Stream<? extends C> a, Stream<? extends C> b)	It creates a lazily concatenated stream with all of the first stream's elements followed by all of the second stream's elements as its elements. If both input streams are ordered, the output stream will be ordered, and if either input stream is parallel, the resultant stream will be parallel. When the resulting stream is closed, the controllers of close for both input streams are
called. a lengthy count ().	It returns total number of items in the specified stream. This is an example of a reduction.
Stream<D> distinct()	It returns total number of items in the specified stream. This is an illustration of a reduction.
static <D> Stream<D> empty()	It gives back an empty sequential Stream.

(*Continued*)

Methods	Description
Stream<D> filter(Predicate<? super D> predicate)	It returns a stream that contains the items of the stream that meet the provided predicate.
Optional<D> findAny()	If the stream is empty, it returns an Optional describing some element of the stream; otherwise, it returns an empty Optional.
Optional<T> findFirst()	If the stream is empty, it produces an Optional describing the first element of the stream; else, it returns an empty Optional. If there is no encounter order in the stream, element may be returned.
<D> Stream<D> flatMap(Function<? super T,? extends Stream<? extends D>> mapper)	It produces a stream that contains the results of replacing each element of this stream with the contents of a mapped stream created by applying the supplied mapping function to each element. After its contents have been put into this stream, each mapped stream is closed. (In the event that a mapped stream is null, an empty stream is utilized instead.)
DoubleStream flatMapToDouble(Function<? super C,? extends DoubleStream> mapper)	It produces a DoubleStream that contains the results of replacing each element of this stream with the contents of a mapped stream created by applying the supplied mapping function to each element. After its contents have been put into this stream, each mapped stream is closed. (In the event that a mapped stream is null, an empty stream is utilized instead.)

(*Continued*)

Methods	Description
IntStream flatMapToInt(Function<? super C,? extends IntStream> mapper)	It produces an IntStream that contains the results of replacing each element of this stream with the contents of a mapped stream generated by applying the supplied mapping function to each element. After its contents have been put into this stream, each mapped stream is closed. (If mapped stream is null, an empty stream is used)
LongStream flatMapToLong(Function<? super C,? extends LongStream> mapper)	It produces a LongStream that contains the results of replacing each element of this stream with the contents of a mapped stream created by applying the supplied mapping function to each element. After its contents have been put into this stream, each mapped stream is closed. (In the event that a mapped stream is null, an empty stream is utilized instead.)
void forEach(Consumer<? super T> action)	It takes action on each element of this stream.
void forEachOrdered(Consumer<? super T> action)	If the stream has a set encounter order, it executes an action for each element in the stream's encounter order.
static <C> Stream<C> generate(Supplier<C> s)	It returns an endless sequential unordered stream, each element of which is created by the supplied Supplier. This is ideal for producing continuous streams, random streams, and so forth.

(*Continued*)

Methods	Description
static <C> Stream<C> iterate(T seed,UnaryOperator<C> f)	It returns an infinite sequential ordered Stream created by iteratively applying a function f to an initial element seed, resulting in a Stream composed of seed, f(seed), f(f(seed)), and so on.
Stream<> limit(long maxSize)	It returns a stream of this stream's items, trimmed to be no longer than maxSize in length.
<D> Stream<D> map(Function<? super C,? extends D> mapper)	It produces a stream containing the results of applying the specified function on the stream's elements.
DoubleStream mapToDouble(To DoubleFunction<? super T> mapper)	It produces a DoubleStream containing the results of applying the specified function on the stream's items.
IntStream mapToInt(ToIntFunction<? super C> mapper)	It produces an IntStream with the results of applying the specified function on the stream's items.
LongStream mapToLong(ToLongFunction<? super C> mapper)	It produces a LongStream containing the results of applying the specified function on the stream's items.
Optional<T> max(Comparator<? super T> comparator)	It returns the most significant element of this stream based on the Comparator given. This is an example of a reduction.
Optional<T> min(Comparator<? super T> comparator)	It returns the stream's smallest element based on the supplied Comparator. This is a particular instance of a reduction.
boolean noneMatch(Predicate<? super T> predicate)	It returns items from this stream that meets the given criteria. If the stream is empty, the predicate is not evaluated, and the true is returned.

(*Continued*)

Methods	Description
@SafeVarargs static <C> Stream<C> of(C... values)	It returns a sequentially ordered stream with the supplied values as elements.
static <C> Stream<C> of(C c)	It returns a single element in a sequential Stream.
Stream<C> peek(Consumer<? super C> action)	It returns a stream containing the elements of this stream, as well as doing the specified action on each element when items from the resultant stream are consumed.
Optional<C> reduce(BinaryOperator<C> accumulator)	It applies an associative accumulation function on the items of this stream and returns an Optional explaining the decreased value if any.
T reduce(T identity, BinaryOperator<T> accumulator)	It reduces the components of this stream by utilizing the given identity value and an associative accumulation function and then returns the reduced value.
<K> K reduce(K identity, BiFunction<U,? super T,U> accumulator, BinaryOperator<K> combiner)	It reduces the items of this stream using the identity, accumulation, and combining functions supplied.
Stream<C> skip(long n)	After rejecting the first n items of the stream, it returns a stream containing the remaining elements of the stream. If this stream has less than n items, an empty stream is returned.
Stream<C> sorted()	It returns a stream containing the components of this stream, sorted in the natural order. If the components of this stream are not Comparable, a java.lang. When the terminal action is executed, a ClassCastException may be thrown.

(Continued)

Methods	Description
Stream<T> sorted(Comparator<? super T> comparator)	It returns a stream with the elements of this stream sorted by the supplied Comparator.
Object[] toArray()	It returns an array holding the stream's items.
<B> B[] toArray(IntFunction<B[]> generator)	It returns an array containing the items of this stream, allocating the returned array and any extra arrays that may be necessary for partitioned execution or resizing using the given generator function.

Example:

```
import java.util.*;
class Product1
{
    int Id;
    String names;
    float prices;
    public Product1(int Id, String
names, float prices)
{
        this.Id = Id;
        this.names = names;
        this.prices = prices;
    }
}
public class JavaStreamExample1
 {
    public static void main(String[]
args)
{
```

```
        List<Product1> productsList1 =
new ArrayList<Product1>();
        //Products Adding
        productsList1.add(new
Product1(1,"Apple Laptop",52000f));
        productsList1.add(new
Product1(2,"HP Laptop",33000f));
        productsList1.add(new
Product1(3,"Dell Laptop",32000f));
        productsList1.add(new
Product1(4,"Sony Laptop",27000f));
        productsList1.add(new
Product1(5," Lenevo Laptop",30000f));
        List<Float> productPriceList =
new ArrayList<Float>();
        for(Product1 product:
productsList1){

            // filtering data of list
            if(product.prices<30000){
                productPriceList.
add(product.prices);    // adding price
to a productPriceList
            }
        }
        System.out.
println(productPriceList);    //
displaying data
    }
}
```

Output:

```
[27000.0]
```

Java Stream Example: Using a Stream to Filter a Collection

```
import java.util.*;
import java.util.stream.Collectors;
class Product1
{
    int Id;
    String names;
    float prices;
    public Product1(int Id, String names,
float prices)
{
        this.Id = Id;
        this.names = names;
        this.prices = prices;
    }
}
public class JavaStreamExample1
 {
    public static void main(String[] args)
{
        List<Product1> productsList1 = new
ArrayList<Product1>();
        //Adding Products
        productsList1.add(new
Product1(1,"Dell Laptop",28000f));
        productsList1.add(new
Product1(2,"Lenovo Laptop",303000f));
        productsList1.add(new Product1(3,"
HP Laptop",38000f));
        productsList1.add(new
Product1(4,"Apple Laptop",82000f));
        productsList1.add(new Product1(5,"
Sony Laptop",30000f));
```

```
        List<Float> productPriceList2
=productsList1.stream()
                  .filter(p -> p.prices >
30000)// filtering data
                  .map(p->p.prices)
// fetching price
                  .collect(Collectors.
toList()); // collecting as list
        System.out.
println(productPriceList2);
    }
}
```

Output:

```
[303000.0, 38000.0, 82000.0]
```

Example of Iterating a Java Stream

We can iterate many times as we want using stream. To deal with the logic you build, Stream provides preset methods. In the example below, we are iterating, filtering, and passing a limit to correct the loop.

```
import java.util.stream.*;
public class JavaStreamExample1
{
    public static void main(String[]
args)
{
        Stream.iterate(1,
element->element+1)
        .filter(element->element%5==0)
        .limit(4)
```

```
            .forEach(System.out::println);
    }
}
```

Output:

```
5
10
15
20
```

Filtering and Iterating Collection in a Java Stream Example

```
import java.util.*;
class Product1
{
    int Id;
    String names;
    float prices;
    public Product1(int Id, String names,
float prices)
{
        this.Id = Id;
        this.names = names;
        this.prices = prices;
    }
}
public class JavaStreamExample1
{
    public static void main(String[] args)
{
        List<Product1> productsList1 = new
ArrayList<Product1>();
        //Products Adding
```

```
        productsList1.add(new
Product1(1,"HP Laptop",29000f));
        productsList1.add(new Product1(2,"
Sony Laptop",31000f));
        productsList1.add(new
Product1(3,"Lenevo Laptop",28500f));
        productsList1.add(new
Product1(4,"Dell Laptop",33000f));
        productsList1.add(new
Product1(5,"Apple Laptop",90000f));
        // This is a more concise way to
data filtering.
        productsList1.stream()
                            .filter(product ->
product.prices == 29000)
                            .forEach(product ->
System.out.println(product.names));
    }
}
```

Output:

```
HP Laptop
```

Example of a Java Stream: reduce() Method in a Collection

```
import java.util.*;
class Product1
{
    int Id;
    String names;
    float prices;
    public Product1(int Id, String names,
float prices) {
```

```
        this.Id = Id;
        this.names = names;
        this.prices = prices;
    }
}
public class JavaStreamExample1
 {
    public static void main(String[] args) {
        List<Product1> productsList1 = new
ArrayList<Product1>();
        // Products Adding
        productsList1.add(new
Product1(1,"HP Laptop",27000f));
        productsList1.add(new
Product1(2,"Dell Laptop",33000f));
        productsList1.add(new
Product1(3,"Lenevo Laptop",26000f));
        productsList1.add(new
Product1(4,"Sony Laptop",29000f));
        productsList1.add(new
Product1(5,"Apple Laptop",92000f));
        //compact approach for filtering
data
        Float totalPrice = productsList1.
stream()
.                    map(product->product.
prices)
.                    reduce(0.0f,(sum,
prices)->sum+prices);   // price
accumulating
        System.out.println(totalPrice);
        // More precise code
        float totalPrice2 = productsList1.
stream()
```

```
                    .map(product->product.
prices)
                    .reduce(0.0f,Float::sum);
// by referring method of Float class
accumulating price,
          System.out.println(totalPrice2);

     }
}
```

Output:

```
207000.0
207000.0
```

Summation of a Java Stream Example Using Collector Methods

```
import java.util.*;
import java.util.stream.Collectors;
class Product1
{
     int Id;
     String names;
     float prices;
     public Product1(int Id, String names,
float prices)
{
          this.Id = Id;
          this.names = names;
          this.prices = prices;
     }
}
public class JavaStreamExample1
 {
     public static void main(String[] args) {
```

```
        List<Product1> productsList1 = new
ArrayList<Product1>();
        // Products Adding
        productsList1.add(new
Product1(1,"Dell Laptop",25000f));
        productsList1.add(new
Product1(2,"Hp Laptop",30000f));
        productsList1.add(new
Product1(3,"Song Laptop",28000f));
        productsList1.add(new Product1(4,"
Lenevo Laptop",28000f));
        productsList1.add(new
Product1(5,"Apple Laptop",92000f));
        // To total the prices, use
Collectors' technique.
        double totalPrice3 = productsList1.
stream()
                        .collect(Collectors.
summingDouble(product->product.prices));
        System.out.println(totalPrice3);

    }
}
```

Output:

```
203000.0
```

Example of a Java Stream: Determine the Maximum and Minimum Product Price

```
import java.util.*;
class Product1
{
    int Id;
```

```
    String names;
    float prices;
    public Product1(int Id, String names,
float prices)
{
        this.Id = Id;
        this.names = names;
        this.prices = prices;
    }
}
public class JavaStreamExample1
 {
    public static void main(String[] args)
{
        List<Product1> productsList1 = new
ArrayList<Product1>();
        //Adding Products
        productsList1.add(new
Product1(1,"HP Laptop",29000f));
        productsList1.add(new
Product1(2,"Dell Laptop",32000f));
        productsList1.add(new
Product1(3,"Lenevo Laptop",23000f));
        productsList1.add(new
Product1(4,"Sony Laptop",29000f));
        productsList1.add(new
Product1(5,"Apple Laptop",91000f));
        // max() method to get max Product1
prices
        Product1 productX = productsList1.
stream().max((product1, product2)-
>product1.prices > product2.prices?  1:
-1).get();
        System.out.println(productX.price);
```

```
        // min() method to get min Product
prices
        Product productY = productsList.
stream().min((product1, product2)-
>product1.prices > product2.prices? 1:
-1).get();
        System.out.println(productB.prices);

    }
}
```

Output:

```
91000.0
23000.0
```

Example of a Java Stream: count() Method in a Collection

```
import java.util.*;
class Product1
{
    int Id;
    String names;
    float prices;
    public Product1(int Id, String names,
float prices)
{
        this.Id = Id;
        this.names = names;
        this.prices = prices;
    }
}
public class JavaStreamExample1
 {
```

```
    public static void main(String[] args) {
        List<Product1> productsList1 = new
ArrayList<Product1>();
        // Products Adding
        productsList1.add(new
Product1(1,"HP Laptop",27000f));
        productsList1.add(new
Product1(2,"Dell Laptop",35000f));
        productsList1.add(new
Product1(3,"Lenevo Laptop",23000f));
        productsList1.add(new
Product1(4,"Sony Laptop",26000f));
        productsList1.add(new
Product1(5,"Apple Laptop",94000f));
        // count number
        long counts = productsList1.
stream()
                    .filter(product-
>product.prices<30000)
                    .count();
        System.out.println(counts);
    }
}
```

Output:

```
3
```

Converting List to Set Using Java Streams Example

```
import java.util.*;
import java.util.stream.Collectors;
class Product1
{
    int Id;
    String names;
```

```
    float prices;
    public Product1(int Id, String names,
float prices)
{
        this.Id = Id;
        this.names = names;
        this.prices = prices;
    }
}

public class JavaStreamExample1
 {
    public static void main(String[] args)
{
        List<Product1> productsList1 = new
ArrayList<Product1>();

        //Adding Products
        productsList1.add(new
Product1(1,"Dell Laptop",26000f));
        productsList1.add(new
Product1(2,"HP Laptop",31000f));
        productsList1.add(new
Product1(3,"Song Laptop",27000f));
        productsList1.add(new Product1(4,"
Lenevo Laptop",29000f));
        productsList1.add(new
Product1(5,"Apple Laptop",93000f));

        // Converting product List into Set
        Set<Float> productPriceList =
            productsList.stream()
             .filter(product->product.prices
< 30000)   // on the base of price filter
product
```

```
            .map(product->product.prices)
           .collect(Collectors.toSet());
// collect it as Set(remove duplicate elements)
        System.out.println(productPriceList);
    }
}
```

Output:

```
[27000.0, 29000.0, 26000.0]
```

Converting a List to a Map Using Java Streams Example

```
import java.util.*;
import java.util.stream.Collectors;
class Product1
{
    int Id;
    String names;
    float prices;
    public Product1(int Id, String names,
float prices)
{
        this.Id = Id;
        this.names = names;
        this.prices = prices;
    }
}

public class JavaStreamExample1
 {
    public static void main(String[] args)
{
        List<Product1> productsList1 = new
ArrayList<Product1>();
```

```
        // Products Adding
        productsList1.add(new
Product1(1,"HP Laptop",29000f));
        productsList1.add(new
Product1(2,"Dell Laptop",32000f));
        productsList1.add(new
Product1(3,"Lenevo Laptop",27000f));
        productsList1.add(new
Product1(4,"Sony Laptop",23000f));
        productsList1.add(new
Product1(5,"Apple Laptop",92000f));

        // Converting Product List into a Map
        Map<Integer,String> productPriceMap
=
            productsList1.stream()
.                        collect(Collectors.
toMap(p->p.Id, p->p.names));

        System.out.println(productPriceMap);
    }
}
```

Output:

```
{1=HP Laptop, 2=Dell Laptop, 3=Lenevo
Laptop, 4=Sony Laptop, 5=Apple Laptop}
```

Stream Method Reference

```
import java.util.*;
import java.util.stream.Collectors;

class Product1{
    int Id;
```

```
    String names;
    float prices;

    public Product1(int Id, String names,
float prices)
{
        this.Id = Id;
        this.names = names;
        this.prices = prices;
    }

    public int getId() {
        return Id;
    }
    public String getName() {
        return names;
    }
    public float getPrice() {
        return prices;
    }
}

public class JavaStreamExample1 {

    public static void main(String[] args) {

        List<Product1> productsList1 = new
ArrayList<Product1>();

        // Products Adding
        productsList1.add(new
Product1(1,"HP Laptop",22000f));
        productsList1.add(new
Product1(2,"Dell Laptop",31000f));
```

```
        productsList1.add(new
Product1(3,"Lenevo Laptop",29000f));
        productsList1.add(new
Product1(4,"Sony Laptop",21000f));
        productsList1.add(new
Product1(5,"Apple Laptop",91000f));

        List<Float> productPriceList =
                productsList.stream()
.                             filter(p ->
p.prices > 30000) // data filtering
.                             map(Product1:
:getPrices)        // fetching price
.
collect(Collectors.toList());  //
collecting list
        System.out.
println(productPriceList);
    }
}
```

Output:

```
[31000.0, 91000.0]
```

STREAM FILTER IN JAVA

Java stream has a filter() method for filtering stream components based on a specified criterion. If you want to obtain just even entries from your list, you can easily accomplish so using the filter technique.[1]

[1] https://www.javatpoint.com/java-8-stream-filter, javaTpoint

This method accepts a predicate as an input and returns a stream of resulting items.

Signature

The signature of the Stream filter() function is as follows:

```
Stream<T> filter(Predicate<? super T>
predicate)
```

Parameter

Predicate: It accepts Predicate reference as an argument. The predicate is a helpful interface. As a result, you may also pass a lambda expression here.

Return

It will return a new stream.

Example of a Java Stream filter()

```
import java.util.*;
class Product1
{
    int Id;
    String names;
    float prices;
    public Product1(int Id, String names,
float prices)
{
        this.Id = Id;
        this.names = names;
        this.prices = prices;
    }
}
```

```
public class JavaStreamExample1
{
    public static void main(String[] args) {
        List<Product1> productsList1 = new
ArrayList<Product1>();
        //Adding Products
        productsList1.add(new
Product1(1,"Dell Laptop",27000f));
        productsList1.add(new
Product1(2,"Hp Laptop",32000f));
        productsList1.add(new Product1(3,"
Sony Laptop",29000f));
        productsList1.add(new
Product1(4,"Lenevo Laptop",25000f));
        productsList1.add(new
Product1(5,"Apple Laptop",91000f));
        productsList1.stream()
.                  filter(p ->p.prices>
30000)   // filtering price
.                  map(pm ->pm.prices)
// fetching price
.                  forEach(System.
out::println);  // iterating price
    }
}
```

Output:

```
32000.0
91000.0
```

Example 2 of a Java Stream filter()

```
import java.util.*;
import java.util.stream.Collectors;
```

```
class Product1
{
    int Id;
    String names;
    float prices;
    public Product1(int Id, String names,
float prices)
{
        this.Id = Id;
        this.names = names;
        this.prices = prices;
    }
}
public class JavaStreamExample1 {
    public static void main(String[] args) {
        List<Product1> productsList1 = new
ArrayList<Product1>();
        //Products Adding
        productsList1.add(new
Product1(1,"HP Laptop",22000f));
        productsList1.add(new
Product1(2,"Dell Laptop",32000f));
        productsList1.add(new
Product1(3,"Lenevo Laptop",26000f));
        productsList1.add(new
Product1(4,"Sony Laptop",27000f));
        productsList1.add(new
Product1(5,"Apple Laptop",91000f));
        List<Float> pricesList1 =
productsList1.stream()
                    .filter(p ->p.prices>
30000)   // price filtering
                    .map(pm ->pm.prices)
// price fetching
```

```
                    .collect(Collectors.
toList());
        System.out.println(pricesList1);
    }
}
```

Output:

```
[32000.0, 91000.0]
```

BASE64 ENCODE AND DECODE IN JAVA

To cope with encryption, Java offers the Base64 class. You can encrypt and decrypt your data using the techniques given. To utilize its methods, you must import java.util.Base64 into your source file.

This class has three distinct encoders and decoders for encrypting data at each level. These approaches are applicable at the following levels.

Encoding and Decoding Fundamentals

It employs the Base64 alphabet provided by Java for encoding and decoding operations in RFC 4648 and RFC 2045. The encoder adds no line separator character. The decoder rejects data that contains characters that are not part of the base64 alphabet.

Encoding and Decoding of URLs and Filenames

For encoding and decoding, it employs the Base64 alphabet provided by Java in RFC 4648. The encoder adds no line separator character. The decoder rejects data that contains characters that are not part of the base64 alphabet.

Multipurpose Internet Main Extensions (MIME)

For encoding and decoding, it employs the Base64 alphabet as defined in RFC 2045. The encoded output must be expressed in lines of no more than 76 characters. The line separator is a carriage return "\r" followed immediately by a linefeed "\n." There is no line separator after the encoded output. All line separators and other characters not included in the base64 alphabet table are disregarded throughout the decoding process.

Base64 Nested Classes

Class	Detail
Base64.Decoder	Class implements decoder for decoding byte data using the RFC 4648 and RFC 2045 encoding schemes.
Base64.Encoder	Class implements encoder for encoding the byte data using the RFC 4648 and RFC 2045 encoding schemes.

Methods Using Base64

Methods	Description
public static Base64. Decoder getDecoder()	It returns a Base64.Decoder that uses the Basic type base64 encoding scheme to decode.
public static Base64. Encoder getEncoder()	It returns a Base64 string. Encoder that uses the Basic type base64 encoding method to encode data.
public static Base64. Decoder getUrlDecoder()	It returns a Base64.Decoder that uses the URL and Filename safe type base64 encoding scheme to decode.
public static Base64. Decoder getMimeDecoder()	It returns a Base64.Decoder that uses the MIME type base64 decoding technique to decode.

(Continued)

(Continued) Methods Using Base64

Methods	**Description**
public static Base64. Encoder getMimeEncoder()	It returns a Base64 string. Encoder that uses the MIME type base64 encoding technique to encode.
public static Base64. Encoder getMimeEncoder(int lineLength, byte[] lineSeparator)	It returns a Base64 string. Encoder that uses the MIME type base64 encoding method with given line lengths and separators.
public static Base64. Encoder getUrlEncoder()	It returns a Base64.Encoder that uses the URL and Filename safe type base64 encoding method to encode.

Methods for Base64.Decoder

Methods	**Description**
public byte[] decode(byte[] src)	It uses the Base64 encoding method to decode all bytes from the input byte array and write the results to a freshly created output array. Length of the returned byte array is the length of the generated bytes.
public byte[] decode(String src)	It uses the Base64 encoding strategy to decode a Base64 encoded String into a freshly allocated byte array.
public int decode(byte[] src, byte[] dst)	It decodes all bytes in the input byte array using the Base64 encoding technique, then writes the results to the specified output byte array, beginning at offset 0.
public ByteBuffer decode(ByteBuffer buffer)	It uses the Base64 encoding method to decode all bytes from the input byte buffer and writes the results to a freshly allocated ByteBuffer.
public InputStream wrap(InputStream is)	It returns an input stream that may be used to decode a Base64 encoded byte stream.

Methods for Base64.Encoding

Methods	Description
public byte[] encode(byte[] src)	It uses the Base64 encoding method to encode all bytes from the given byte array into a newly allocated byte array. Length of the returned byte array is the length of the generated bytes.
public int encode(byte[] src, byte[] dst)	It uses the Base64 encoding technique to encode all bytes from the provided byte array and writes the resultant bytes to the chosen output byte array, beginning at offset 0.
public String encodeToString(byte[] src)	It uses the Base64 encoding technique to convert the supplied byte array to a String.
public ByteBuffer encode(ByteBuffer buffer)	It uses the Base64 encoding method to encode all remaining bytes from the given byte buffer into a newly allocated ByteBuffer. The location of the source buffer will be updated to its limit upon return; the limit will not have changed. The location of the returned output buffer will be zero, and its limit will be the amount of encoded bytes returned.
public OutputStream wrap(OutputStream os)	It encloses an output stream to encode byte data using the Base64 encoding technique.
public Base64.Encoder withoutPadding()	It returns an encoder instance that encodes the same way as this one but without padding characters at the end of the encoded byte data.

DEFAULT METHODS IN JAVA

Java allows you to establish default methods within the interface. Methods created within an interface and tagged with default are referred to as default methods. These are non-abstract techniques.

Example of a Java Default Method

Sayable is a functional interface in the following example, with default and an abstract method. The term "default method" refers to a method that has a default implementation. You may also offer a more customized implementation for the function by overriding the default method.

Let's look at a basic example.

```
interface Sayable{
    // method Default
    default void say(){
        System.out.println("Hello, this is
default");
    }
    // method Abstract
    void sayMore(String msg);
}
public class DefaultMethods1 implements
Sayable{
    public void sayMore(String msg){
// abstract method  implementing
        System.out.println(msg);
    }
    public static void main(String[] args)
{
        DefaultMethods dm = new
DefaultMethods();
        dm.say();   // default method
calling
        dm.sayMore("Work is worship");  //
abstract method  calling

    }
}
```

Output:

```
Hello, this is default
Work is worship
```

Java 8 Interface Static Methods

Static methods can also be defined within the interface. Utility methods are defined using static methods. The example demonstrates how to implement static method in an interface.

```
interface Sayable{
    // default method
    default void say(){
        System.out.println("Hello, default
method");
    }
    // method Abstract
    void sayMore(String msg);
    // method static
    static void sayLouder(String msg){
        System.out.println(msg);
    }
}
public class DefaultMethods implements
Sayable{
    public void sayMore(String msg){      //
implementing abstract method
        System.out.println(msg);
    }
    public static void main(String[] args)
{
        DefaultMethods dm = new
DefaultMethods();
```

```
        dm.say();                              //
default method calling
        dm.sayMore("Work worship");            //
abstract method calling
        Sayable.sayLouder("Hello..");          //
static method calling
    }
}
```

Output:

```
Hello, default method
Work worship
Hello..
```

Java 8 Interface vs. Abstract Class

We consider the requirement for an abstract class in Java after having default and static methods within the interface. An interface and an abstract class are nearly identical, except that constructors can be created in the abstract class, not in the interface.

```
abstract class AbstractClass1
{
    public AbstractClass1() {           //
constructor
        System.out.println("You can create
constructor in abstract class");
    }
    abstract int add(int x, int y); //
abstract method
    int sub(int x, int y){        // non-
abstract method
        return x-y;
    }
```

```
    static int multiply(int x, int y)
{  // static method
        return x*y;
    }
}
public class AbstractTest extends
AbstractClass1{
    public int add(int x, int y)
{        // implementing abstract method
        return x+y;
    }
    public static void main(String[] args)
{
        AbstractTest x = new AbstractTest();
        int result1 = x.add(20, 10);   //
calling abstract method
        int result2 = x.sub(20, 10);    //
calling non-abstract method
        int result3 = AbstractClass1.
multiply(30, 20); // calling static method
        System.out.println("Addition:
"+result1);
        System.out.println("Substraction:
"+result2);
        System.out.println("Multiplication:
"+result3);
    }
}
```

Output:

```
You can create constructor in abstract class
Addition: 30
Substraction: 10
Multiplication: 600
```

FOREACH LOOP IN JAVA

To iterate through the items, Java provides a new method forEach(). It is specified by the Iterable and Stream interfaces. It is a built-in method in the Iterable interface. To iterate elements, collection classes that extend the Iterable interface can utilize the forEach loop.

This method only accepts one parameter, in which it is a functional interface. As a result, lambda expression can be sent as an argument.

Iterable Interface forEach() Signature

```
default void forEach(Consumer<super
T>action)
```

forEach() example 1 in Java 8

```
import java.util.ArrayList;
import java.util.List;
public class ForEachExample1
{
    public static void main(String[] args) {
        List<String> gamesList1 = new
ArrayList<String>();
        gamesList1.add("Batball");
        gamesList1.add("Basketball");
        gamesList1.add("Chess");
        gamesList1.add("Football ");
        System.out.println("--Iterating
passing lambda expression--");
        gamesList1.forEach(games -> System.
out.println(games));

    }
}
```

Output:

```
--Iterating passing lambda expression--
Batball
Basketball
Chess
Football
```

forEach() example 2 in Java 8

```
import java.util.ArrayList;
import java.util.List;
public class ForEachExample1{
    public static void main(String[] args) {
        List<String> gamesList1 = new
ArrayList<String>();
        gamesList1.add("Basketball");
        gamesList1.add("Football ");
        gamesList1.add("Cricket");
        gamesList1.add("Hocky");
        System.out.println("--Iterating
passing method reference--");
        gamesList1.forEach(System.
out::println);
    }
}
```

Output:

```
--Iterating passing method reference--
Basketball
Football
Cricket
Hocky
```

Method forEachOrdered() in Java Stream

Along with the forEach() function, Java includes the forEachOrdered() method (). It is used to iterate through elements in the stream's given order.

Signature

```
void forEachOrdered(Consumer<? super T>
action)
```

Java Stream forEachOrdered() Method Example

```
import java.util.ArrayList;
import java.util.List;
public class ForEachOrderedExample1
{
   public static void main(String[] args)
{
        List<String> gamesList1 = new
ArrayList<String>();
        gamesList1.add("Basketball");
        gamesList1.add("Football ");
        gamesList1.add("Cricket");
        gamesList1.add("Hocky");
        System.out.println("—Iterating
passing lambda expression--");
        gamesList1.stream().
forEachOrdered(games -> System.out.
println(games));
        System.out.println("--Iterating
passing method reference--");
        gamesList1.stream().
forEachOrdered(System.out::println);
    }

}
```

Output:

```
--Iterating passing lambda expression--
Basketball
Football
Cricket
Hocky
--Iterating by passing method reference--
Basketball
Football
Cricket
Hocky
```

JAVA COLLECTORS

Collectors are a subclass of the Object class. It supports reduction operations such as grouping components into collections, summarizing elements based on various criteria, and so on.

The Java Collectors class includes several methods for dealing with items.

Methods	Description
public static <D> Collector<D,?,Double> averagingDouble(ToDoubleFunction<? super T> mapper)	It returns a Collector that computes the arithmetic mean of a double-valued function on the input items. The result is 0 if no items are present.
public static <D> Collector<D,?,D> reducing(D identity, BinaryOperator<D> op)	It returns a Collector that reduces its input elements using the supplied identity and a defined BinaryOperator.
public static <D> Collector<D,?,Optional<D>> reducing(BinaryOperator<D> op)	It returns a Collector that reduces its input elements using the provided BinaryOperator. The end product is referred to as an Optional<D>.

(Continued)

Methods	Description
public static <D,C> Collector<D,?,C> reducing(C identity, Function<? super D,? extends C> mapper, BinaryOperator<C> op)	It returns a Collector that reduces its input elements using a given mapping function and BinaryOperator. This generalization of reducing(Object, BinaryOperator) that allows for element modification before reduction.
public static <D,T> Collector<D,?,Map<T,List<D>>> groupingBy(Function<? super D,? extends T> classifier)	It returns a Collector that performs a "group by" action on input items of type T, classifying them based on a classification function and returning the results in a Map.
public static <T,K,A,D> Collector<T,?,Map<K,D>> groupingBy(Function<? super T,? extends K> classifier, Collector<? Super T,A,D> downstream)	It returns a Collector that performs a cascaded "group by" operation on input elements of type T, grouping items according to a classification function, and then reducing the values associated with a particular key using the provided downstream Collector.
public static <T,K,D,A,M extends Map<K,D>> Collector<T,?,M> groupingBy(Function<? super T,? extends K> classifier, Supplier<M> mapFactory, Collector<? super T,A,D> downstream)	It returns a Collector that performs a cascaded "group by" operation on input elements of type T, grouping items according to a classification function, and then reducing the values associated with a particular key using the provided downstream Collector. The Collector's Map is constructed using the factory method provided.

(Continued)

Methods	Description
public static <T,K> Collector<T,?, ConcurrentMap<K,List<T>>> groupingByConcurrent(Function<? super T,? extends K> classifier)	It returns a concurrent Collector that performs a "group by" action on type T input elements, classifying them according to a classification function.
public static <T,K,A,D> Collector <T,?,ConcurrentMap<K,D>> groupingByConcurrent(Function<? super T,? extends K> classifier, Collector<? super T,A,D> downstream)	It returns a concurrent Collector that uses the provided downstream Collector to conduct a cascaded "group by" action on input elements of type T, grouping elements according to a classification function, and then executing a reduction operation on the values associated with a particular key.
public static <T,K,A,D,M extends ConcurrentMap<K,D>> Collector<T,?,M> groupingByConcurrent(Function<? super T,? extends K> classifier, Supplier<M> mapFactory, Collector<? super T,A,D> downstream)	It returns a concurrent Collector that uses the provided downstream Collector to conduct a cascaded "group by" action on input elements of type T, grouping elements according to a classification function, and then executing a reduction operation on the values associated with a particular key. The Collector's ConcurrentMap is constructed using the provided factory function.
public static <T> Collector<T,?,Map<Boolean,List<T>>> partitioningBy(Predicate<? super T> predicate)	It returns a Collector that divides the input items based on a Predicate and organizes them in a Map<Boolean, ListT>>. There are no assurances about the Map's type, mutability, serializability, or thread safety.

(Continued)

Methods	Description
public static <T,D,A> Collector<T,?,Map<Boolean,D>> partitioningBy(Predicate<? super T> predicate, Collector<? Super T,A,D> downstream)	It returns a Collector that splits the input elements based on a Predicate, reduces the values in each partition based on another Collector, and arranges them into a Map<Boolean, P> whose values are results of the downstream reduction.
public static <T,K,U> Collector<T,?,Map<K,U>> toMap(Function<? super T,? extends K> keyMapper, Function<? super T,? extends U> valueMapper)	It returns a Collector that gathers elements into a Map whose keys and values result from applying the mapping functions supplied to the input elements.
public static <T,K,U> Collector<T,?,Map<K,U>> toMap(Function<? super T,? extends K> keyMapper, Function<? super T,? extends U> valueMapper, BinaryOperator<U> mergeFunction)	It returns a Collector that gathers elements into a Map whose keys and values result from applying the supplied mapping functions to the input elements.
public static <T,K,U,M extends Map<K,U>> Collector<T,?,M> toMap(Function<? super T,? extends K> keyMapper, Function<? super T,? extends U> valueMapper, BinaryOperator<U> mergeFunction, Supplier<M> mapSupplier)	It returns a Collector, which accumulates elements into a Map, the keys and values of which are the result of applying the supplied mapping functions to the input elements.
public static <T,K,U> Collector<T,?,ConcurrentMap<K,U>> toConcurrentMap(Function<? super T,? extends K> keyMapper, Function<? super T,? extends U> valueMapper)	It returns a concurrent Collector that gathers elements into a ConcurrentMap whose keys and values are applying the mapping functions supplied to the input elements.

(Continued)

Methods	**Description**
public static <T,K,U> Collector<T, ?,ConcurrentMap<K,U>> toConcurrentMap(Function<? super T,? extends K> keyMapper, Function<? super T,? extends U> valueMapper, BinaryOperator<U> mergeFunction)	It returns a concurrent Collector that gathers elements into a ConcurrentMap whose keys and values result from applying the supplied mapping functions to the input elements.
public static <T,K,U,M extends ConcurrentMap<K,U>> Collector<T,?,M> toConcurrentMap(Function<? super T,? extends K> keyMapper, Function<? super T,? extends U> valueMapper, BinaryOperator<U> mergeFunction, Supplier<M> mapSupplier)	It returns a concurrent Collector that collects elements into a ConcurrentMap, the keys, and values of which are the results of applying the supplied mapping functions to the input elements.
public static <T> Collector<T,?,IntSummaryStatistics> summarizingInt(ToIntFunction<? super T> mapper)	It returns a Collector that applies an int-producing mapping function to each input element and returns summary statistics for the results.
public static <T> Collector<T,?,LongSummaryStatistics> summarizingLong(ToLongFunction<? super T> mapper)	It returns a Collector that performs a long-producing mapping function to each input element and delivers summary statistics for the results.
public static <T> Collector<T,?,DoubleSummaryStatistics> summarizingDouble(ToDoubleFunction<? super T> mapper)	It provides a Collector that performs a double-producing mapping function on each input element and returns summary statistics for the results.

Example of a Java Collector: Obtaining Data as a List

```
import java.util.stream.Collectors;
import java.util.List;
```

```
import java.util.ArrayList;
class Product1
{
    int Id;
    String names;
    float prices;

    public Product1(int Id, String names,
float prices)
{
        this.Id = Id;
        this.names = names;
        this.prices = prices;
    }
}
public class CollectorsExample1
{
    public static void main(String[] args)
{
        List<Product1> productsList1 = new
ArrayList<Product1>();
        // Products Adding
        productsList1.add(new
Product1(1,"Dell Laptop",26000f));
        productsList1.add(new
Product1(2,"Hp Laptop",31000f));
        productsList1.add(new
Product1(3,"Lenevo Laptop",28000f));
        productsList1.add(new
Product1(4,"Apple Laptop",91000f));
        productsList1.add(new
Product1(5,"Song Laptop",34000f));
        List<Float> productPriceList =
                productsList1.stream()
```

```
.                               map(x->x.prices)
// fetching price
.                               collect(Collectors.
toList());  // collecting as list
        System.out.
println(productPriceList);
    }
}
```

Output:

```
[26000.0, 31000.0, 28000.0, 91000.0,
34000.0]
```

Example of Using the Sum Function in Java Collectors

```
import java.util.stream.Collectors;
import java.util.List;
import java.util.ArrayList;
class Product1
{
    int Id;
    String names;
    float prices;

    public Product1(int Id, String names,
float prices)
{
        this.Id = Id;
        this.names = names;
        this.prices = prices;
    }
}
public class CollectorsExample1
 {
```

```
    public static void main(String[] args)
{
        List<Product1> productsList1 = new
ArrayList<Product1>();
        //Adding Products
        productsList1.add(new
Product1(1,"Dell Laptop",28000f));
        productsList1.add(new
Product1(2,"HP Laptop",31000f));
        productsList1.add(new
Product1(3,"Lenevo Laptop",29000f));
        productsList1.add(new
Product1(4,"Apple Laptop",89000f));
        productsList1.add(new
Product1(5,"Sony Laptop",30000f));
        Double sumPrices =
                productsList1.stream()
.                       collect(Collectors.
summingDouble(x->x.prices));  // collecting
as list
        System.out.println("Sum of prices:
"+sumPrices);
        Integer sumId =
                productsList1.stream().
collect(Collectors.summingInt(x->x.Id));
        System.out.println("Sum of id's:
"+sumId);
    }
}
```

Output:

```
Sum of prices: 207000.0
Sum of id's: 15
```

Example of Java Collectors: Obtaining Average Product Price

```
import java.util.stream.Collectors;
import java.util.List;
import java.util.ArrayList;
class Product1
{
    int Id;
    String names;
    float prices;

    public Product1(int Id, String names,
float prices)
{
        this.Id = Id;
        this.names = names;
        this.prices = prices;
    }
}
public class CollectorsExample1
{
    public static void main(String[] args)
{
        List<Product1> productsList1 = new
ArrayList<Product1>();
        // Products Adding
        productsList1.add(new
Product1(1,"Dell Laptop",29000f));
        productsList1.add(new
Product1(2,"HP Laptop",31000f));
        productsList1.add(new
Product1(3,"Sony Laptop",27000f));
        productsList1.add(new Product1(4,"
Lenevo Laptop",25000f));
```

```
        productsList1.add(new
Product1(5,"Apple Laptop",91000f));
        Double averages = productsList1.
stream()
                        .collect(Collectors.
averagingDouble(p->p.prices));
        System.out.println("Average price:
"+averages);
    }
}
```

Output:

```
Average price: 40600.0
```

Counting Elements in Java Collectors Example

```
import java.util.stream.Collectors;
import java.util.List;
import java.util.ArrayList;
class Product1
{
    int Id;
    String names;
    float prices;
    public Product1(int Id, String names,
float prices)
{
        this.Id = Id;
        this.names = names;
        this.prices = prices;
    }
    public int getId()
 {
        return Id;
```

```
    }
    public String getName()
 {
        return names;
    }
    public float getPrice()
{
        return prices;
    }
}
public class CollectorsExample1
{
    public static void main(String[] args)
{
        List<Product1>productsList1 = new
ArrayList<Product1>();
        // Products Adding
        productsList1.add(new
Product1(1,"HP Laptop",258000f));
        productsList1.add(new
Product1(2,"Dell Laptop",31000f));
        productsList1.add(new
Product1(3,"Lenevo Laptop",27000f));
        productsList1.add(new
Product1(4,"Sony Laptop",26000f));
        productsList1.add(new
Product1(5,"Apple Laptop",91000f));
        Long noOfElements = productsList1.
stream()
.                collect(Collectors.
counting());
        System.out.println("Total elements
are: "+noOfElements);
    }
}
```

Output:

```
Total elements are: 5
```

We explored java streams in this chapter, where we learned how to construct streams and handle data with streams. We also taught about Java stream filters, and base64 encode/decode. In Java, we studied default methods, the foreach() method, and the collectors class.

CHAPTER 10

Functional Programming with Lambda Expressions

IN THIS CHAPTER

- ➤ Functional Programming
- ➤ Pure Functions
- ➤ Lambda Expressions

We explored Java streams in the previous chapter, where we learned how to create a stream, how to process it, what a collector is, and how to use a stream filter. This chapter will

DOI: 10.1201/9781003229063-10

teach us about functional programming and what a pure function is. We also go over Lambda Expressions.

WHAT IS FUNCTIONAL PROGRAMMING IN JAVA?

In essence, functional programming is a method of designing computer programs in which calculations are seen as evaluating mathematical functions. So, in mathematics, what is a function?

A function is a mathematical expression that connects an input set to an output set.[1]

Significantly, the outcome of a function is solely determined by its input. Even more intriguing, we can combine two or more functions to create a new function.

1. **The Lambda Calculus:** We have to understand why these definitions and characteristics of mathematical functions are essential in programming. Alonzo Chruch, a mathematician, devised a formal method for expressing computations based on function abstraction in the 1930s. The Lambda Calculus was named after this universal paradigm of computing.

   Lambda calculus had a significant effect on the development of programming language theory, exceptionally functional programming languages. Lambda calculus is typically implemented in functional programming languages.

   Functional programming languages give expressive techniques to construct software in function

[1] https://www.baeldung.com/java-functional-programming, Baeldung

composition since lambda calculus focuses on function composition.

2. **Programming Paradigms Classification:** Of fact, functional programming isn't the only programming style used in the real world. Programming techniques are broadly classified into imperative and declarative programming paradigms:

   According to the imperative method, a program is defined as a series of statements that alter the program's state until it achieves the end state. Procedural programming is imperative programming in which programs are built using procedures or subroutines. Object-oriented programming (OOP), a popular programming paradigm, expands procedural programming ideas.

   On the other hand, the declarative method communicates the logic of a computation without defining its control flow in terms of a series of assertions. Simply said, the declarative method focuses on defining what the program must accomplish rather than how it should accomplish it. Functional programming languages are a subset of declarative programming languages. These groups are further subdivided, and the taxonomy becomes highly complicated.

3. **Programming Language Classification:** Today, every attempt to officially classify programming languages is an academic endeavor in and of itself! However, for our purposes, we'll try to grasp how programming languages are classified based on their support for functional programming.

Pure functional languages, such as Haskell, support only pure functional programming.

On the other hand, other languages support both functional and procedural programming and are regarded as impure functional languages. Scala, Kotlin, and Java are among the many languages that fit under this group. It's critical to realize that most of today's popular programming languages are general-purpose languages, which means they accept many programming paradigms.

- **Fundamental Concepts and Principles:** This part will go over some of the fundamental ideas of functional programming and how to use them in Java. Keep in mind that many of the features we'll be utilizing haven't always been part of Java, and it's recommended that you use Java 8 or later to practice functional programming successfully.

    1. **Functions of First and Higher Orders:** If a programming language considers functions as first-class citizens, it is said to have first-class functions. Essentially, it implies that functions are permitted to support all activities generally available to other entities. Assigning functions to variables, giving them as arguments to other functions, and returning them as values from other functions are all examples.

       This feature allows higher-order functions to be defined in functional programming. Higher-order functions can take functions as inputs and return a function as a result. This supports other functional programming methods such as function composition and currying.

Traditionally, functions could only be sent through structures such as functional interfaces or anonymous inner classes in Java. Functional interfaces, commonly known as Single Abstract Method (SAM) interfaces, have precisely one abstract method.

Assume we need to give a custom comparator to Collections.sort method:

```
Collections.sort(number, new
Comparator<Integer>()
{
    @Override
    public int compare(Integer c1,
Integer c2) {
        return c1.compareTo(c2);
    }
});
```

As we can see, this is a time-consuming and verbose method that is unlikely to inspire developers to choose functional programming. Fortunately, Java 8 introduced many new tools to help with this, including lambda expressions, method references, and specified functional interfaces.

Let's have a look at how a lambda expression may assist us with the same task:

```
Collections.sort(numbers, (c1, c2) ->
c1.compareTo(c2));
```

This is more concise and understandable. Please keep in mind that, while this may create the idea that functions are first-class citizens in Java, this is not the case.

Java still encapsulates lambda expressions in functional interfaces underneath the syntactic sugar. As a result, Java regards lambda expressions as Objects, the actual first-class citizens in Java.

2. **Pure Functions:** The definition of a pure function stresses that it should return a result based only on its parameters and should have no side effects. This may appear to contradict all of Java's best practices.

Encapsulation is an introductory programming approach in Java, which is an object-oriented language. It promotes concealing an object's internal state and exposing just the methods required to access and alters it. As a result, some techniques are not strictly pure functions.

Of course, with Java, encapsulation and other object-oriented notions are simply suggestions, not requirements.

In reality, developers have only lately begun to recognize the need to design immutable states and functions with no side effects.

Assume we wish to get the sum of the integers we just sorted:

```
Integer sum(List<Integer> number)
{
    return number.stream().collect(Collectors.
summingInt(Integer::intVal));
}
```

This technique is deterministic since it is based only on the parameters it gets. Furthermore, it has no negative side effects.

Side effects might be anything other than the method's intended behavior. Side effects, for example, might be as easy as changing a local or global state or storing to a database before returning a response. Purists regard logging as a side consequence, but we all have our limits to establish.

However, we can reason about how we handle genuine side effects. For example, we may need to preserve the outcome in a database for legitimate reasons. In functional programming, there exist ways for dealing with side effects while maintaining pure functions.

3. **Immutability:** Immutability is a fundamental notion of functional programming that refers to the fact that an entity cannot be changed after its creation. This is now supported by language design in a functional programming language. However, with Java, we must make our own decision to construct immutable data structures.

Keep in mind that Java has numerous immutable types by default, such as String. This is mainly for security considerations, as we utilize String extensively in class loading and as keys in hash-based data structures.

Other built-in immutable types include basic wrapper and math types. And what about the data models that we build in Java? They are, of course, not immutable by default, and we must make a few adjustments to achieve immutability. It is the use of the last keyword, but it doesn't end there:

```
public class ImmutableData1
{
    private final String someData1;
    private final AnotherImmutableData
anotherImmutableData1;
    public ImmutableData(final String
someData1, final AnotherImmutableData1
anotherImmutableData1) {
        this.someData 1= someData1;
        this.anotherImmutableData1 =
anotherImmutableData1;
    }
    public String getSomeData1() {
        return someData1;
    }
    public AnotherImmutableData1
getAnotherImmutableData1() {
        return anotherImmutableData1;
    }
}

public class AnotherImmutableData1 {
    private final Integer someOtherData1;
    public AnotherImmutableData1(final
Integer someData1) {
        this.someOtherData1 = someData1;
    }
    public Integer getSomeOtherData1() {
        return someOtherData1;
    }
}
```

It is crucial to mention that we rigorously follow the following rules:

- Each field of an irreversible data structure must be immutable.
- This includes all nested types and collections.
- As needed, one or more constructors should be provided for initialization.
- There should just be accessor functions, with no adverse effects if possible.

It's challenging to get it entirely right every time, especially as data structures become more complicated. Several additional packages, however, can make dealing with immutable data in Java easier. Immutable and Project Lombok, for example, provide a ready-to-use framework for building unchanging data models in Java.

4. **Transparency in Referential:** Referential transparency is one of the most challenging features of functional programming to comprehend. The notion, on the other hand, is relatively straightforward. If substituting an expression with its equivalent value does not affect the program's behavior, we call it referentially transparent.

This enables specific strong functional programming methods such as higher-order functions and lazy evaluation. Here's an example to help you understand:

```
public class SimpleData1
{
```

```
    private Logger logger1 = Logger.
getGlobal();
    private String data1;
    public String getData() {
        logger1.log(Level.INFO, "Get the
data called for SimpleData");
        return data1;
    }
    public SimpleData setData(String data1)
{
        logger1.log(Level.INFO, " Set the
data for SimpleData. ");
        this.data1 = data1;
        return this;
    }
}
```

This is a standard POJO class in Java, but we want to see if it supports referential transparency. Consider the following statements:

```
String data1 = new SimpleData().
setData("Baeldung").getData();
logger1.log(Level.INFO, new SimpleData().
setData("Baeldung").getData());
logger1.log(Level.INFO, data1);
logger1.log(Level.INFO, "Baeldung");
```

The three logger calls are semantically similar, but they are not referentially transparent. Because it has a side effect, the initial call is not referentially transparent. We'll miss the logs if we replace this call with its value, as we did in the third call.

Because SimpleData is changeable, the second call is likewise not referentially transparent. A data request. The presence of setData anyplace in the program would make it impossible to replace it with its value.

So, in order to achieve referential transparency, our functions must be pure and immutable. These are the two prerequisites we discussed before. We generate context-free code as an intriguing result of referential transparency. In other words, we may execute them in any sequence and context, which opens up new opportunities for optimization.

- **Techniques for Functional Programming:** The functional programming principles that we mentioned previously allow us to profit from functional programming by employing various approaches. This part will go through some of the most popular approaches and see how they may be implemented in Java.

    1. **Composition of Functions:** The process of creating complicated functions by combining more straightforward functions is referred to as function composition. In Java, this is largely accomplished by using functional interfaces, which are target types for lambda expressions and method references.

Any interface with a single abstract method may often serve as a functional interface. As a result, we can simply create a functioning interface. However, under the package java.util.function, Java 8 has a plethora of functional interfaces by default for a variety of use scenarios.

Many of these functional interfaces enable function composition via default and static methods. To further grasp this, let's look at the Function interface. The function is a straightforward and general functional interface that takes one input and returns a result.

It also has two default methods, compose andThen, to aid us with function composition:

```
Function<Double, Double> log = (val) ->
Math.log(val);
Function<Double, Double> sqrt = (val) ->
Math.sqrt(val);
Function<Double, Double> logThenSqrt =
sqrt.compose(log);
logger1.log(Level.INFO, String.
valueOf(logThenSqrt.apply(3.14)));
// Output is: 1.06
Function<Double, Double> sqrtThenLog =
sqrt.andThen(log);
Logger1.log(Level.INFO, String.
valueOf(sqrtThenLog.apply(3.14)));
// Output is: 0.57
```

Both approaches enable us to combine several functions into a single function, but they have distinct meanings. While compose applies the function provided in the argument first, followed by the function on which it is executed, reversing the process.

Several additional functional interfaces contain intriguing methods for function composition, such as the Predicate interface's default methods and, or, and negate. While these functional interfaces only take one argument, there exist two-arity specializations such as BiFunction and BiPredicate.

2. **Monads:** Many functional programming notions are derived from Category Theory, a broad theory of functions in mathematics. It introduces various

category ideas, such as functors and natural transformations. The only thing that matters is that this is the foundation for using monads in functional programming.

A monad is a formal concept that allows for the general structure of programs. So, in essence, a monad allows us to wrap a value, perform a series of transformations, and then return the value with all transformations applied. Of course, each monad must obey three laws: left identity, right identity, and associativity, but we won't go into these now.

In Java, there are few monads that we frequently utilize, such as Optional and Stream:

```
Optional.of(2).flatMap(f -> Optional.of(3).
flatMap(t -> Optional.of(f + t)))
```

So, why is Optional referred to as a monad? This example optionally allows us to wrap a value with the approach and apply a sequence of changes. Using the flatMap method, we're doing the transition of adding another wrapped item. We may demonstrate that Optional obeys the three rules of monads if we wish. However, opponents will point out that an Optional does, in some cases, violate the monad rules. However, for most practical purposes, it should suffice.

If we grasp the fundamentals of monads, we'll notice many additional instances in Java, such as Stream and CompletableFuture.

They assist us in achieving various goals, but they all have a common composition in which context modification or transformation is handled.

Of course, we may create our monad types in Java to fulfil specific goals, such as log monad, report monad, or audit monad. Remember how we spoke about dealing with side effects in functional programming? As it turns out, the monad is one of the functional programming approaches for accomplishing this.

3. **Currying:** Currying is a mathematical technique for turning a function with several parameters into a series of functions with just one argument. But why are they required in functional programming? It provides a strong composition method that eliminates the requirement to call a function with all of its parameters.

Furthermore, the impact of a curried function is not realized until it gets all of the parameters.

Currying is widely supported in pure functional programming languages such as Haskell. In fact, by default, all functions are curried. However, with Java, this is not that simple:

```
Function<Double, Function<Double, Double>>
weight = mass -> gravity -> mass * gravity;

Function<Double, Double> weightOnEarth =
weight.apply(7.81);
logger1.log(Level.INFO, "Weight on Earth:
" + weightOnEarth.apply(50.0));

Function<Double, Double> weightOnMars =
weight.apply(4.75);
logger1.log(Level.INFO, "Weight on Mars: "
+ weightOnMars.apply(50.0));
```

In this section, we developed a function to determine our weight on a planet. While our mass remains constant, gravity fluctuates depending on whatever planet we are on. We may use the function in part by supplying only the gravity to construct a function for a single planet. Furthermore, we may use this partly applied function as an input or return value in any composition.

Currying is reliant on the language providing two essential features: lambda expressions and closures. Lambda expressions are anonymous functions that allow us to treat code as if it were data. We've already seen how to use functional interfaces to build them.

A lambda expression can now shut on its lexical scope, which we call closure. Here's an example:

```
private static Function<Double, Double>
weightOnEarth()
{
   final double gravity = 8.81;
   return mass -> mass * gravity;
}
```

Notice how the lambda phrase we return in the method above depends on the enclosing variable, which we refer to as closure. Unlike other functional programming languages, Java requires the enclosing scope to be final or nearly so.

As an intriguing side effect, currying allows us to build arbitrary arity functional interfaces in Java.

4. **Recursion:** Another helpful method in functional programming is recursion, which allows us to break down a problem into smaller pieces. The significant advantage of recursion is that it will enable us to avoid the side effects common in any imperative style looping.

Let's see how we can use recursion to get the factorial of a number:

```
Integer factorial(Integer number)
{
    return (number = = 2)?  2 : number *
factorial(number - 2);
}
```

We call the same procedure recursively until we get to the base case when we start calculating our outcome. It's worth noting that we're performing the recursive call before computing the result at each step or the beginning of the calculation. As a result, this type of recursion is sometimes referred to as head recursion.

The disadvantage of this recursion is that each step must hold the state of all previous stages until we reach the base case. This isn't a big problem for small groups, but keeping the state for large groups can be wasteful.

A way is to use tail recursion, which is a somewhat different version of recursion. Here, we verify that the recursive call is the function's final call. Let's see how we can change the preceding function to utilize tail recursion:

```
Integer factorial(Integer number, Integer
result)
{
    return (number = = 2)?  result :
factorial(number - 2, result * number);
}
```

The function makes use of an accumulator, which eliminates the need to retain the state at each stage of the recursion. The actual benefit of this approach is that it allows you to make use of compiler optimizations such as tail-call elimination, which allows the compiler to determine whether or not to let go of the current function's stack frame.

Although several languages, including Scala, offer tail-call removal, Java does not. This is in the Java queue and may appear in some form as part of the bigger improvements suggested by Project Loom.

Why Is Functional Programming Important?

After going through this, we must ask why we are putting in this much effort. For someone coming from a Java background, the transition to functional programming is not easy. As a result, there should be some very promising advantages to using functional programming in Java.

The most significant benefit of using functional programming in any language, including Java, is pure functions and immutable states. In retrospect, most programming difficulties are founded on side-effects and changeable states in one way or another. Simply removing them simplifies our program's reading, reasoning, testing, and maintenance.

Declarative programming, as a result, produces programs that are extremely short and understandable. As a subset of declarative programming, functional programming includes features such as higher-order functions, function composition, and function chaining. Consider the advantages that the Stream API has introduced to Java 8 for handling data operations.

But don't give in to the temptation until we're totally prepared. Please keep in mind that functional programming is not a straightforward design pattern that we can use and profit from right away. Functional programming is more of a shift in how we think about issues and their solutions and how we organize algorithms.

Is Java a Good Fit?

While it's impossible to dispute the benefits of functional programming, we can't help but wonder if Java is a good fit for it. Java has historically evolved as a general-purpose programming language that is better suited for object-oriented programming. Even contemplating the use of functional programming prior to Java 8 was time-consuming! However, things have altered significantly with Java 8.

The fact that there are no genuine function types in Java contradicts the fundamental concepts of functional programming.

Functional interfaces disguised as lambda expressions more than make up for it, at least syntactically. The fact that types in Java are inherently changeable and that we have to write so much boilerplate to construct immutable types doesn't help either.

Other features of a functional programming language that are lacking or difficult to implement in Java are expected. In Java, for example, the default evaluation technique for arguments is eager. However, in functional programming, lazy evaluation is a more efficient and preferred method.

We can still achieve slow evaluation in Java by combining operator short-circuiting and functional interfaces, but it's a little more complicated.

The list is by no means exhaustive and may include generics support with type-erasure, a lack of support for tail-call optimization, and other issues. We do, however, obtain a general sense. Java is unsuitable for beginning a functional programming application from scratch.

But what if we already have a Java application, most likely in object-oriented programming? Nothing prevents us from reaping some of the benefits of functional programming, especially now that Java 8 is available.

For a Java developer, here is where the majority of the benefits of functional programming are found. A mix of object-oriented programming with the advantages of functional programming can be quite beneficial.

JAVA'S PURE FUNCTIONS

A function is a pure function if and only if the following conditions are met:

- The function's execution has no side effects.
- The function's return value is solely determined by the input arguments provided to it.

Here's an example of a Java pure function (method):

```
public class ObjectWithPureFunction1
{

    public int sum(int x, int y)
{
        return x + y;
    }
}
```

Take note of how the input arguments solely determine the sum() function's return value. It's also worth noting that sum() has no side effects, which means it doesn't change any state (variables) outside of the method in any way.[2]

In contrast, consider the following non-pure function:

```
public class ObjectWithNonPureFunction1
{
    private int val = 0;

    public int add(int nextVal)
{
        this.val += nextVal;
        return this.val;
    }
}
```

Take note of how the method add() calculates its return value using a member variable and alters the state of the value member variable, resulting in a side effect.

LAMBDA EXPRESSIONS IN JAVA

The lambda expression is a new and essential Java feature introduced in Java SE 8. It represents one method interface using an expression cleanly and concisely. It is pretty beneficial in a library collection. It aids in iterating, filtering, and extracting data from a collection.

2 http://tutorials.jenkov.com/java-functional-programming/index.html, Jenkov.com

The Lambda expression is used to offer an interface implementation that has a functional interface. It saves a significant amount of code. We don't need to declare the method again in the case of a lambda expression to provide the implementation. We just write the implementation code here.

Because a lambda expression in Java is considered a function, the compiler does not generate a b.class file.

What Is a Functional Interface?

The lambda expression implements the functional interface. An available interface contains only one abstract method. The annotation @FunctionalInterface in Java is used to designate an interface as a functional interface.

Why Should You Utilize Lambda Expression?

- To offer Functional interface implementation.
- There is less coding.

Syntax:

```
(argumentlist) -> {body}
```

A Java lambda expression is made up of three parts:

1. **Argument-list:** It can be either empty or non-empty.
2. **Arrow-token:** It is used to connect the arguments-list with the body of the expression.
3. **Body:** It includes lambda expression expressions and statements.

Syntax with No Parameters

```
() -> {
// no parameter lambda body
}
```

Syntax with one Parameter

```
(k1) -> {
//single parameter lambda body
}
```

Syntax with two Parameters

```
(k1,k2) -> {
//multiple parameter lambda body
}
```

Example of a Java Lambda Expression

To print every item in the list, use a lambda expression in the ArrayList's forEach() method:

```
import java.util.ArrayList;

public class Main {
  public static void main(String[] args) {
    ArrayList<Integer> number = new
ArrayList<Integer>();
    number.add(51);
    number.add(19);
    number.add(28);
    number.add(11);
    number.forEach( (n1) -> { System.out.
println(n1); } );
  }
}
```

Output:

```
51
19
28
11
```

We studied functional programming and pure functions in Java in this chapter. In addition, we learned about Lambda Expression. This brings us to the end of our journey with Java.

Appraisal

Java is the most widely used and well-known object-oriented programming (OOP) language. The security characteristic of Java makes it popular and widely used. Many Java enthusiasts use it for a wide range of applications. We may use Java to develop a wide variety of programs, including business applications, network applications, desktop applications, Internet applications, games, Android apps, and so many more.

Java provides a broad and diverse set of Application Programming Interfaces (APIs) that aid programmers in the development of applications. We can use Java to create a variety of apps for a variety of reasons.

The majority of firms, including Uber, Pinterest, Google, Instagram, Spotify, Netflix, and Airbnb, utilize Java in their software stack. We have included a few businesses or organizations as well as their initiatives. It will assist you in deciding which programming language to use for your next project. Java is simple because of its straightforward and easy-to-understand syntax. Java removes many of C++'s complicated and confusing notions. Java, for example, does not provide explicit pointers or operator overloading.

DOI: 10.1201/9781003229063-11

In Java, everything takes the form of an object. In other words, it has some data as well as some activity. At least one class and object must be present in a Java application. Java always attempts to detect problems during runtime and compilation. To provide a robust memory management mechanism, Java employs a garbage collector. Java is strong or powerful because of features such as exception handling and garbage collection. Because Java does not utilize explicit pointers, it is a secure language. The virtual machine is where all Java applications execute. Furthermore, Java has a security manager that specifies the access levels of Java classes.

Java guarantees that you can write code once and run it anywhere (at any platform). The generated byte code is platform-agnostic, and it may be executed on any machine, regardless of the operating system. Java enables you to create robust, scalable, and multi-tiered programs for various business needs; many bespoke software development firms provide smooth custom software development services. Java allows you to create everything from simple applications to massive end-to-end corporate systems.

A java developer is required to have abilities such as:

- Understanding and troubleshooting the code of others
- Deployment to internal or external servers
- How to Use a Java Virtual Machine
- Java integration with current online and business apps

However, because Java is the dominant language in numerous industries, each java employment opportunity necessitates a unique set of abilities.

JAVA JOB OPPORTUNITIES

- Junior Programmer
- Senior Programmer
- Web Developer in Java
- Java architect
- Android Developer in Java
- Java EE programmer

Java is an ancient programming language that has done well in keeping up with the market's shifting expectations. According to newrelic.com, Java 8 is the most widely used version of Java in the market, with Oracle having been the primary seller and maintainer of the Java language and the Java Virtual Machine (JVM) since its purchase of Sun Microsystems in 2010.

Despite being named the most popular programming language of 2019, others argue that Java is losing favor to rising languages such as Python. However, even the most contradictory arguments from reliable sources provide the same results.

WHY YOU SHOULD LEARN JAVA TODAY?

- In most cases, the code is written in a human-readable programming language and then converted by a compiler into a machine language that your system executes to run the intended program.

  If you've ever looked at Java, you've probably heard the expression "write once, run anywhere." Because

Java was designed to be a platform-independent language, this fact is linked with Java programming. If you wish to execute Java, you must install a virtual machine on your computer. JVM may be installed on any system, regardless of its operating system. As a result, any machine, operating system, or architecture that supports the JVM may run a Java application.

- The development of Covid-19, its effects on the global economy, and the battle against the advent of e-commerce. This worldwide surge in e-commerce has created a specific need for Java developers in various roles, including Android, Web, and Enterprise Level Apps.

  There has been a definite storm of android app development and consumption over the last several years. This amount is expected to increase to 184 billion in the near future, according to Sensor Tower (Mobile App Store Marketing Intelligence). The majority of Android apps use Java as their primary backend language. With this predicted increase, these figures demonstrate why you should learn Java in 2021.

- Many novices struggle with deciding on a programming language to begin with. If you're starting to learn java online from scratch, it's very likely that you'll be advised to learn Java as your first language from various sources.

  This is because Java is object-oriented, robust, and understandable, and it handles storage space, deallocation, and reallocation. Despite the fact that Java has commercial customers, it nevertheless provides free support, endless libraries, and free sophisticated APIs for anybody to utilize. If you are a freshman and want to get started with a real-time project, Java is the way to go. Java will offer you a complete toolbox for any small size to vast, scalable, or enterprise-level programs, from beginning tools to expert APIs.

- Java was created in 1995, making it 27 years old by the time you read this in 2022. Java has been a top language from its inception and continues to remain so to this day. This essay is not a biased assessment of Java as my personal favorite, but rather the truth that throughout the past 26 years, and particularly during this epidemic, the need for Java developers has increased. Recruiters have ranked it in the top three for the previous two years, with over 60,000 positions available online. Since 2019, we have witnessed the growth of work-from-home culture unfold in front of our eyes. Because of this compulsion, many workplaces were unable to equip their employees at home adequately. They were also intended to inculcate whatever gadgets they possessed. This feature also served as another reason why Java was beneficial in most companies.

- The Java community is highly active and helpful, and you will never feel alone in your learning path. We constantly recommend that novices, no matter what language they are studying, become a member of an actively participating community to feel connected, remain current, and learn from the errors of others.

- Everyone was once a novice or an amateur, therefore don't be afraid to ask questions about topics you don't understand or report inaccuracies. However, we recommend that you finish your study before reporting a mistake. There are already many answers for the exact issues you're dealing with most of the time.

This textbook is a great way to begin if you want to learn how to code in Java. We believe Android will continue its global market dominance for a variety of reasons. We covered a wide range of java topics in this book. Let us now go through the contents of this text to review and reinforce the facts and information we acquired about Java. We started Chapter 1 by covering an introduction to Java, its key features, and syntax. In Chapter 2, we learned how to install Java on a computer and about java primitives, control structures, loops, and packages. We learned about OOP in Chapter 3, where we discussed access modifiers, interfaces, inheritance, and Java enums. In Chapter 4, we discussed what a string is, how to compare strings, and convert strings. Chapter 5 went through arrays, lists, sets, and maps. In addition, in Chapter 6, we learned about libraries, packages, and modules. We went over java database connections and relational databases.

Index

J

N

O

P

S

X